CTOs at Work

Scott Donaldson
Stanley Siegel
Gary Donaldson

Stanley Siegel
23 FEB 2012

Apress®

CTOs at Work

ISBN-13 (pbk): 978-1-4302-3593-4

ISBN-13 (electronic): 978-1-4302-3594-1

President and Publisher: Paul Manning
Lead Editor: Jeffrey Pepper
Editorial Board: Steve Anglin, Mark Beckner, Ewan Buckingham, Gary Cornell, Morgan Ertel, Jonathan Gennick, Jonathan Hassell, Robert Hutchinson, Michelle Lowman, James Markham, Matthew Moodie, Jeff Olson, Jeffrey Pepper, Douglas Pundick, Ben Renow-Clarke, Dominic Shakeshaft, Gwenan Spearing, Matt Wade, Tom Welsh
Coordinating Editor: Rita Fernando
Copy Editors: Mary Sudul, Nancy Sixsmith
Compositor: Mary Sudul
Indexer: BIM Indexing & Proofreading Services
Cover Designer: Anna Ishchenko

Distributed to the book trade worldwide by Springer Science+Business Media New York, 233 Spring Street, 6th Floor, New York, NY 10013. Phone 1-800-SPRINGER, fax (201) 348-4505, e-mail orders-ny@springer-sbm.com, or visit www.springeronline.com.

For information on translations, please e-mail rights@apress.com, or visit www.apress.com.

Apress and friends of ED books may be purchased in bulk for academic, corporate, or promotional use. eBook versions and licenses are also available for most titles. For more information, reference our Special Bulk Sales–eBook Licensing web page at www.apress.com/bulk-sales.

To my growing family: Shelly, Melanie, Manoli, Nick, Stephanie, David, Laura, and Ashleigh.
—Scott Donaldson

To Bena, my wife, and our grandchildren: Eva, Ezra, Avi, Raffi, Tal, Eli, Zoe, Sarah, and Emma.
—Stan Siegel

To Gail Winston, my wife, for her support, encouragement, and keen wit throughout the process; and my Golden Retriever Colby, who always knew just the right time to take me for a walk.
—Gary Donaldson

To the memory of Susan Marie Donaldson Leddy who was taken too soon from her loving family, Phil, Chris, Andrew and Remy.
—Gary and Scott

Contents

Foreword

CTOs at Work is a terrific contribution that breaks the mold for books of its type. There are three traditional structures for harnessing the collected wisdom of CTOs and CIOs. The most scholarly treatments involve interpreting the results of some survey or surveys of CTOs. The resulting numerical data is then crunched through various mysterious but important looking formulae to obtain, purportedly, surprising conclusions. The authors, usually academics then include their own insights and recommendations for the reader. I like these kinds of books the least because they are sterile and devoid of real CTO insight. Surveys can provide some important data for researchers, but generally, when you aggregate the responses of a large number of CTOs, each in a unique situation, no real usable information ensues. For example, so what if the average budget of a CTO is $1 million dollars? How can this information really be used?

Another approach to CTO mindshare books involves case studies of failed (and sometimes successful) projects, occasionally featuring commentary from the CTOs involved. In many cases, the editors/authors of these texts have never held the role of a CTO. Yet case study books tend to include self-righteous second guessing by the editors/authors. Or the case studies take information out of context to support some hidden agenda. The reader, then is put in the position of having to decide whose insight is better—the real CTO, or some professor assessing the situation from the bleachers, and with the benefit of hindsight.

Until I discovered *CTOs at Work*, my favored template for CTO wisdom type books involved collecting essays from CTOs themselves. This third approach has the advantage of presenting information in the CTO's own "voice," relatively unfiltered. I co-edited a book using this approach and I was pleased with the results. The downside to this structure, however, is that contributions can be uneven and sometimes haphazard, making it hard to discern any thematic content.

Now there is a fourth and vastly superior framework for harvesting the wisdom of CTOs. This book, *CTOs at Work* uses a series of in-depth, sit-down interviews with active CTOs. Editors/interviewers, Scott Donaldson, Stanley Siegel, and Gary Donaldson ask all the questions that you would want to ask if you had access to these CTOs. But the questioning is not formulaic, like some telephone survey. It's lively, informal, and the interviewers adapt each question to the previous response, giving the dialogue a much more conversational feel. It's like watching "Inside The Actor's Studio" hosted by James Lipton.

By virtue of this informal style, the CTOs open up and provide raw, unfiltered insights. You learn about their organization, role, and most challenging projects and colleagues. You also get to know the CTOs themselves, as human beings, not executives in gray flannel suits. For ten years I led a community of practice of CIOs/CTOs in the Philadelphia metropolitan area, and the dialogues you will see in CTOs at Work replicate the honest, intimate discussions we had in these community of practice meetings.

CTOs at Work contains valuable information for experienced CTOs, in their own words, unfiltered, and uninterpreted not spun to fit the agenda of some researcher or consultant pedaling the panacea du jour. This book is fascinating, inspiring, sometimes surprising and an invaluable resource for CTOs, CIOs, anyone working for these executives or anyone who wants to be a CTO or CIO one day. *CTOs at Work* is not a text book, yet I think it is as valuable as any CTO/CIO text book that professors use in their courses. In fact, it probably should be supplemental reading for any technology management course.

—Phillip A. Laplante
Professor of Software Engineering
Pennsylvania State University

About the Authors

Scott Donaldson has more than 30 years of experience managing complex programs (ranging from 10's of millions to 100's of millions); expertise in systems development, process improvement, and technical cultural change. He is a Senior Vice President for Science Applications International Corporation (SAIC) and is the Chief Technology Officer (CTO) for its multi-billion dollar Health, Energy and Civilian Solutions Group.

He teaches graduate courses in software engineering, software process improvement, and information technology at Johns Hopkins University, Whiting School of Engineering. Johns Hopkins honored him in 2009 with an Excellence in Teaching Award. He has a B.S., Operations Research from the United States Naval Academy and a M.S., Systems Management from the University of Southern California.

Mr. Donaldson co-authored the software engineering books *Successful Software Development: Making It Happen*, Prentice Hall PTR, 2nd Edition; *Successful Software Development: Study Guide*, Prentice Hall PTR; and *Cultivating Successful Software Development: A Practitioner's View*, Prentice Hall PTR. He has contributed to the *Encyclopedia of Software Engineering: Project Management—Success Factors*, CRC Press and the *Handbook of Software Quality Assurance: Software Configuration Management—A Practical Look*, 3rd Edition.

Dr. Stanley Siegel has more than 35 years of progressive experience as a systems engineer, mathematician and computer specialist. He started his career with the U.S. Government in the Department of Commerce and then the Department of Defense. After his government service, he was with Grumman for 15 years and Science Applications International Corporation (SAIC) for 20 years. He helped SAIC grow to a $11 Billion leader in scientific, engineering and technical solutions by helping win hundreds of millions of dollars of new business.

He earned a nuclear physics doctorate from Rutgers University. Physicists solve problems. He has served as a senior technical advisor and director on a wide spectrum of projects in areas such as software engineering methodology assessment, software requirements analysis, software testing and quality assurance, mathematical support for software-algorithm development, and technology assessment.

He has taught graduate courses since the mid 1990s. He teaches both in-class and online software systems engineering courses at the Johns Hopkins University Whiting School of Engineering. Johns Hopkins honored him in 2009 with an Excellence in Teaching Award.

Dr. Siegel has co-authored four software engineering books including the seminal software engineering textbook *Software Configuration Management: An Investment in Product Integrity*, Prentice Hall PTR. He has contributed to a number of books including the *Encyclopedia of Software Engineering: Project Management—Success Factors*, CRC Press and the *Handbook of Software Quality Assurance: Software Configuration Management—A Practical Look*.

 **Gary Donaldson** has more than 35 years experience in executive, program, project and consultant leadership positions across federal, state, DoD, commercial, university-affiliated, health care, non-profit, and technology sectors, including 10 years with SAIC. His expertise is strategic organizational change, user-adoption, and workforce performance improvement. Mr. Donaldson served as graduate faculty at Johns Hopkins University, School of Professional Studies in Business and Education, and consultant faculty to numerous universities throughout the United States. He holds Masters Degrees from Boston College and American University with a combined focus in organizational behavior, workplace learning, and performance improvement.

Mr. Donaldson is author of "Creating and Adding Value: Redefining the Organization", in Quality Performance in Human Services: Leadership, Values and Vision (G. Gardner & S. Nadler, eds.), Baltimore: Paul H. Brookes Publishing; "Work Programs for Enhancing Cognitive Performance Components," in Work Practice: International Perspectives (Jacobs & Pratt, eds.), Oxford: Butterworth Heinemann; and Toward Supported Employment: A Process Guide for Planned Change (Gardner, J., Chapman, M., Donaldson, G., Jacobson, S), Baltimore: Paul H. Brookes Publishing.

Acknowledgments

We thank Jeff Pepper for proposing this project to us. We also thank him for his prodigious efforts down the homestretch of this project.

We thank Jessica Belanger, Rita Fernando, and Mary Sudul for helping to produce the book.

We thank Joe Craver of Science Applications International Corporation for encouraging us and supporting our work on this project.

We thank Leadership Maryland, Leadership Montgomery County Maryland, and William Ballard, President of Location Age Geographic Information and Technology for supporting our efforts to identify key leaders in the local technology community.

We thank Jack Speer, newscaster and journalist for National Public Radio (NPR), for providing guidance on effective interviewing strategies and techniques.

We thank Mike Starling, Executive Director of NPR Labs, for introducing us to the Vice President of Technology Operations and Broadcast Engineering.

We thank David Wright, software engineer, for making our interview possible with the Gerson-Lehrman Group while we were on a journey half-way around the world.

We thank Phillip Laplante, Professor of Software Engineering, Pennsylvania State University, for graciously agreeing to write the book's foreword.

We thank our family and friends for their encouragement and support.

Finally, we thank the interviewees for taking time from their busy schedules to give us insight into their day-job worlds.

Introduction

CTOs at Work is a series of interviews from many leading Chief Technology Officers from an array of companies. Their perspectives on their roles, and most often the job itself, vary considerably from industry to industry. These candid discussions will give the reader a unique glimpse at how technology plays a role in the company and how the company makes its decisions, investments, and the software that drives every aspect of the business.

The interviewees talk about how they tackle their day-to-day CTO work. They explain what their role is in their organization. They provide insight into how they interact with internal business units to assure that the organization leverages:

- Investments
- Technologies
- Teamwork

They detail how they help automate, integrate, and drive business growth (and profit) through innovative technologies that align with business needs. They provide insight into how they allocate investments and manage projects. They explain how they assess technologies in the near-term, mid-term, and far-term. Finally, you will hear what keeps them up at night.

The interview population comes from the following industries:

- Science and Applied Technology
- Commercial Software Products
- Energy Research and Development
- Defense Research and Development
- Intelligence Community Consulting
- Commercial Energy Products
- Public Broadcasting
- Information Technology Research and Advisory Consulting
- Worldwide eBook Publishing
- Image Search Technology

- Investment and Advisory Consulting
- Pharmaceutical Information Technology.

The CTOs interviewed work for companies that span the size spectrum from a dozen employees to thousands of employees. The CTO role varied across industries. One thing they had in common is they all drive their organizations efforts to compete in a competitive, innovative yet cost-effective manner.

There is no one way to define the CTO role. They are managers, researchers, visionaries, entrepreneurs, developers, deployers, project leaders, advisors, and administrators all rolled into one. However, there are similarities and overlaps among these characteristics; the primary one being that they are innovators who look to meet the needs of their customers through the use of the technologies they control.

> *Please accept our invitation to meet these CTOs who enable their businesses through technology.*

Amy Alving

SAIC

Amy Alving, Ph.D., is the CTO and senior vice president at Science Applications International Corporation (SAIC). She is responsible for the creation, communication, and implementation of SAIC's technical and scientific vision and strategy.

Alving joined SAIC in 2005 as CTO for the Engineering, Training and Logistics Group and later served as corporate Chief Scientist. Prior to joining SAIC, Alving was the director of the Special Projects Office at DARPA. In this role, she was responsible for strategic planning, operations, finance, security, program development and execution.

Alving was a White House Fellow (1997-98) serving at the Department of Commerce. Prior to that, she was an associate professor of aerospace engineering at the University of Minnesota.

She serves on the Board of Directors for Pall Corporation and, previously, the Fannie and John Hertz Foundation. She is also a member of the Georgia Institute of Technology Advisory Board and has been a member or advisor to the Naval Research Advisory Committee, Army Science Board, Defense Science Board, and National Academies studies. She is a member of the Council on Foreign Relations.

Alving has a B.S. in mechanical engineering from Stanford University and a Ph.D. in mechanical and aerospace engineering from Princeton University. She also carried out post-doctoral research in Berlin, Germany.

Siegel: Amy, we'd like to begin with your journey to CTO, and it's my understanding that you have multiple technical degrees. The question is, given when you went to school, what motivated you to develop a career in science and technology because at that time, if memory serves me correctly, there was a glass ceiling for women regarding getting into science and technology?

Alving: I am a very curious person. I like to know how the world works. I didn't actually know what engineers did growing up because my whole family was in medicine. So I knew a lot about what physicians did. We talked about that at the dinner table. When I got to college, I actually started in physics because I like basic science and stayed a physics major for a little over a year while I figured out what I really wanted to do. I wound up in engineering because I decided that, although I like physics, I like the discipline of it, what I really wanted to do was solve problems. Physics is an important element of that, but it's a little bit more upstream than where most of our practical problems are. So I wound up in engineering.

I got my bachelor's at Stanford. The summer between my junior and senior years of college, I went to work in industry as an intern at a company that has since been acquired and merged and changed its name, but even then it was a large aerospace engineering company. I knew I was just there for the summer, so I wasn't making career decisions based on what my summer job was, but I watched what the people with bachelor's degrees did. They seemed to be working on very small pieces of somebody else's problem, and they didn't get access to the big picture. I found it hard to be interested in that, and so I decided to go on and get a Ph.D. I didn't know in particular what I was getting into. At Princeton, I got my Ph.D. in mechanical and aerospace engineering, and then I needed to decide what to do after that because I had kind of used up my earlier career decision.

I decided to do a postdoc overseas to see the world and learn about other cultures. It's always a broadening experience to step out of your comfort zone. I didn't speak German when I decided to do my postdoc at the Technical University in Berlin. On the one hand, that might seem very reckless, but on the other hand, in the technical community—the Europeans certainly, and pretty much around the world—the professionals speak English. So I was pretty fortunate and could get along just fine. I learned a lot during my postdoc. I took ownership of a technical investigation and we made some advances and discoveries. That was very rewarding. In my personal life, I learned German, which was, of course, a great benefit from living overseas. Also on a personal level, it was an exciting time to be in Germany. I started out in West Germany and by the time I left, a couple of years later, I was in Germany because the Iron Curtain had come down. I had started in West Berlin and then Berlin unified. So it was certainly a very interesting time from a geopolitical perspective. It was also important to live in a different culture. Germany, being part of Western Europe, in some ways is very similar to the United States, but it's still not the same. I really gained an appreciation for the importance of culture, the differences and similarities. I gained an appreciation for the experience of people who move to another country. There's always a transition into a new culture, and I'm glad I got the chance to understand that better.

Siegel: Let's switch gears now and go to your career as an associate professor at the University of Minnesota.

Alving: I started as an assistant professor on the tenure track, and I worked my way up. The environment was very familiar to me, because I had spent my whole life in an academic environment. So, in that sense, it was very comfortable. What was really valuable from that experience is the ability to go really deep in a particular technical area, to create new knowledge that, by definition, nobody has known before. You're adding to the amount of wisdom, so to speak, in the world. The intellectual rigor of academia is extraordinary. I really value the way it prizes intellectual integrity—the process of peer review, transparency around experiments and results, the way the data are analyzed and deciding what you can and can't conclude based on the evidence... That whole level of discipline associated with the pursuit of truth is extraordinary. So, to your question: I got tenure, with the rank of associate professor. And I enjoyed that.

In my last few years of being an academic, I was actually starting to branch out. I valued the depth that academics afforded, but I also had the opportunity to work with and then later join the Army Science Board, which is one of the scientific advisory boards of the Defense Department. It advises the secretary of the Army and the senior leaders in the Army about how technology can help or may not be able to help address some very important real-world issues that the Army or the Defense Department is facing. What I liked there was almost just the opposite, that it was very broad and you have to deal with the world the way it is. You can't carve off just a narrow slice that you're going to pursue. You have to deal with the whole world in all its complexity. And you're working on real-world problems that matter.

Siegel: But what was the spark that caused you to leave the university environment?

Alving: So at that point, I hadn't left. I still was a faculty member at the University of Minnesota. Service is one of the three components of an academic role, and in that capacity I was working with the Army Science Board. I was broadening my experiences, my contacts, my perspectives, but I was a full-time professor. In fact, at the next step of my career, when I became a White House Fellow, I still did not leave the university permanently. I went on academic leave, so I was not at the university, but I still had the tenured position. I decided to become a White House Fellow because some very good friends put it on my radar screen and it sounded great! The program is designed to allow people who are not part of the government to spend a one-year term sitting at the very highest levels of government as a special assistant to a Cabinet secretary or senior people in the Executive Office of the president. I went through the application process and was fortunate enough to be selected. What I liked about the White House Fellows program, again, is that it's very broadening. It puts you into a completely different venue, by design well out of the comfort zone. I served as the special assistant to the deputy secretary of Commerce and got to work with him on all sorts of long-term, far-reaching policies on things that affect everyday life. It was a fascinating view of things that have a technology component in them, but were much broader than just technology per se.

Siegel: So that provided you a way to transition into the real world then?

Alving: Well, "real" is in the eye of the beholder. But it was definitely broadening. For example, at the time Commerce was heavily involved in the policy of opening up satellite imaging to commercial providers. The discussions were about shutter control, and were we risking our national security, and how did that balance against the commercial potential? Those decisions have now played out. Now we have commercial mapping industries, like Google Maps that we all take for granted. We were working on things that have a technology component, like satellite technology, like imaging, etc., but they also have a much broader play.

We were also just starting up the decennial census. Every 10 years Commerce is responsible for trying to count every person in the United States. That's mandated by the Constitution, and it's a really hard job. It's also something that by definition happens only periodically. So there's always a core census capability in Commerce, but every 10 years it has to ramp up suddenly for the largest peacetime mobilization the country does. I was fortunate enough to be working for the deputy secretary of Commerce when he was just starting to ramp up, figuring out how we were going to count all of the people in the country, including those who don't trust the government, don't want to be counted, or couldn't be bothered to turn in their census form. This is why it's such a difficult undertaking. If everybody responded to the mail-in form, it wouldn't be so hard. Census results affect everything from where Congressional lines are drawn to where schools and hospitals are built and so forth. There are technical issues around the census, especially around statistical techniques for counting large populations, but there are also very broad policy implications. What I found fascinating was how things that have a technology core have much broader impact than simply the technology element. That's what I had hoped to get out of being a White House Fellow, and, in fact, I had a great experience doing that. But at that point I was still on leave.

Siegel: From the university?

Alving: Yes. The White House Fellowship is a one-year term, and after you leave the fellowship, you either go back to what you were doing or you do something else. As much as I had loved the experience working at Commerce, I wanted to work in the government with more of a technology-centered focus. I ended up being the deputy director of one of the offices of DARPA (Defense Advanced Research Projects Agency), which, of course, is a heavily technology-oriented organization. I eventually rose to become the director of the office. So, Stan, to answer your question, after I had been at DARPA for one year, I left the University of Minnesota, and the reason for that in some ways was very tactical. At a university, when you're tenured, you can go on leave for two years without too much difficulty. But after that time, they either want you to come back and engage in research and teaching, or they want you to give up the tenure seat. And so I decided that I was having such a great time at DARPA that I gave up my tenured position at the university and remained at DARPA. I had been there for a year when I made that decision.

Siegel: Well, that really showed some guts to leave the comfort of the university environment, which is lifetime employment.

Alving: That's an interesting point, and this was very much a topic of conversation as I was going through tenure. I've always viewed tenure as being about academic freedom, and lifetime job security happens to be the means to guarantee academic freedom. Around that time, there were conversations at the University of Minnesota and other universities about how to make sure that lifetime job security didn't turn into people being less than dynamic and energetic about their jobs. But for me, I didn't have to struggle with the job security part because that wasn't, in my mind, the purpose of tenure. And anyway, I was having so much fun at DARPA that it just seemed like a natural decision. I've never regretted giving up tenure, although certainly I had some very good colleagues and enjoyed the environment at the University of Minnesota. But, you know, I was giving it up for other things that were also very good.

Siegel: Can we roll the videotape forward a little now and talk about the transition from a research environment to the SAIC scientific engineering and technology environment? What caused you to make that shift?

Alving: At DARPA, the intention is to bring in the technical leaders – the office directors, program managers, and agency directors—temporarily, have them spend a few years and then leave. You know, a little secret: by the time I left DARPA, I had the equivalent of tenure in the government. I was a career SES (Senior Executive Service), but again, I didn't view the administrative element that said I could stay there forever as determining my career. Part of what really makes DARPA special is that it brings in technical people, gives them a chance to make a difference, and then lets them move on to something else. Even though I had a permission slip to stay in the government forever, that was not my focus. I was interested in the broadening aspect. I'd been in academia and I'd been in government. There are many other roles I could do in either, but my heart was really in working in the private sector, and in particular, the defense industry since that's where I felt I had the most to offer. What I liked about SAIC was what I now know, internally, we call our "entrepreneurial culture." As a government customer I had always seen SAIC come to DARPA with a lot of good ideas. SAIC took those ideas and had a disciplined process for turning them into solutions. And they had integrity. They really cared about solving the problem, not just about getting the contract. So I found those very attractive characteristics. I talked to a number of different potential employers, but in the end, I decided to come to SAIC fundamentally for those reasons.

Siegel: Okay, so as a segue to where you are now, was there a time when you decided that you wanted to be a CTO?

Alving: The short answer is no, and I have to say that my career path has had a couple of stages to it, but it has never had a clear definition from me of, "First, I want to do this, and then I want to do that, and then X amount of time later do something else." I try to do the best job I can at what I'm doing, and then pick opportunities as they come along that offer some broadening experience, that give me a chance to use the skills I've developed in a way that brings value, and in return, offer me the opportunity to do something different. So I was not looking for a CTO role per se. Once I decided that I wanted to work in industry, I wanted to be in a position that had as broad a spectrum of technologies and problems as possible. To me that's been the constant as I've moved from one role to another, going from very narrow and very deep—and being narrow is what allows you to be very deep—into ever-broader areas, looking at more challenging problems.

Siegel: Along that path, did you have mentors who helped you shape your career?

Alving: I did. For instance, Wilson Talley was an early mentor, and he called me one day to announce without preamble, "Amy, you need to become a White House Fellow." That was the first I ever heard of the White House Fellows. Over time, he and other former Fellows told me about the program. None of them had the power to make me a Fellow, but they did have the power to open my eyes about what was possible, to help me set goals for myself and to think about how to reach them. That's why mentors are so powerful in a young person's career, because they share perspectives and expand horizons.

When I became an assistant professor, in my first grown-up job so to speak, I had another mentor who was the associate dean of the college. He was extremely helpful to me in understanding, as an assistant professor, what's important and what's not. He gave me some advice that I think he gave to a number of high-achieving people. He said, "You have to learn to say no sometimes. You can't say yes to everything you're asked to do." He meant that you have to be selective about your focus, that you have to channel your energy into a handful of things where you're committed to making a difference. Because otherwise you won't get anything done.

I had other mentors. For example, I ended up at DARPA because another mentor was coming in to be Director, Defense Research and Engineering, which is the position that DARPA reports to. He suggested that after I left my White House Fellowship, DARPA might be a good fit. When I was looking for jobs in industry, I talked to other mentors about having a resume that resonates within industry or about specific job opportunities. So I haven't had one single mentor; I have had a number of people who have played different roles at different times and were really key to helping find and recognize opportunities and make the right decisions.

Siegel: Did that mentor group also include your parents?

Alving: Definitely. Since I was a kid, my dad played an important role in the way I look at the world. He implicitly conveyed a belief that the world makes sense and it's up to us to try to understand how it works—especially on the physics and technology side, maybe a little less so when you get to human nature. He was a key person in developing my inquisitive nature. I tend to learn by asking questions, building out a mental model of the world, and I know I got that from him because people tell me that. When you're four years old, you don't understand what's shaping you, but in retrospect, I realize he was really a critical factor.

And my mom just had a passion and commitment for getting stuff done. She was tenacious, and some of that rubbed off on me.

Siegel: So just before we talk about your day-to-day job, we'd like to ask you what you enjoyed most in the various positions along your career path?

Alving: I got different things out of each position. As I said, out of the academic positions, I got the joy of learning new things that nobody else had figured out yet, the time and the expectation to pursue intellectual rigor, to really know what's right and what's wrong and to spend time sorting it out. In the government jobs, I enjoyed the connection between very high-level policy decisions and things that affect people's lives every day. And in the CTO role here at SAIC, again, in a similar vein, it's about how the company's strategic decisions end up affecting the direction of the company and the solutions we can deliver to our customers.

Siegel: Let's talk about your real-world day-to-day job at SAIC. What's a typical day? What are your main responsibilities, whom do you report to, and who reports to you?

Alving: Okay, I'll spend some time talking about what I do, but I probably can't describe a typical day.

S. Donaldson: There are no typical days.

Alving: Right! I report to the CEO. As far as who reports to me, I have a small staff, but I also have, throughout the company, a network of CTOs at several levels, from the groups down to the business units and sometimes, depending on how strong the technology focus is within an organization, there may be CTOs at further subdivisions. All the CTOs together play related roles, although each is a little bit different depending on the level. As the Corporate CTO, I spend a lot of time on the strategy. In particular, I work with the Group CTOs as part of our strategic planning process, the integrated business planning process, or IBPP. It takes a very disciplined approach to identifying the strategic directions for the company. Once those strategic directions are identified, then we as CTOs need to figure out what that really means? What are the technology imperatives? What technologies do we need to own, or be masters of, or where do we need to work with others if we want to execute that strategy? Then we assess where we stand today, relative to those aspirations. That defines the gaps, and we have to figure out how we are going to fill the gaps, whether it's by hiring or technology development or teaming agreements or acquisitions or whatever the right tactic may be. The group CTOs tend to be strong leaders in this part of the cycle. The answers to these questions fold into the annual operating plan, which includes things like investment portfolios for technology development, a strategic roadmap of potential acquisition targets, etc., etc. And then as the fiscal year begins, the plans shift into execution and the business unit CTOs play a lead role for their parts of the business.

As execution issues start to cross business units, the groups will be involved. As they start to cross groups, then the corporate CTO will be involved. So, for example, I would be directly involved with an acquisition if it's of strategic importance across the company. For smaller acquisitions, the chief technology officers at the appropriate levels are more involved in doing the due diligence, looking at the technology, and so on. At my level as the corporate chief technology officer, in the spectrum from strategy to execution, I spend a lot more of my time on the strategy. As you go through the levels of the organization, the CTOs shift the mix of how they spend their time. Some of the CTOs, as you go down in the organization, are not full-time CTOs. They may be on direct jobs in some cases, or they may wear a couple of hats, doing a mix of technology, strategy, and business development for their part of the organization. So there really is not a one-size-fits-all solution in the company, because this is not a one-size-fits-all place. As you know, it's a very complex organization. We do lots of things for lots of different customers.

S. Donaldson: And it reflects in part, too, the collegial nature of an academic setting, because sometimes you have to get very deep and narrow.

Alving: Right.

S. Donaldson: Fortunately, there are places where you can go to do that.

Alving: So that brings me to another key role of the CTOs, and, again, this plays out differently at different levels. And that is synchronizing the technology, both the technology development efforts, and the technology capabilities we already have, synchronizing those across the different parts of the company. So, for instance, if we have technology that exists in one part of the company that is needed by a customer served by another part of the company, the CTO network is critical in making sure that we get that capability transferred from point A to point B. We have a strong focus on collaboration within the company. We recognize that the simple act of what we call "cross-selling," taking something we've developed for one customer or one market and selling it to a different customer or a different market, is a really important way to leverage one of SAIC's strengths. That strength is our incredible breadth of technologies, of capabilities, etc. So the CTOs have to be involved in recognizing what technologies exist and what may be useful to others.

Siegel: That's a very good point.

Alving: Another area where the technologists are important is in developing new solutions that rely on the expertise of many different parts of the company. In that case it's the CTOs who recognize who has what capabilities, what are the gaps, and who can stitch it all together into a solution. An example of that is what we're doing in the next generation of information technology and in particular what we're doing in designing, developing, building, and instantiating a secure private cloud. These are fundamentally technology issues, and the expertise to do that comes from across the company. The CTOs are figuring out what that solution should look like, where our technical capabilities are, and what we need to do in terms of development to actually instantiate that. And so the CTOs, again, play a really important role in connecting our aspirations to what we're actually producing today.

Siegel: Okay, now you've been a CTO at SAIC for how many years?

Alving: For about four years.

Siegel: How does your role during that period of time match with the expectations you had before coming on board?

Alving: I'd say it's consistent with it, but doing the job now day-to-day, I have a much better understanding of what the job really is. You asked: is it management, administrative, communication? Yeah, it's all of those things. In fact, I like to tell technologists that life is a lot more about communication than many of us who were raised doing problem sets necessarily appreciate. You can't do management—or technology—without being a good communicator; it's an undervalued skill. It's critical, for instance, to be able to talk across the company, to bring networks together, to get people speaking in the same language, understanding the same problem, not talking past each other. Communication is one of the most important skills. It's not what we think of as a core for technologists, but I think that's a mistake.

Siegel: When you came on board to take this position, was this collaboration role and this ability to facilitate communication part of the job description?

Alving: SAIC has been on a journey about collaboration. Historically our company was maybe not as integrated as it is today. So over the last several years, we've really been focused on how we do a better job of collaboration within the company. I think we've been making great strides there. We've changed the mindset, we've changed the expectations of our leaders, and people have seen the benefit of that. So I think we're a much more collaborative organization than we've been in the past. We're also changing some of our internal processes. For example, one of the ways I work with the CIO is on information technology systems that allow us to do a better job of sharing our electronic documents internally. In the outside world we have things like Facebook and so forth. Those are great, but they're not appropriate for a company that not only has proprietary data but also has customer data that's very sensitive and not everybody within the company is allowed to see everything that people have. So we have to be very thoughtful about the way we collaborate and share electronic documents. As the CTO, I'm the executive sponsor of our initiative to do a better job of spreading internal awareness about our broad capabilities. I partner with our CIO, who's converting our IT systems to allow us to share documents within the constraints that are appropriate to an enterprise as complex as SAIC.

S. Donaldson: In the four years that you've had this role, there's a lot of change and the CTO role has evolved. It's becoming more visible in the organization. Do you see a continuation of that as SAIC moves forward and gets more disciplined in the business planning process, investment processes, and linking those processes together going forward?

Alving: I do see that role as becoming, as you say, more visible and more integrated. Just the fact that we have a clearly defined planning process means that the opportunities for engagement are very well defined and that engagement by the CTOs is a necessary thing to keep that process moving along. SAIC has been on a journey throughout its existence. Early on it was a number of essentially small organizations that each grew up locally around a customer, solving that customer's needs, and doing an excellent job of that. As the company grew in scale, those independent organizations started to bump into each other and merge, and now that we are such a large company, we're operating differently. Articulating a strategic direction and having the technology to back it up resonates within a company focused on science applications. These things are critical to our future, so it's an exciting time to be a CTO.

Siegel: Despite all of the organization change we have been discussing, SAIC's tag line says "From Science to Solutions." Do you feel that that accurately portrays what SAIC is trying to provide? How does the CTO position help the company make the transition from science to solutions?

Alving: I interpret the tagline in perhaps a slightly different way than some people. "From Science to Solutions," doesn't necessarily mean that SAIC starts with the science, does the science, takes it through ever-increasing levels of maturity, and eventually brings it into a solution. We do that sometimes, but I think we're actually much stronger when SAIC thinks about all sources of science and technology invention and figures out, "How do we turn those inventions into solutions?" Those inventions may come from within SAIC; they may come from technology teammates in small companies;

they may come from big companies; they may come from universities. And that's why the CTO is the executive sponsor of our university relations program. We're looking for relationships with universities in part because they're one of the great sources of technology development, and we can help turn those inventions into innovations, into solutions. So the CTOs should be looking at all sources of invention, all sources of new technology, and figuring out how to couple it with another element of our secret sauce: our deep mission or domain expertise. So we're not just technologists inventing a new widget and trying to make people care about it. We're looking at the problems within a mission area, using our domain understanding of how things actually work in that area, looking at inventions, whether they're SAIC-invented or invented elsewhere, and figuring out, "How do we bring those together using a disciplined process to actually make a solution?" And to me, that's what we mean by "From Science to Solutions."

Siegel: Okay, could you illustrate those points with a collaboration example?

Alving: A good example is what we're doing in health information technology. To us, the solution to that problem is not an IT solution on its own. You also have to understand the domain that you're working in. You have to understand why electronic medical records or electronic health records are so complex. You have to understand the medical language and codes that exist in those electronic health records and the multiple translations from one language to another language in order to solve that problem. We were the first, for instance, to connect the DoD (Department of Defense) electronic medical records to the VA (Veterans Administration) medical records and make them talk to each other. We think not just about an IT problem, we think not just about a medical language problem, we think not just about an electronic records problem… We think about all of those things at the same time, as well as the service-oriented architecture to connect those two systems in a flexible and scalable way. So, again, to get to the solution, you need the technology as well as mission domain understanding and a disciplined process to bring it all together. The CTOs are critical to making all of that happen.

Siegel: What makes SAIC different from the competition, without revealing any company secrets here?

Alving: I think a couple of things make SAIC different. One I just talked about is the intersection of deep technical knowledge with domain and mission understanding, because you can't solve problems, you can't get to the best solutions, having just one or the other. Otherwise, you turn into a technology looking for a problem or a problem with no good way to solve it. Actually, I draw a lot of analogies there to my work at DARPA. It was much the same thing. To invent new programs at DARPA, in my mind, you need to be working on a problem that really matters, understanding all of the constraints and boundaries that go along with that problem, and you have to have an idea about technologies that could solve that problem. In industry, it's really the same problem, viewed a little bit differently. What makes SAIC so capable is that it has in-house expertise in both that deep technical knowledge over a broad set of different areas, and that domain expertise so that we understand, "What problem are we really trying to solve?"

I would say that another important aspect of SAIC is that we work at the intersection of the physical and the information domains. We have expertise in both, and we really shine when the solution requires both because that dual expertise is pretty rare. There are IT companies; there are physics-based companies. We really have both at scale. For example, in the ISR (intelligence, surveillance and reconnaissance) domain, we produce sensors that generate the bits, transfer those bits through networks, wireless or wired, convert the bits into data, into knowledge, and into decisions through the processing, exploitation, and dissemination chain. With a teammate we developed a brand-new type of biological sensor that we called "TIGER" (Threat ID through Genetic Evaluation of Risk). That technology won *The Wall Street Journal* "gold" Technology Innovation Award in 2009 for the best invention of the year. It relies on a combination of advanced biotech hardware with groundbreaking bio-informatics techniques that were based on our radar signal processing expertise. Information from a sensor like that can feed into our epidemiology and disease tracking work. That's an example of a sensor at the front end through information flow at the back end. In the cyber security domain, our subsidiary, CloudShield, has a very special piece of hardware that enables real-time, deep packet inspection of network traffic at network line speeds, and that allows you to find cyber threats embedded in the traffic. We build those physical devices into information architectures and services that allow information gathered from a number of different sources and fed back in real time to give a much more proactive, forward-leaning cyber security posture. So in a lot of different examples, part of what makes SAIC unique is that we operate at this intersection between the physical and the information.

Siegel: Okay, so given that uniqueness of SAIC, where do you look to recruit to make those things happen?

Alving: Recruiting happens all over the place. Traditionally, the company recruited by luring away the best and the brightest from other companies.

S. Donaldson: Or each other.

Alving: That didn't grow the enterprise. [Laughter.]

S. Donaldson: That's true.

Alving: Recruiting away from other companies is not a sufficient source of talent moving into the future, in part because we've gotten to be so large that we're now an attractive target for others to recruit from, so that's at best a zero-sum game. But also, if you want to maintain freshness in technology, you've got to make sure you're not only talking to the experienced technologists, but, in fact, you're recruiting those with the freshest ideas, the kids coming out of school, who have been living and breathing social networking, mobile technologies, etc., since they could talk. So, over time, we've been increasing our emphasis on universities. Earlier I mentioned that we look to universities as an important source of technology invention, to make sure we're working with some of the smartest people out there and developing new solutions for our customers. We're also working with universities for recruiting. Over the years, we had a thin stream of students coming in from the universities, but we're recommitting at the enterprise level to really increase that pipeline because we think it's important for our growth, not only in terms of sheer numbers, but also in terms of the diversity of thoughts and ideas and experiences that come with recruiting straight out of college and graduate school.

Siegel: Switching topics slightly, what do you see as important issues confronting your customers today and also in the future?

Alving: Certainly money is a concern, whether it's the decreasing budgets or the economy. I think we all recognize that our customers will be trying to do more with less in the future, and we have to help them be successful with that. So as we look at developing solutions, we're very conscious of the cost-effectiveness of the solutions. For defense customers, who are our biggest customers today, they face a lot of changes in force structure, in mission, in their own expectations as we come back from Afghanistan and Iraq. We've got a lot of equipment that was tailored to those particular conflicts. We bought that equipment very quickly, so we didn't have the usual processes in place to figure out how to sustain it and maintain it and figure out how it fits in the bigger picture. So the Defense Department has a number of challenges.

I would say for all of our customers and all of us as individuals, we're facing an information deluge, sometimes called a "data tsunami." That's true in the ISR realm, where there's a lot more data being generated than people can look at very carefully. But it's true in every other realm, as well. It's true in the health world. As we transition to electronic medical records, that will cause a data tsunami in the medical community. This will be a good thing in the end, but first our customers are going to have to learn how to deal with that data deluge. The same thing is happening in the energy domain. Think about the smart grid. I call the smart grid "social networking for the power grid" because it's got a lot of distributed sensors networked together, it's going to be information-aware, sending a lot of data back and forth, it's going to use real-time data to make decisions, whether at a central command and control level about which assets and resources to bring online or offline or decisions made by consumers about when to turn on their appliances, whether to buy an electric vehicle, and if so, when and where they recharge it, and so on. This information deluge is facing customers in different ways, but it's here to stay.

And related to all that data is the question of cyber security. People are starting to become aware that it's an issue. We haven't yet seen the cyber security "Pearl Harbor," a single event that fundamentally changes people's perspective. But, on the other hand, we see lots of evidence in a lot of different ways that cyber security is a problem that we haven't sufficiently solved, and it affects all customers in all domains. It affects all of us.

Siegel: How do you help the customers realize that these are things that they have to be worried about as an entrée to generating new business?

Alving: Thought leadership is an important piece of that. We do a lot of educating of the customer. But, frankly, nobody likes to just be told they should be really scared without being offered something to do about it. And on the other hand, if we offer them a solution that they don't think is needed, then that's not going to resonate either. So when we talk to customers, we talk to them about as much as we can, given what the classification level is, about what the threat is, and we also talk to them about what potential solutions are. We try to come to the table with some good news in addition to the bad news. We talk at conferences and discuss, as appropriate for the forum, both why the challenges are real and, again, provide some thoughts about how people might address the problem.

Siegel: Okay, so to follow up with that, how does SAIC monitor and assess evolving technologies to identify potential applications for expanding business opportunities, products, or services?

Alving: SAIC is so broad that that's really a contact sport; there are a lot of people involved in it. Nuclear phenomenology is where we got our start many decades ago, and now we cover a huge range of technologies—signal processing, data analytics, neurological and behavioral science, biometrics, cancer, geospatial information, image analysis, positioning including GPS

(Global Positioning System), language translation, high-energy lasers, architectural engineering for complex processing plants, energy efficiency, environmental cleanup… and that's just a piece of it! There's no single, go-to source for innovations or for customers. We have a breadth of technology experts in so many different areas. Those people are out there every day not only working in those fields, but making contacts with their peers in other companies, in universities, etc., and staying abreast of what's going on. So the trick is how do we take that widely distributed set of knowledge and information gathering and connect it in a meaningful way at the enterprise level, so that we're not all running off in different directions. And that gets back to the integrated business planning process, which provides the strategic thought about what direction we're going in and how we get there. That's why the CTOs are so important in that process, because they're the connection between that local, individual technology perspective on where things are going and what it might mean to the company. That needs to feed back into a larger discussion to identify those things across the enterprise that are going to be important so that, for those enterprise-wide things, we can make the big bets and make sure that they get executed. So, again, the CTOs as a network are important to providing that connectivity, from the frontlines of the individual technologies and innovation areas all the way up to the strategic direction of the company.

Siegel: Okay, let's shift gears. Are there any big technology projects on the horizon now?

Alving: One area of focus is on the cloud. When we look at the transformation that's taking place in cloud, we recognize there's a lot of hype. People have been talking about cloud for a couple of years now, and it's gone through its hype cycle and it sort of remains all things to all people. Then people say, "Wait, does it really mean anything to me?" There's no doubt the cloud is coming, for all the reasons that people talk about, including the financial imperative, because it's part of the solution to the budget issues that people are facing: we need a different paradigm for who owns, who operates, and who uses IT, and that's what the cloud offers. It's coming, but for our customers, national security customers and other customers with very sensitive data, we have to address the security question, the data integrity question, both for data at rest and for data on the move. We have to make sure the systems in the cloud are connected in a way that's secure.

So that's one of our enterprise priorities, to make sure that we have an offering there that's unique and capable because, until our customers start to hear a solution they believe is going to satisfy their security requirements, they're not going to move very much to the cloud. We believe that the right answer, again, lies at the intersection between the physical and the information. You cannot solve this problem only by new protocols or new software or new after-the-fact fixes. We believe that there is a hardware component of this, and so we're working with our CloudShield folks to make sure that we get that hardware component right. Our goal is to make sure that a cloud doesn't have to operate either as an efficient cloud or a secure cloud, but, in fact, we can have the efficiencies of the cloud and security at the same time. And here, again, our deep mission experience in protecting highly classified information is critical in our ability to develop these solutions.

Siegel: Let's talk now about technology investments. You mentioned CloudShield. Are there other examples that illustrate how SAIC invests in technology?

Alving: We invest in technology in a couple of ways. We do acquisitions. For example, we did an acquisition of CloudShield. We did an acquisition around the language expertise that I mentioned. But we also do a lot of organic investment. In fact, our CEO believes that organic investment has the highest return on investment, and so we've been making a big push over the last couple of years to increase our investment levels. Since I took over as the CTO, our investments have been rising. The CEO at the time had been putting an emphasis on internal research and development (IRAD) funding. We are on a path towards quadrupling our investment in less than a decade.

We also invest in our people. For example, five years ago there weren't a lot of people who had cyber security degrees or the deep training that you really need to develop cyber security solutions. SAIC had not been investing much in that. Now we're investing with university allies to help develop new courses and new degree programs in cyber security. We've been hiring out of those programs just as fast as people are coming out. We're also investing in people we already have within SAIC to get them training and qualifications in cyber security.

So we really look at a mix of different types of investments, and that gets back to this strategic planning process, identifying the gaps and then figuring out the best ways to fill them.

S. Donaldson: As you think through the breadth of the company, its challenges, issues, etc., what keeps you up at night?

Alving: Well, not much. I mean, honestly.

S. Donaldson: You leave work at work?

Alving: Well, yeah, as much as I can. But when I think about that question, I think about something at the national level. I don't know if that's of interest to you...?

S. Donaldson: Yeah.

Alving: It's the question of what identity means in the 21st century. If you think about discussions about cyber security and privacy, all of that implies that you're keeping private what should be private and allowing to be public what should be public. Security is, in part, helping make private data secure at the same time that you're making public data public. That implies that we have a construct for what is private and what is public that comes from an understanding of what defines an individual's identity, and who owns that. I believe we need a more sophisticated construct of identity for the 21st century, and it probably needs to be not monolithic, but nuanced with various facets for different purposes and different types of information. In the 1970s, identity was about physical presence, and it was pretty much proven with a driver's license. To the extent that there was an electronic identity, people in the U.S. used a Social Security number. By the way, when that was created, it was explicitly intended *not* to be an identification number. But as people needed electronic identification, there was nothing else, so it kind of fell into becoming an electronic ID that served to "prove" the identity of a person.

Now we need a new paradigm. We're living in a world where massive amounts of data are being generated, especially personal data of many different types—your health information or your financial or banking data or photos of you—where that data is stored essentially forever, where it's connected through high-bandwidth links to essentially everyone, where there are extraordinarily sophisticated analytic tools to analyze all that data. I think these questions, about what is identity, what are its dimensions and who controls them, need to be addressed, and we're not, in my mind, really thinking about the whole problem. We're thinking about pieces of it, like we're thinking about cyber security or HIPAA (Health Insurance Portability and Accountability Act) for privacy of medical records. But we're not looking at the whole problem. All data are not created equal, and access to data may be either good or bad, depending on its purpose. It's good for my doctors to share my medical information and for credit agencies to provide financial information if I apply for a loan... but I sure don't want that sharing to get mixed up! That's what I mean when I say there's no monolithic solution. We need something better than a single electronic ID number.

And people are contributing to the size of this problem every day through vehicles like Facebook. They're putting a lot of private information out and then coming to the realization that, well, that data lives forever, and if it was an embarrassing photo, maybe that's not so good 20 years later in your life. And what if a friend posts a photo of you on his social networking site? Do you have any rights to control how you're portrayed, forever, in those databases?

There are questions like biometrics. I joined the CLEAR program (i.e., biometric identification to bypass long security waits at airports) back when it started. I voluntarily gave up some biometric information about myself to a private company because I travel a lot and the benefit to me was worth the risk. But once they went out of business, who owns "my" biometric data? There's not really any way to get it back.

You also see this question about identity and who owns identity coming up at the intersection of the physical and the information domains again. Recently in *The Wall Street Journal,* there was an article about technology that comes out of the military community and is now used by the police to track cell phones, not to listen to cell phone conversations but to track where they are, even when they're not in use, by actively pinging cell phones so their location can be triangulated. And that information can be used by the police to find people who own those cell phones. Was that part of their identity? Is that part of who they are, where they are at a particular time as revealed through a physical device?

So I think the issue of identity raises profound questions. I don't hear this conversation at the fundamental level on the national stage. We're dealing with issues that arise from it every day, mostly through the courts, but we're doing it in the absence of a larger philosophical construct about what identity means. And I think that construct needs to be created as part of a national conversation that includes the government; includes industry, which uses or generates this information; and includes academia, which can contribute great thinking about where these boundaries should be and what we should value.

S. Donaldson: The ethical nature of it.

Alving: Yes. And there is a place for not-for-profit organizations and so forth. So that, to me, is a great, unaddressed question. It's far beyond the scope of any one company. I think it affects all of us.

S. Donaldson: Right.

Alving: There's another thing I didn't talk about, and I don't know whether it fits into your concept for the book. And that's about being on the board, being a director of a public corporation.

S. Donaldson: Sure, let's talk about it.

Alving: I'm on the board of the Pall Corporation, and I've been on the board for something like a year and a half now. I bring it up because the reason I was invited to join the board was that this company is a very technology-centric company. They have a core set of technologies around filtration and separation, and they're the largest stand-alone player in that space right now. Being a very technology-centric company, they decided that they wanted to make sure that the technology core of the company was healthy. So they did two things: they created a corporate-level chief technology officer, which they had not had before, and they went out looking for somebody to put on the board who is a CTO who understands some of the issues that we've been talking about.

My participation on the Pall Corporation board is only possible because our CEO supports such outside activities with what he calls "3-2-1." That's a little mantra to remind our senior executives that engagement with the outside world is important. "3-2-1" refers to an annual goal of three high-level engagements, two speeches, and one board participation from each of the senior executives. It's important for leaders to remember that engagement with the outside world is part of what makes us all successful... and that's just as true for CTOs as for other executives.

Siegel: Amy, thank you for a great discussion today. Thank you for your time, insights, and participation.

Alving: Thanks. I enjoyed our conversation.

Don Ferguson

CTO, CA Technologies

Dr. Donald F. Ferguson *is executive vice president and chief technology officer at CA Technologies. Tasked with promoting technical excellence at CA Technologies and further developing the company's technical community, Don chairs the company's Architecture Board and a newly-formed Distinguished Engineer Board. He also serves on the Executive Leadership Team, which supervises the business and technology strategies for the company as a whole. Before assuming the position of CTO, Don was corporate senior vice president and chief architect. In this role, he defined the direction and technical evolution for products.*

Prior to joining CA Technologies in 2008, Don was a Microsoft Technical Fellow working in the Office of the CTO. He worked on various projects exploring the future of enterprise software, with a special emphasis on Web services and Internet application platforms.

Don began his career at IBM, where he worked for twenty years. In 2001 Don became an IBM Fellow, IBM's highest technical honor. IBM has approximately 50 IBM Fellows in their 150,000 person engineering team.

Scott Donaldson: So let's begin with your journey here to the CTO position. How did you get to be CTO?

Don Ferguson: That's a good question. It wasn't my cunning plan. I got a Ph.D. in computer science from Columbia University, and when you did that back in '87, '88, you went one of two places: you went to become a professor or you went to an industrial research center. I didn't want to have to deal with the stress of trying to get tenure and getting funding, so I went to

IBM Research, which is about 40 miles from Columbia. And a lot of people from IBM Research took courses at Columbia, so I had connections there, and I was a summer student and an intern there during most of my Ph.D. So I joined IBM Research, and I did research on various projects. I wrote papers. It was industrial research.

Then IBM had the near-death experience, and they concluded that one of the causes was that research was not linked enough with products and product development. My favorite example of that was that IBM invented RISC technology. IBM invented relational databases. IBM was the last company that had relational databases on RISC technology. There's something wrong with this picture. So I pitched in and worked on advanced technology for products. My philosophy was just to grab an oar and row. And my work made a difference because of the group I was in. I actually worked on modern mainframe software despite the fact that working on mainframe projects made you look like a troglodyte in academic research.

But there was actually some interesting research. I actually got two or three papers and patents out of it. And it was kind of funny at that time because before the death experience, when you would go to a meeting, all of the people from the products team would have jackets and ties and all of the research guys would be like in business casual. And the company had concluded that product research needed to be more helpful to product development and product development needed to be more like Silicon Valley. So after that, whenever you went to a meeting, people from the research division would be in a suit and tie and people from product development would be in business casual.

So I did a couple of projects on the mainframe, and they were quite successful actually. And that was the thing that, using a Mafia term, that made my bones. I did some technology back then that helped us sell mainframes because of the extended storage architecture, and then I worked on transaction management and as we transitioned from really fast bipolar uniprocessor to parallel, large memory mainframe systems. I actually got a paper and patent out of that one, so there was really a lot of innovation there.

Then IBM was getting a lot of investment in distributed UNIX RISC System/6000, so I started running some projects on distributed systems management for a commercial data processing systems; it was Power Parallel System V2. So we were doing this type of project. We had produced some frameworks to do a highly productive system infrastructure using distributed object technology. I used to present to the executives. So periodically, executives from product teams would come in and go, "Hey guys, you know, show us what we're getting from research." And one of the executives,

Irving Wladawsky-Berger brought in a CIO, Barry Lynn, who was the CIO of Wells Fargo. And before the meeting, Barry sent a question, "We're trying to solve this problem. Can you tell us how you'd do it?" I thought about it and I came in and presented how we would do it with our technology.

And they loved it, so that created a project called "First of a Kind." Research used to do First of a Kind with customers. We would work on this idea with a customer and then it would evolve into a product. It was really kind of successful. The executives would come in and I'd go, "Your current approach to distributed-objects process doesn't make sense. Here's an example of something we're doing that does make sense." I'd do this all the time. So one day I'm sitting in my office—fat, dumb, and happy. Two guys walk into my office, Mark Bilger and Mark Wegman, who eventually became an IBM Fellow. And they said, "Come with us," which I found vaguely ominous. I said, "Where are we going?" They said, "Come with us." And then we got in the car—it was getting worse. "Where are we going?" "Somewhere." Okay, it could be worse. It could be a dumpster in Jersey.

S. Donaldson: That's right.

Ferguson: Somers was the IBM business unit headquarters. We go in and I walk in an office and saw Robert LeBlanc, who was in charge of a lot of the application development and middleware. Robert said to me, "Yesterday we transitioned the object technology over to me. And I want you to come in and be the technical lead for turning your ideas into products."

S. Donaldson: Excellent.

Ferguson: And I said to him, "Robert, I'm not sure that's such a good idea, 'cause I'm a research guy. I don't have product experience and my wife's having a baby in a month." So he said, "Oh, okay. So you just shoot your mouth off. You don't actually do anything, do you?" At which point I responded, "Screw you. I'm on the job." So we pulled together a team of five or six people, defined what we could do based on what we had been doing, and that project became an IBM product; a product that started WebSphere. When I started that project, we started it with five people. When I left IBM about 10 years later, there were 5,000 people working on WebSphere and it was a billion dollar business.

S. Donaldson: That's fascinating. I did a little of the research on that work and I coined a new phrase for you: "Parents of WebSphere." This team did some remarkable work. One of the things that we were curious about is what was really unique about this team? How did they come together? What made it click to go from 5 people to 5,000?

Ferguson: After WebSphere started to take off, it eventually became a multimillion-dollar business. At one point WebSphere was the fastest-growing product in IBM history. There was a magazine that came out, WebSphere Developers' Journal, and marketing decided that the first issue of WebSphere Developers' Journal should be an interview with the "Father of WebSphere". And so they were going to interview me. And the first thing I said during the interview is, I said, "I don't like the title of 'Father of WebSphere.' I have two daughters. I'm their father, not WebSphere's. And victory has a thousand fathers, defeat is an orphan."And they said, "Well, that's nice, but we're going to sell more magazines if we say 'The Father of WebSphere,' plus marketing said it was going to be 'The Father of WebSphere', so shut up."

So people often ask me, how did WebSphere succeed? And I will say three things. The first one is that at that time and even now, there was a small group of executives that were running the Software Group that were, in my opinion, some of the best executives in the software industry: Steve Mills, Danny Sabbah, Robert Leblanc, John Swainson (who used to be the CEO of CA) and Ambuj Goyal. There's no executive software management team in the world that's better than these guys. And they were willing to take technology risks. Danny Sabbah and Ambuj Goyal were also from the research division. They were executives in research. They were good technologically. Steve Mills came up through sales and marketing, but he has an eerie ability to understand the technology and how it's going to help customers. It's spooky. The guy's not an engineer. He never studied computer science. But Steve has an awesome gift.

S. Donaldson: But he bridges that gap.

Ferguson: And John Swainson was the same. When John Swainson retired from CA, we actually voted him distinguished engineer emeritus, which is the CA equivalent of an IBM Fellow. At IBM there was a cluster of executives who were deeply technical who were willing to take risks, had the courage to take risks, and understood that we needed to do this. John Swainson helped build a similar team at CA Technologies, which is why the company has become amazingly innovative. Bill McCracken is another example. Bill spent his career in sales and management in IBM. Bill majored in physics in college and started as a Systems Engineer in IBM. I love having technology conversations with Bill. David Dobson, Ajei Gopal (my former manager), Russ Artzt, Jacob Lamm, Peter Griffiths, Adam Elster and the others.

The second thing is if you talk to any senior military leader, they will tell you that the backbone of the Marine Corps is the noncommissioned officers and the junior officers.

S. Donaldson: Right.

Ferguson: There was a nucleus of technical leaders, senior engineers, STSMs, Distinguished Engineers, etc., and we basically held that organization together. We collectively made decisions that were in the best interests of the IBM Software Group and company. Not individual and parochial interests. It was, you know, product development managers; product managers will tend to make parochial decisions. It's not that they're bad people. It's just their perspective.

S. Donaldson: Right.

Ferguson: But there was this core of people who—STSMs, DEs worked together and pushed decisions that were right for the company as a whole. The analogy is—you know, my father was in the Marines and he was in an air wing. He became a sergeant and was an ordinance man. Dad taught me how to make booby traps, but let's not go there.

S. Donaldson: Semper Fi. Yeah, I was in the Corps.

Ferguson: I wasn't because I grew up during Vietnam and my father said, "You're not going into the Marines." I always regret that I didn't. Anyway, but Marines are obsessed with using Marine close-air support. They don't want it from anybody else, and the reason is that the first lieutenant that is rolling in on the target probably knows the first lieutenant who's commanding the platoon and calling in the air strike.

S. Donaldson: Right.

Ferguson: The pilot's not going to let that guy down.

S. Donaldson: Right.

Ferguson: So, anyway, managers came and managers went, and we were reorg'd again and again. I worked with the same technical guys, Tom Storey, Tim Holloway, Rob High, Jerry Cuomo, Eric Herness, Martin Nally for years. They were my brothers in arms. I would do anything for them and vice versa.

S. Donaldson: So these folks made decisions to advance shareholder value for the whole corporation – they had that thought in mind?

Ferguson: Yep. We were a team, and no matter how the company reorg'd, it was the same people. We'd be in different roles, but we were a team. We were the constant.

And then the third thing for our success was communication—I am with customers all the time. So unlike a lot of technical people and many engineers in development, I spend as much time with customers as I can. Every good idea I ever had I've stolen from a customer.

S. Donaldson: Right.

Ferguson: Now, so WebSphere sprang out of this; partly out of this conversation with Barry Lynn and then a couple of others. It's kind of funny. Barry Lynn retired and then he went into the VC (virtual cloud) business and he became the CEO of a company 3Tera, that we acquired about two years ago when cloud wasn't an easy thing to explain, but Barry explained it to me. I got it, and I drove and drove and drove, and I gave a presentation to the Executive Leadership Team, and it clicked. The acquisition was a gutsy, technology driven call the Bill McCracken, Jacob Lamm, Russ Artzt and others made. I will always admire that call. 3Tera AppLogic is now at the heart of everything we're doing in cloud computing.

S. Donaldson: Let's shift gears just a little and talk about what you do day-to-day. What are your main responsibilities, who do you report to, who reports to you, where do you spend your time? Do you spend your time mainly on management, administrative, communications, research, getting out with the customers? Those sorts of things.

Ferguson: I am the worst manager and administrator in the world. It's important to know your strengths and weaknesses. And my goal in life is to not be a manager. There have been many people who have come to me and said, "You know, I'd like to come and report to you." I say, "Well, I don't hate you, so I don't think that's a good idea."

So I take a step back and I think about what I do and I do five things. The first thing is advise and consent on the design and implementation of our products. I advise which features should go into products, how we should build them, where they should go. And I consent to the design, to make sure it's a good design and it winds up with basic principles, etc. Advice and consent; we have a review process for that. We call it the architecture technical review. We did that in IBM.

When I became an IBM Fellow, I moved up and was the chief architect for the IBM Software Group as a whole. About two days after that, I get called in to review a project to build a B2B (business to business) system based on WebSphere and Software Group products. It took 14 physical machines to build and run the "Hello World" business process. I didn't know what the right answer was, but I knew it was less than 14. When I left, it would all run on a ThinkPad. It was a big ThinkPad, but it would all run on a ThinkPad. And that was all just advice and consent, and the fact that when I gave advice and consent, my technical colleagues would hash it out and figure out how to do it; then it was game time. Let's go and let's do it.

S. Donaldson: Right.

Ferguson: In the entire time I was the chief architect for Software Group, I only once in four years had to say the words, "I've heard all the people, but we're going to do it this way." We would talk about it, we would form a consensus, and then we would go. And I only held a vote in the Software Group Architecture Board once. It was a disaster, because I asked what we were going to do. "Are we going to do XForms or Java, Java Server Faces with tag libraries?" I wrote it on the board, and I went around voting, and everybody suggested another option. And I said, "You don't understand. You get to vote for one of these two. There were no write-in candidates in this election."

We were able to make it happen. In Software Group, I called the architecture reviews a "peer review", which had all your peers and colleagues, look at your design and make suggestions and hash it out. It was meant to be very collegial. I want it to be like that here because, CA never had that before. When John Swainson was asking me to come here, I asked him, "Well, how do you do your architectural reviews?" He said, "We don't." I was like, "What do you mean you don't? You must." Then we had this conversation for about five minutes, and he said, "Look, Don, focus. We don't do it." I was like, "Okay." But it's advice and consent.

S. Donaldson: Okay.

Ferguson: The second one is innovation. My folksy story for that is, product management, competitive analysis, these things are all-important for marketing, you know, market intelligence. But in 1880, if you did standard product management, market analysis for illumination, you would have gotten cheaper candles, you know, scented whale oil.

S. Donaldson: [Laughing] Right.

Ferguson: You wouldn't have gotten light bulbs. It's my job to figure out what the light bulbs are. And so we actually have a couple of projects that I think are revolutionary that we showed at CA World 2011 in November. It's partly my job—looking for innovation.

S. Donaldson: So how do you do that? Your focus appears to be on reaching out to the customers and the community, your peers within the industry, sitting down and just thinking, "What takes us to the next level?"

Ferguson: Knowing your personal strengths and weaknesses; this is one of the most important things that people should know. And I have three gifts, and they're gifts. I don't know where they came from, but the first one is I have an eerie ability to look at a complex environment and figure out how to build a system that will solve it. I don't know where that comes from. I look at it, and it comes. It's spooky.

I have an eerie ability to pick things up. People will come in and will start talking to me about the system they're building or something, and three minutes into it, I can explain to them, "You know, you must be building this way or doing that." And it's just – it's a gift.

The second gift is that I can ask myself extreme questions. An example is one of the last products we did when I was at IBM was something called Web-Sphere Extended Deployment. And we had all this complicated load balancing, cluster support stuff with WebSphere. And it was really good stuff. I mean, it was one of the competitive advantages. But one day I was thinking, and I said, "What would we do if hardware were free?" And the answer was: we wouldn't do what we were doing. You've got a performance problem? Instead of doing spooky load balancing, just throw hardware at it. And that question—what would we do if hardware were free—that was where Web-Sphere ED came from.

One of the innovative products that we're doing at CA Technologies is intuitive, model based IT management. If you look at our products, you'll see over and over again—icons connected by lines—and then you can click on an icon and get a property sheet up. "Wow that looks like PowerPoint." What would the world look like if you could manage IT with PowerPoint and clip art? That's where the model-driven design came from. I'll look at a problem and I'll think about it for a second, and I'll say, "There is a problem in a completely different domain, and if you apply the principles from that problem to this one, this is what you'll get." An example is people will say, "A 10X improvement in IT management? That's not possible." And my response is, "Well, relational databases did it for data. Why can't we do it for IT management? How did they do it? They did it in domain-specific languages for data management."

And the third gift I have is for understanding a business problem, converting it into technology, and then explaining back to business people in business terms. I don't know where that came from. And I'm just very grateful for those gifts. Whenever I see something new, my first reaction is, "How do I make money with this? How I do make it a good idea?" It's never, "Is this a good idea?" My job is to make it work. If somebody came to me and presented some story about a new technology for getting chickens to lay more eggs, my job would be to figure out how use it to make more money for CA. Now we will go and do the next step, which is the pro-and-con analysis. It's my job to make it work.

When people tell me something won't work, I'll say, "Why?" The most common answer is, "We tried it before and it didn't work." My response is, "Well, if we gave up every time something didn't work, we wouldn't have fire. We'd be wet and cold in a cave, eating rocks. So we're going to try again." And the second thing is, "You don't understand. It's your job. You don't know it won't work until you try."

S. Donaldson: So advice and consent, innovation, make things work.

Ferguson: Right. Well, innovation is part of making things work.

S. Donaldson: Okay.

Ferguson: Number three is consult with business executives. We're inherently a technology company. Technological considerations factor into our business decisions. I'm their trusted advisor on technology.

Number four is care and feeding of the technical team. Although some CTOs actually are also the VP of Engineering, I'm not. All the engineers are in line development organizations. They have management chains. I have an ethical responsibility to support those people. To be somebody they can come to when they have a problem. I've often told people, "Any one, any technical professional, in any part of CA can come to me at any time for any reason and I will try to help them. I may not be able to, but that's my job."

S. Donaldson: Do they take you up on that?

Ferguson: Not as much as you might think. Because for reasons that I don't completely understand, many people have told me that I'm scary and unapproachable. I'm not quite sure why, but they don't.

When I was going through a leadership development program, they do these 360 reviews. And one of the questions was, "Is Don helpful when you come to him with a problem?" And there were like 20 respondents. A 5 rating was "the most helpful person I've met." One was "completely useless." Ten people rated me 5 and 10 people rated me 1, and the guy who was coaching it said, "I've never seen anything like this. How is it possible?" And I said, "Ten of the people came to me, and 10 of them haven't yet." [Both laughing]

I went out to dinner with my family, and we were sitting down at the table and there was a box where you could take questions out to stimulate conversations, which I actually thought was kind of pathetic, that you would need a box with your family to stimulate conversation. Using a box to stimulate conversation is solving the wrong problem. And my daughter took out a card and said, "What one word would most people use to describe you?" And she thought for a minute and said, "For me I don't know what it is, but for Dad it would be 'dangerous'." I nearly fell on the floor.

[Both laughing]

Ferguson: Giving an example, in IBM and in CA Technologies, I hold office hours. I'm on the phone for an hour at least once a week. Anyone can call in and talk about anything they want. If we were all on one site, I would just sit in my office, but I have telephone office hours. I blog. I write an internal blog, which people tell me is great. I have been giving webcasts on various topics. And I've been getting—when most of the time when somebody gives a webcast, it's only 50, 100 people—I routinely get over 1,000.

So when we had switched strategy, we were starting to focus on virtualization and cloud, my manager called me in my office and said, "Don, we've got to get this done in six months. You've got to quarterback this. We've got to get this done by CA World." So I started reviewing the project. I'm talking to these guys, Kouros Esfahany and Greg Bodine. I mean, these guys are as good as anyone I've ever known. I realize two hours into the meeting that they've got this situation under control. I said, "You don't really need me to quarterback, do you?" They said, "No." "Oh, okay. Now my job is to block for you."

S. Donaldson: Yeah, so they can get it done.

Ferguson: And even some of it is just mundane stuff. I was on a call and somebody said, "Well, you know, we want to have a design meeting on the portal, but because we're getting to the end of the quarter, we have a travel freeze." I said, "Well, you should take the trip. I'll pay for it out of my budget." "And if I can't, I'll pay for it with my personal credit card".

[Both laughing]

S. Donaldson: Get it done?

Ferguson: The next one is communication; both internal and external. I give a lot of keynotes at conferences. I do the internal webcasts. The internal communication is important. Every single day, every engineer in this company is going to make two or three decisions. Our technology development group has 5,000 people. That's 15,000 decisions in a day. I can't review all of those. They need to know the play. They need to be in the huddle, because there are a number of things that break because not everybody was in the huddle.

And then there is communication with customers, visits, conference keynotes, etc. We need to understand and explain where the world is going. So communication, care and feeding of the technical team, executive advice, innovation, and governance are all important.

S. Donaldson: Do you ever have an opportunity to get the technology people together?

Ferguson: Yes, we do it several ways. One way is through site visits and I do town halls there. We also have an architects' conference where 200 people come together every year. We have an organization called the "Council for Technical Excellence," which spans the company and meets once a year. We get them together; periodically, we have meetings.

S. Donaldson: So, given all that, how do you define success for yourself? When you get something to the market, or you've helped somebody solve through a very complicated problem?

Ferguson: That's a really good question. It varies tremendously from topic to topic. Whenever I review something, whenever I suggest something, I almost always focus on three observations. If you do fewer than three, you're not trying. If you do more than three, "He who tries to do ... everything fails." Whether it's a customer problem, a product we're trying to build, a business problem we need to solve, a competitive situation. I pick three things. And the success is, "Did we do the three things or not?" But they can be anything that's relevant to the problem at hand.

S. Donaldson: Okay.

Ferguson: But I do have a list of goals. These are the things I want to get done. I just bang-bang-bang-bang-bang against the goals. But the most important thing is, I mean, the key to happiness in life is lowered expectations. You know, if I have 100 things on my list and I get 51 of them done, it was a good year.

Donaldson: Right, right.

Ferguson: Ted Williams got into the Hall of Fame, but his career batting average was .340. Because of the nature of my job, there are indirect things I have influence on and obviously, it's hard to measure the effect of what I do. It's not like I manage a product, or a development team. It's got to be the list of goals.

The other part of it is—I used to say it in a very negative way. I used to say my career was over. Now, what I meant to say was, "I have the best job in the world for a person like me. I'm never going to have a better job than this." Even though I said, "I'm never going to have a better job," is a negative way of saying it; I do feel I have the best job in the world.

I don't need to worry about my career. I don't want another job. I don't want to advance. I'm the chief technology officer of a large software company that is trying to completely revolutionize an industry. It doesn't get any better than that for me. And when I had that realization, I was reading a book on Buddhism, and the author wrote, "The key to happiness in life is trying to make other people happy." I came to the conclusion that my job is to help other people.

S. Donaldson: So inside the corporation, is there a CIO organization?

Ferguson: Yes.

S. Donaldson: Do you guys overlap? What's the interface, what's the structure?

Ferguson: Well, the thing that you have to remember is, unlike a bank, which has a CTO, we are a company that builds software. So, the CTO/CIO relationship here is slightly different than the relationship in other industries. You know, CTO and the CIO in a bank or in a pharmaceutical company, they work together to make better drugs. Here we make software.

Now having said that, we have a CIO now, who joined us about a couple of months ago, and he's great. His name is Greg Valdez. I need to do a better job of spending time with Greg. We don't meet enough. I want his advice, talk to him, because he runs an IT department. We sell software that runs IT departments, so talking to him is probably a pretty good idea.

S. Donaldson: So is he primarily internally facing with respect to keeping the infrastructure online going?

Ferguson: Yeah, he runs global information systems (GIS).

S. Donaldson: But you're eating your own dog food, so to speak, in the sense that you're selling software to that industry as well.

Ferguson: People will say, "We have to eat our own dog food, and so we need to help the CIO use our own stuff." We also sometimes say, "Global Information Systems and the CIO, it should be there first—they should be our first best customer." I think that's shooting too low. My attitude is they should be helping us figure out what we should do. Greg and his team need to be part of defining our direction, not consuming our technology. The GIS team is stepping up. Not helping us figure out how customers will perceive what we've done. They should be helping us figure out where to go and all that. Validating and assessing what we've done.

S. Donaldson: You've provided an excellent description of the journey to CTO. If you had a key lesson to pass along, what might you pass along?

Ferguson: Again, that's a good question. I've been very successful. When I was became an IBM Fellow, I used to do roundtables all the time. And when I would sometimes get interviewed by magazines, they would ask me, "What skill do you think is the most important?" My answer is, "You've got to be able to plausibly take credit for the work of others."

S. Donaldson: [Laughing]

Ferguson: My real answer is, "I don't know. It's not like I planned this." I sort of fell down the stairs, and this is where I landed. Your life pivots on these things that just seem so insignificant at the time. If I had been sick on the day that Barry Lynn had come to IBM, my life would have been completely different. I had no way of knowing that at the time. So people say, "Well, that's not a good answer. I've got a magazine. Let's come up with some good ones."

So, I picked three things. The first one is you've got to spend time with your customers. You just have to do it. The second one is what I tell customers all the time is, "Even if you don't buy my product at all, I'm still committed to helping you succeed. My job is to help you succeed."

S. Donaldson: We have a saying back home: "Our only success is your success when you're talking to the customer."

Ferguson: Yeah, my job is to make customers succeed. So the second thing is you have to say what you mean and mean what you say, even if it's unpopular. You just have to be willing to do that. And if you say you're going to do something, you have to do it. It's just the way it's got to be.

S. Donaldson: Keep your commitments.

Ferguson: Right. And the third thing, which is probably not a particularly good one, is that I am amazingly competitive. In a leadership development program, we took a personality profile test. The sample population was 8,000 senior executives in the United States. I scored 98th percentile on competitiveness. The guy who ran the course said, "I've never seen anything higher than 85 in my entire life. I think Klingons are like 87. And Genghis Khan is like 90."

[Both laughing]

Ferguson: I went home and I showed it to my girlfriend. And she said, "I don't know how you didn't get 100. You must have inadvertently answered a question incorrectly."

On compromise, I scored in the 6th percentile. The leadership development guy said, "Dead people get a 10." And then he looked at me and said, "But on collaboration you get a 40. How is that possible?" I said, "Well, collaboration means work together. As long as everyone does it my way, we're fine."

[Both laughing]

So, I told my family this and they looked at me like, "You don't think you're competitive? You're the most competitive guy we know."

You know, I have a black belt in karate.

S. Donaldson: Really?

Ferguson: When I took my test, I took it with a 17-year-old. I'm 50; I was like 45 at the time. I'm one of three people in this system over 40 to pass a black belt test. It was 90 degrees. I took it with a 17-year-old. It was a four-hour test. And I was so dehydrated, I went home and I drank like, I don't know, three gallons of water—that's how dehydrated I was.

The second part of the test was sparring 12 rounds; each time with a new opponent. In about the fourth or fifth round, I thought, "I can't make it another six rounds." I was just dragging, and one of the other guys—you're not supposed to make full contact with the head even though we wear helmets—one of the guys I was sparring with hit me in the head really hard. And I got really mad, and I made it through the next six rounds. And I said to him, "You know, Tommy, you're not supposed to hit people on the head." He said to me, "Don, you were really dragging. I knew that if I hit you in the head hard, you were going to get pissed off and you were going to finish the test, and I could see when I hit you in the head, I could see the lights come on in your eyes." I thought, "Yeah, actually, it's true."

S. Donaldson: Very interesting.

Ferguson: I take Krav Maga now, which is Israeli martial arts. And you don't need to be crazy to take Krav Maga, but it helps a lot. The first 20 minutes are like really intense cardio and then 20 minutes of techniques and practice. But the last 20 minutes—like, if you're learning defenses against chokes, they'll put you in the middle of the room, turn the lights out, blare music, people will spin you around, and somebody will choke you, but you've got to open your eyes and do a defense, and as soon as you're done, you—I mean, it's like—you look at this and it's like, "Man, these guys got to be crazy."

S. Donaldson: And you're paying somebody for this?

Ferguson: And I'm paying, but, you know, I love it. It's just that I'm really competitive.

S. Donaldson: Well, let's shift gears again here and maybe talk about the company a little bit. What makes this company differentiated in the marketplace?

Ferguson: Well, there are several ways to answer that question. One is just pretty straightforward. We sell business software, which is what I did at IBM. We sell business software, but we sell IT management and security software, so we don't have products like WebSphere or Oracle databases or SAP R3. We sell software that manages IT environments, basically to the CIO.

Now, we're actually going to the next tier down, emerging enterprises, SMBs (small & medium businesses), because they're becoming increasingly driven, and increasingly relying on IT. It's very hard to describe what I do, what our company does, because most people are consumers of technology. It's not like they work for the CIO.

So people keep probing me. After a while I say, "The last time you went to the bank and used the ATM, did you get your money?" And they say, "Yes," and I go, "You're welcome. Did anybody else get your money?" "No." "You're welcome." There are very few pure IT management/security companies and we are one of them. So that's one thing that I think is kind of unique about us.

The second one is we decided about a year and a half ago to change the world in terms of how IT works. And not a lot of companies do that. And I sometimes joke, "We're either going to succeed beyond our wildest expectations or go down in a giant ball of flames, but it's not going to be anything in between."

We decided to change the world. It's about cloud computing and managing cloud computing. The realization I came to is 98% of what you need for cloud computing is IT management and security. Historically, if you look at the way IT has worked, it has been application platforms, software development tools, pre-built applications, but if I'm using the Amazon relational database I don't need a database platform. I need to manage the Amazon RDS (relational database service).

S. Donaldson: Right.

Ferguson: If you look at Salesforce.com, people don't actually write Salesforce.com applications. There's the actual application and then there's another application that allows you to customize the application. That's the beauty of Salesforce.com; it is that there are really two applications. There's the Salesforce app and then the app you use to customize it. The thought experiment I had on this one is – my girlfriend's an attorney. She's got basic computer skills. She could go subscribe to Salesforce.com and tailor the app so that it was a Salesforce app for a law firm. You don't write any software. You don't have a platform.

S. Donaldson: Right.

Ferguson: The elevator speech for SOA was, "Put all your APIs and your web service registry and then string them all together." When we do that today (string business processes and portals), we call it the Internet.

There's a site that's really cool, www.programmableweb.com. They've got, I don't know, 2,500 web-callable APIs. And they're not just the things teenagers use. FedEx has got callable API services.

Most people who look at Amazon and their web services, they focus on elastic cloud computing. Amazon has a relational data service. They've got a simple queuing and messaging service. They have APIs to get historical information about the prices of things. Dun and Bradstreet publishes APIs. There's another site that's cool. These are just examples. It's Drupal.org. It's an open-source content-management system. It's got 8,500 plug-ins.

My thought experiment is: can I actually come up with an application that's going to require me to write code or install software? I can't come up with one. You can't—it is find the API, decide whether to use it, then use it, secure it and manage it. Application platforms, application development tools, all of the hardware—that stuff is all gone. The only thing that's left is, "Is the damned thing running?"

There was a famous case recently where Amazon EC2 was having hiccups. People had cobbled together business apps really quickly and used Amazon EC2, but they didn't find out for five days that their app wasn't working, because Amazon was having problems. Our job is to solve that.

So my view is that we're trying to change the world with the things we're doing, model-driven IT management, aligning IT with the business, because 90% of the value in enterprise IT is going to move to IT management and security, so we're trying to change the world. And I think we're the only one that has that vision, and so I think that's one thing that makes us unique.

Another one is domain expertise. IT management is a very, I mean, it's not an arcane, but it's a highly specialized domain. It's unlike most other kinds of software. The engineering team here is as good as anywhere else. We also have extraordinarily good management here. Bill McCracken, Peter Griffiths, Jacob Lamm, David Dobson are the people on EMT. There's no better management team in the world.

Bill McCracken spent most of his life at IBM in Sales and was very successful. People assume because he's in Sales he doesn't get technology. Bill McCracken was a physics major in college, and his first job at IBM was a systems engineer. The guy understands technology.

S. Donaldson: The first-order principles are still there.

Ferguson: Yeah. And I remember I was talking to him about how we discover systems on a network, and I suddenly realized he didn't really know much about TCP/IP. He basically said, "Oh, so it's like this," and we started talking, and I thought, "Oh crap, he's going to start talking about SNA (an old IBM networking protocol). I've got to remember all that SNA stuff." And it suddenly dawned on me, he wasn't going there. He was talking about how channels work and channel command words and CSWs. I explained discovery in these terms and Bill picked it up right away.

So we have really good management here. Lots of companies want programs to improve the culture, make people work better together, etc. Our guys mean it. It's not just smoke. They're just not going through the motions. They really mean it.

S. Donaldson: The people are the engine that feed what you need.

Ferguson: Right, when EMT says we're going to improve the culture, lots of places have heard that. These guys mean it.

S. Donaldson: Okay. So now, let's take a look at some of the technologies that you use. What technologies are important? What programming languages? What databases? How many people are working this issue?

You did mention earlier there are some 5,000 people on the engineering team. Do you outsource a lot of this? Is it all done in-house? Is it some kind of combination?

Ferguson: We do product development in a few places. We have a core development team in the Technology and Development group (TDG). I'm the corporate CTO, but for various reasons I'm actually in TDG. That doesn't matter. My rule of life has been, you know, my influence is because of who I am. It's not where I report. It's personal credibility, not organizational.

S. Donaldson: Right.

Ferguson: There are about 4,000people in TDG. We have two other development teams that are in the product side. One of them is in a customer solution unit focused on midmarket. There is an engineering team focused on security. So we have about altogether 6,000 people in development, which includes very technical people in Sales and CA Services. So I would imagine maybe half the company is people I would consider technologists.

S. Donaldson: Are the products being built primarily within that group? Do you outsource some development overseas?

Ferguson: Some of it, yeah. We have development teams in Prague, Hyderabad, and China. But those are CA. And then we do some outsourcing of various parts of development.

S. Donaldson: What kind of things get outsourced?

Ferguson: It falls into three categories. If the product's mature and if you're mostly focusing on sustaining and support, you'll tend to outsource that.

S. Donaldson: Okay.

Ferguson: The second category is certain cases where an outsourcing partner has the main expertise. They're just an expert in that space, and we rely on them. So there are cases where we rely on them for innovation.

S. Donaldson: Okay.

Ferguson: Or they already have an existing asset that we use and we also use it for variable capacity. I mean, we may have to have a surge in development to do a product. So I would say it's variable capacity, some low cost, and then some domain expertise.

S. Donaldson: So when you do the capacity piece, are they coding to your standards? Or do they have their own standards and you treat their product as a black box?

Ferguson: No, they code—they basically have to code to our standards.

S. Donaldson: The other thing that we were curious about has to do with the trend to mobile today. Everybody's either mobile or they're social networking somehow. Are those two aspects impacting the types of products that you're producing here or are those trends not in the equation right now?

Ferguson: I got on Facebook about a year and a half ago. I don't know why I did it. Been on there about six months and there was a Facebook game, where you were supposed to write 25 little-known facts about yourself. And then tag 25 people and they were supposed to do the same. So basically it was a Facebook chain mail, chain letter. So my girlfriend tagged me. And my first fact was, "I don't play tag." My second tag was, "If you tag me, I tag you back. You stay it." And my third fact was, "I don't have 25 friends, and this doesn't bother me."

[Both laughing]

But the answer to your question, to both of them, is yes.

S. Donaldson: Okay.

Ferguson: In terms of social networking, at CA World in 2008, we announced something that we call CA Open Space, which is a collaboration-centered approach to management. For instance, if you are working at a service desk and you hover on a ticket, you basically look at a popup saying who's been involved in this ticket, if they are online, or if they have they commented on it. Basically, CA Open Space is a federated service.

Historically, if you've got a problem and you log onto a service desk, the first thing the service desk person asks is, "Would you like to search the knowledge base?" And you humor the service desk, because you know the answer's not there, and they know you're humoring them, but they have to have the knowledge base.

S. Donaldson: Right.

Ferguson: And what you actually do is you go Google the web, so our knowledge base does federated search on the web. You can decide which sites, which places you are willing to search, which data—and it also publishes. There's a lot of social stuff around the product, so we do a lot of "social" collaboration.

In CA Labs, our research group, we did a research project that analyzed email and internal SharePoints and built a social network. Big deal—we built a social network. But it doesn't really matter who your friend is. It matters what skills that person has. So how many degrees of separation are there between you and somebody who knows how to use a Mac inside CA? That's what matters.

So the network is weighted by skills. Like, who are the people closest to you that can help you with this problem? You can figure that out from reading email and instant messaging and internal posts. So, yeah, we do a lot of that.

Mobile, yes, we've got several products that have mobile. So there are several aspects to mobile. One of them is mobile device interfaces to our products. People will have iPads. Why do they have to go find a PC to log on? The second one is managing mobile devices. Employees and customers have an iPhone and if they can't submit their transaction, they're not happy. So the question is, how do you manage them?

And then the third one, which is really interesting, is that mobile computing is going to change business IT in ways people don't fully appreciate. There are things you can do that weren't possible before. An example is user authentication, which is if I'm in England and I try to log onto my bank, it can detect that I'm in England. Well, how does it tell that it's really me? It can send me an SMS message on my iPhone asking me to respond. The chances of somebody having stolen both my password and my iPhone are pretty small. And if they can pass those two security challenges, they have probably kidnapped me and beaten the information out of me and their getting into my bank accounts is the least of my problems now.

Another example is related to video/image. We did this video that was kind of funny. It was a spoof of "Star Wars," and one of the things we did was about QR [quick response] codes.

Suppose a device stopped working. Well, what I would normally have to do is go look at the device number, go log on. Basically, we had an app where you could take a picture of the QR code with your cell phone, and it would go into the asset management system, pull up the record, and then you could take a picture of your badge, which had a QR code on it, and then that would tell you who the submitter was. My advanced technology group team did a proof of concept of using facial recognition with a cell phone camera for authentication. So it allows things like this that you would never have been able to do before.

But one trend that is really profound has two facets. Facet number I is that enterprises are going to lose control of the user interface. I'll pick on American Airlines because I use it a lot. American Airlines assumes that when I interact with them, I'm using aa.com. However, my favorite app is this thing called FlightStats, which aggregates data from all over the place, FAA, SeatGuru.com, etcetera. People are going to start accessing American Airlines through that app versus aa.com. American Airlines has lost control of its user interface.

S. Donaldson: Right.

Ferguson: They don't have a website. They have APIs that they publish to the world. And there are going to be hundreds, thousands of apps like my daughter writes that access their APIs. They're losing control of their interface. And I don't think they fully realize that.

If you think about the web revolution, it really was a different kind of user interface. It stopped being people in call centers, so terminals started being browsers, but the app developer still controlled the user interface. Sorry, this isn't the case anymore; this interface control is gone.

As soon as you surface HTML/HTTP, you have effectively provided a REST interface and any guy can build an iPhone app and put it in the app store that takes over your interface. I'm sorry. Get over it. Now what are you going to do? I mean, your whole business, your whole transactions are routed by kids who put apps in the app store. Man, that's scary.

Another one is that a huge percentage of transactions are going to be based on location. A lot of things I do are going to be based on what's the nearest store that has the thing I want.

S. Donaldson: Right.

Ferguson: The other one enables a completely new type of application. The industry sometimes uses the term "situational application" or ad hoc application. A simple example of this is when Hurricane Irene hit, I thought about that for a minute and I said, "What's probably going on in insurance companies right now is there are people who are going and looking at the weather forecast trying to figure out where there's danger. They're proba-bly going to places that can estimate where the flooding is going to be. They're probably pulling information out of the corporate property man-agement, putting it into a spreadsheet, and estimating risk and then mailing it to the executives." Well, weather.com emits a feed and has a callable inter-face. There's a callable interface from a company ESRI [Environmental Sys-tems Research Institute] that if you give it rainfall forecasts, it will estimate flooding because it's got historical data.

And your property management system has got callable APIs and so stitch-ing this stuff all together is just basically using Excel-like programming. I don't need to do this manually anymore. I can cobble this thing together in 40 minutes, 30 minutes, and then this thing can do automate the task and update itself. I can go watch TV and my boss thinks I'm amazingly produc-tive. I mean, "Wow, look at this guy. He's producing great stuff."

[Both laughing]

When I worked for Microsoft I used to fly backandforth from Seattle to New York. Six times in a row I missed my connection in Dallas. It's nothing. This stuff happens. And then I would have to sit down and rebook; do I need a car and do I tell my friends? The idea around the new app model is that I could write an app that did this. It could subscribe to the feed; it could get an RSS feed that I missed my flight; it could go in my calendar and send email. It couldn't get everything right, but it could get 80% of it done before I ever landed, you know? Today, the kids entering the workforce can do this kind of stuff.

S. Donaldson: Right.

Ferguson: Today, if you're in a data center, the CIO might have 20 apps, each one's used by thousands of people. They pray to God the apps don't change faster than every nine months. You know, CIOs are going to have to continue to support such apps, and, oh, by the way, there's going to be 40,000 applications. They change every day and each one's used by six people. It sucks to be you. People say, "Oh no, that's never going to happen. You're never going to get that kind of explosion in apps." And it's like, "Do you guys ever use the app store?"

S. Donaldson: Right.

Ferguson: Do you have web access? It's like, do you guys understand? I mean, seriously dudes. There are 500,000 apps in the app store that didn't exist three years ago. So if it's happening there, it's going to be happening. So those are some things that are going to completely change the world.

S. Donaldson: Let me ask with respect to investments that you make in technology, do you get involved in such things as mergers and acquisitions? Can you describe that a bit?

Ferguson: It tends to have two facets. The relatively straightforward one is we do technical due diligence when considering an acquisition. So we review the architecture. We review the code. There have been companies where we have decided not to do the deal because it was just too much at variance with our engineering, our platform, our architecture. There have been other cases where there were several candidates and we picked the one that was most aligned.

S. Donaldson: Is this a long process? Or can you get to the bottom of it pretty quick?

Ferguson: Historically, it's tended to be a long, a long process. We were doing an acquisition that was a relatively big one. There were other companies that were interested. These companies' processes took months. Bill McCracken challenged us to do the deal in 30 days. It's like, you've got to kidding—normally, it takes four months.

S. Donaldson: Easy.

Ferguson: Right, "You can't get it done in 30 days."

S. Donaldson: Right.

Ferguson: But we got it done. So now it doesn't have to be a long process. We acquired a company that had a SAS–based service desk. We already had

Nimsoft, but we went ahead and bought the company. Then, within six months we had the two products integrated, and they have extended our capability. Nimsoft and the InfraDesk team worked really hard. They did a great job. The fact that they were able to do that wasn't an accident. This was not an example of being lucky. This was due to architecture review in due diligence.

S. Donaldson: Essentially, you take a look at the strategy of a corporation—its growth, its targets and where it's going—and then the supporting technologies to go along with that assessment.

Ferguson: Yeah.

S. Donaldson: So, how do you do that technology-gap assessment between where you are today and where you think you want to be? Do you look at the inventory of what you have? Do you identify some key technologies you are missing?

Ferguson: From an innovation point of view, you make a hypothesis about how the world's going to be and then you see whether there's a company out there that will jumpstart it. So it starts with a hypothesis and then you determine whether there's somebody.

The second one is you do an analysis of customer wants or needs or competitors' capabilities. And, then perform again a gap analysis. We actually do this in a systematic way: here's what the customer wants; here's what we have, red, green, yellow; here's what our competitors have; go fix the red ones.

S. Donaldson: Are you on an annual cycle of review?

Ferguson: No, no.

S. Donaldson: Sliding? Just do it all the time? If you need to do it, do it?

Ferguson: Just do it all the time. But, we had defined a strategic roadmap of what we want. I mean there's a process that John Swainson put in place, but we're flexible. So there's just that standard stuff.

And then the third one is generate lots of customer scenarios, synthesize what they need, and then figure out what's missing. So those tend to be the three ways.

S. Donaldson: As we're getting toward the end here, we'd like to probe a little bit about what you see as the future. You've alluded to a couple of things here. And I know you've got some announcements coming down the road, but where do you see the industry that you're in 5 years from now, 10 years from now versus where we are today?

Ferguson: The enterprise business software, IT management is going to change more in the next 5 years than it's changed in the previous 50 years combined. And that's a pretty bold statement—client, server, RISC, web.

There are three or four tipping points that are happening. I give them simple taglines: Everyone can program. It's never happened before. I've seen high school kids write programs that years ago would have required core CO-BOL programmers. These people are entering the workforce.

So then the question is, and people say, "Well, they can program. The question is will they?" The answer is, "If there's a reason to." It's happening.

Historically, there have been more people than applications. It's going to turn around; there are going to be more applications than there are people. It's a completely different world. It's never been like that. For example, 15 years ago if you said, "You know, there are going to be more IP addresses than there are people," people would have looked at you like you were crazy. "There are going to be more telephone numbers than there are people?" They'd look at you like you're nuts. "Sorry, it's happening." There are going to be more applications than there are people. It's going to be a quantum cloud of applications coming and going. That's going to be completely different.

The second point is, even to this day, if you take a step back and think about it and watch what goes on around you, it's staggering the amount of things that aren't automated that could be that are still automated by people. Go into a shoe store, you want a pair of shoes; the shoe store doesn't have it. They call another shoe store, they schedule a delivery, and it comes over. They call you back when it gets delivered and you have to come and get it. Seriously? There's an app for that.

S. Donaldson: Right.

Ferguson: It doesn't need to be this way. My favorite example was about four years ago when I got pneumonia. I went to the Emergency Room. Every time some doctor came in or they ran a test, they would go and they had a clipboard with a piece of paper on it. And they would go and check something or write notes. Unfortunately, the piece of paper wasn't the same size as the clipboard, so they would fold it around and then they would tape it on the back of the clipboard. So they would have to turn the clipboard around every time they would do something. You know, it's a pain. I went to my physician. I went in for the follow-up. When he opened my chart, he had one of the copies.

Now, my father ran a printing company. And those no-carbon-required things typically have at most three copies. What if I had four doctors? What were they going to do? Photocopy a copy? Seriously, guys, this is the way Dickens would have done it. Yeah, you know, "Here's a nickel, buddy. Go buy yourself a real computer." So, that's one thing that's going to be amazingly different. It's something we can't even begin to imagine. The second one is the concept of not being connected. Everything is going to be connected to everything.

S. Donaldson: I forgot my cell phone on a business trip three or four weeks ago. I felt totally lost the entire time, disconnected. I couldn't wait to get home so I could get my machine up so I could plug back in.

Ferguson: Well, I can top that. I have four cell phones, and I also have about five GSM/GPRS [global systems for mobile communications/general packet radio service] devices like computers, so all of those have telephone numbers, so I have like 11 telephone numbers. But I have four cell phones. I use two of them on a regular basis.

I went on a trip. I managed to forget both cell phones. This is not good. Plus my wife and my daughter had gone. They were ahead of me and now I've got to synchronize with them when they get there. What did I do? I went to a vending machine and bought a cell phone.

S. Donaldson: Right.

Ferguson: You're probably going to take that thing (digital recorder) back and stick a cable in it and move it to a computer.

S. Donaldson: That's exactly right.

Ferguson: Five, two years from now, you are going to push the button. It's going to go up to a sky drive.

Even the basic concept of a computer is a cell phone. I carry a cell phone and a laptop. Why do I carry a cell phone and a laptop? Well, there tend to be three reasons. The first one is the display on a cell phone isn't big enough. The second one is there's not enough storage or power to run my apps. And the third one is it must have a mouse and a good keyboard. On the other hand, you walk into a hotel room and there's an Internet-enabled TV that's got a keyboard attached to it. And if all my apps were cloud-based, I don't need to bring a computer. I just need to bring my cell phone and the computer assembles itself around me wherever I am. What if you're on an airplane? JetBlue's got monitors on the back of their seats. They're pretty frigging close, dude.

I was telling my girlfriend this story about renting a car. It's kind of annoying when you're renting a car. You know what's going to happen in the future. You're going to get a car; it's going to connect to your mobile phone; it's going to get your calendar and all your contacts in it; it's going to preload the GPS routes; and it's just going to have to do this, that, and the other thing. Basically, you walk into the car with a cell phone and it personalizes the entire environment—it's going to adjust, your seats are going to be adjusted the way you like them. And she says, "Well, what happens when I turn the car back in?" I said, "Well, it just gets rid of the data." And she said, "Well, I don't trust technology for that kind of security." Seriously? Do you like mail stuff? Are you telling me that the US postal system is going to be better at security than Hertz? Why?" I asked her, "Do you have like an accountant or something?" And, she said "Yeah." I said, "I think he's got stuff you wouldn't want others to get—and, you're more concerned about Hertz having your Outlook calendar than you are about Bank of America having your money?" I would focus on the money part. You know the fundamental basis of security is trust, and my point is it's just going to be completely different.

S. Donaldson: So one last question.

Ferguson: Sure.

S. Donaldson: What keeps you up at night?

Ferguson: The main thing that keeps me up at night is the fact that I have 10 times as many things to do as I can actually get done, and I worry about them. You know, it's like being in college. You know the set of stuff that's going to be on the final is 10 times more than you can actually know. And so you worry about it.

What keeps me up at night is I just have so much stuff that I can't do. And another one is—what have I missed? 'Cause when you're in my level, if you miss something, if you forget something, if you don't realize a trend, it can affect your company.

You know, it's just like—with the number of candle companies that went out of business—what have I missed?

S. Donaldson: Right.

Ferguson: Then another one is—I was going on a trip, and my admin booked my flight from LaGuardia. The car service took me to Kennedy instead. I fell asleep in the car because I was leaving at 3 o'clock in the morning.

When I got there, it was a little hard to check in, so I couldn't get to LaGuardia in time. I missed my flight and I couldn't go to the meeting. She made herself scarce for the rest of the day. When I finally caught up with her, she said, "Oh my God. I'm so sorry." It's like, "Amanda, relax." When I make a mistake, it's 100 million dollars. There are no small mistakes in my job.

S. Donaldson: How do you attack that problem and try not to overlook things?

Ferguson: When I was in graduate school, we would be thinking about mathematical models—my Ph.D. thesis was "Economic Models for Resource Allocation. We used to joke, "I can sit in a room and stare out a window, and you can't prove I'm not working."

S. Donaldson: That's true.

Ferguson: And, unfortunately, if that's your definition of work, I do it all the time. And I do have two processors in my brain. One of them is processing what I'm doing; the other one is running background tasks. I'm just thinking work all the time. And, also, it's acceptance. I mean, I'm going to make mistakes. There's nothing I can do about it.

S. Donaldson: From your earlier description, you're plugged in a lot to levels, internally, externally, etc. There are constant checkpoints going on.

Ferguson: Well, that's where the openness comes in. Bill McCracken likes to say, "None of us is as smart as all of us." The number of times somebody, even a junior person, has come to me and asked me a question and I've gone, "Oh my God, how could I have forgotten that?"

S. Donaldson: Right.

Ferguson: There are six, seven thousand technical professionals in this company. It's unlikely all of us are going to miss it. The reason companies don't pick up on those things is that some junior guy comes and talks to some senior guy and the senior guy goes, "Who is this?" How could I have forgotten this, you know? The bottom line is we must have coverage.

S. Donaldson: Well, on behalf of all of us, I want to say thank you. We appreciate it.

Ferguson: The unexamined life isn't worth living. When you have a conversation like this, you actually think about your life, and it's very helpful.

Craig Miller

The MAPA Group

Dr. Craig Miller is a technologist with extensive background in the physical sciences, information technology, and systems engineering. He has developed new technology and cutting-edge systems for more than 30 years, within and for both startup and established corporations. His particular strength is the conceptualization, tuning, and positioning of new technology products. More than 2000 companies in the U.S. use systems or technology he has architected or developed.

Dr. Miller serves as the Chief Technology Officer (CTO) of the MAPA Group. In this role, he is the lead technologist, responsible for the assessment of new technologies, technical development, and commercialization, supporting projects across the company.

Dr. Miller's many accomplishments deserve mention: his participation in seven startups; serving as SAIC's Chief Scientist (during which time he was granted the "Heroic Achievement in Information Technology" award from the Smithsonian Institution); and wide experience in technical and financial media as a key investor relations expert, technologist, inventor, and analyst on behalf of diverse companies such as Proxicom, GridPoint, DiData, and Aguru Images, a high-end digital imaging company that he started. More recently, Dr. Miller has achieved a national reputation in the advanced smart grid and cyber-security arenas.

Scott Donaldson: A scientist, an entrepreneur, an innovator, and a technologist.

Miller: Dang.

S. Donaldson: So there's a lot to talk about.

Miller: Okay. Good.

S. Donaldson: What we'd like to talk about today is your journey through your career with respect to technology, and your role as a CTO.

Miller: Sure.

S. Donaldson: So could you provide us an overview of your journey to where you are today?

Miller: Absolutely. I started out in physics. I wanted to be a pure scientist. I was working on my dissertation in physics when the University of Virginia hired a new dean of the engineering school, who was the most charismatic, brilliant, inspirational person I ever met. He said, "Why don't you come on over and be my advisee over in the engineering school?" And I thought that was pretty cool, having the dean as your advisor, especially when he's a rock-star dean. So I ended up getting my doctorate in systems engineering, but I was working on my dissertation in physics when all this started. This was back in the mid-'70s, and I was working on energy systems engineering. As I'm sure everybody remembers, at that time we had a couple of energy embargos.

The dean said to me, "Why are you working on energy systems at UVA [University of Virginia] when they're writing the first national energy plan up in Washington, DC?" So he told me to go to Washington and get my foot in the door there. At the time, it was very early in the arena of energy policy, so I was able to walk in and meet the guy who was running Project Independence, a guy named Al Alm, who said, "It's pretty cool." Al Alm is famous, of course. He said, "I can't hire you, but the way we work is with these contractors." So he sent me over to a firm called Energy and Environmental Analysis, and they hired me instantly. I walked in the door thinking I'm going to do a job interview, and they said, "When do you start and what is your salary?" I hadn't thought about this because I'd never really worked before, and I said, "A lot, you know, and right away! So let's do this."

But the cool thing was that it was such a virgin territory, energy policy in those days, and particularly for somebody who was at a doctoral level in energy, I got way more responsibility than I was ready for. They put me to work building humongous models, doing policy analysis, actually working on some of the early designs of the Department of Energy. So I ended up being an absolutely wet-behind-the-ears kid in an extremely responsible position; about 30 people working for me a year out of college, which was interesting. Didn't realize I had the best job I would ever have in my life, up until my current one.

I went off and started my own engineering company with a few friends in Boulder, Colorado, and that was pretty successful. Then when we decided to sell that and go in the direction of economics, I joined SAIC [Science Applications International Corporation], which was a phenomenal graduate school in management. You learn how to win work, not just from how to write a proposal, but really the theory of it. How do you capture somebody's imagination? How do you align yourself with their objectives and become part of it? I stayed with SAIC for 14 years, eventually becoming a chief scientist. And about two thirds of the way through that tenure, the internet got interesting; this was 1995 or so. I really started to pursue internet-type applications. We started a different model within SAIC, where we would develop a dotcom company for equity, as opposed to just simply doing contract work. The first one I did was CATEX, which was a catastrophe risk exchange. I would say that was my first CTO role because the partners we had were experts in insurance, but the theory was that the internet would provide a ubiquitous 24/7 platform for people to negotiate reinsurance contracts. Reinsurance contracts are very complicated. You are looking at a particular catalog of risks and saying, "How much will I reinsure that for? What is the rate?" And they're large, in general, and so it's frequently necessary to syndicate them out to other people as soon as you get them. You don't want to place your own money on a bet; you want to just manage it.

So, typically, the fees were on the order of 10% of the value of the policy. So for, say, Tyson's Corner Mall, the insurance premium is $200 million; the fee for placing the program was $20 million. At that scale, it might go down to $5 million. We felt that there was an advantage to doing this online, bringing everyone together in the same space. The opposite of what people were thinking of as the internet. They were thinking of the internet at that time as selling commodity things, simple instruments like sneakers, you know, something of that sort.

We saw the greatest potential in complex instruments, things where every parameter had to be negotiated because there was a lot of information exchanged, and the ubiquity of it, the 24/7 nature, the ability to do cash-complex information, like books of business or financial statements for people to analyze later. The internet actually fits very well with the time constant of complex instrument trading.

So, working with the people who were brilliant in the insurance industry, I designed the technology for negotiating reinsurance contracts over the internet. We launched it pretty successfully. SAIC ended up owning 40% of it and then selling a piece of its share, but the market cap hit $110 million in 18 months. So the chairman was Bob Beyster, a wonderful guy.

I have to tell a Beyster story. When we started with the insurance industry, and I was looking for some money to finance this idea—you know, how do I pay people to do it? People who I talked to said, "You have to talk to Bob Beyster." I said, "Okay." I didn't know him. They said, "This guy is an executive. All he cares about is money," which, by the way, is exactly not Bob Beyster. I mean, the guy has a passion for the real grit of business.

S. Donaldson: Right.

Miller: So, I went to see him and I started pitching the concept and he said, "What do you know about the insurance industry?" I said, "I read up on it. It's pretty cool." The first sentence said, by the way, "The $3.2 trillion dollar United States reinsurance industry," and after the word "trillion," the first time I ever saw it printed, I knew I was hooked. I was an insurance dude from that point on. I said, "Well, it's the largest industry in the United States." He said, "No, it isn't. Health care is," and I said, "Well, excuse me, but every check the healthcare industry gets is written by an insurance company. Half of our health care is subsidiary." He thought about it and then he just laughed. And we veered off from talking about money to talking about the opportunity. After that things just went well. When we sold our share, it was at a market cap of $110 billion, so we didn't do badly. I got a really cool award, and this got me on the radar screen.

We started a couple of other dotcoms in green energy and environmental applications and things of that sort. The model was working, so I was recruited by Proxicom, which was one of the hottest of all the dotcom integrators at the time. I was recruited there and I became their first chief technology officer. That was a wonderful gig between 2000 and 2003, only a three-year period, but it was amazing. I mean, there were staggering amounts of money and the technology was changing monthly.

S. Donaldson: I bet.

Miller: Keeping up with it and trying to put the company where it needed to be was a huge challenge. Raul Fernandez, who was the CEO and founder of Proxicom, was one of the owners of the Washington Capitals, so he's a hockey fan, and he used to say that what made Wayne Gretzky wonderful was that he skated to where the puck was going to be. If I have a definition of what a CTO is, it's helping the company skate to where the puck is going to be.

The company's underlying technology was changing rapidly and the world's vision of the dotcom business was changing; it was phenomenal. It was a great experience trying to keep up and trying to lead them. The company was bought by Dimension Data, one of the largest integration firms in the world. They're based in Africa. Most of the executives at Proxicom weren't running their own show anymore and they wanted to get out. I fell in love with being a global chief architect of a multibillion-dollar integration firm. Très cool. All of a sudden, there were just infinite resources and infinite opportunity there.

So I stayed there until I got very, very sick. I was working in Africa. I got a tropical disease. I came home. I was laid up for most of the year, and basically was doing a little bit of work for DiData from home, but not very much. I came out of retirement when a company called GridPoint came along. I walked in and looked at them, and it was a very interesting company. Still is; they're still there. But they were searching for direction, and as part of the executive team there, I tried to reposition them to a specific area.

S. Donaldson: Right.

Miller: There was no unanimity of opinion on the direction among management, and I was outnumbered, so I left on favorable terms. They're friends and they're good people; it's a great company and I still endorse them.

S. Donaldson: Right.

Miller: It wasn't a fit for me. Throughout my career people with advanced technology will come to me and ask me, "Does this work? Does this not work? How would you modify this? Can you fix this? Would you adjust its market? Who would buy this? Who doesn't?"

So I went to MAPA, which is the consulting firm that I am a partner in and CTO of right now. These guys walked in the door and said, "Here is some wonderful imaging technology that we built and the patents," just raw patents. They were a VC [venture capital] firm. They say, "Can you do due diligence on these?" I said, "Sure." I started reading up on imaging, which sounds like, "Well, what do you know about imaging, Craig?" And the answer is...

S. Donaldson: About as much as you knew about insurance.

Miller: Pretty much, yeah. So I read the book anyway. [Laughter] I was pretty quick. The cool thing about modern cameras is that they are all digital. There is no image in the camera. There are just 60 million voltage measurements.

S. Donaldson: Right.

Miller: And turning 60 million voltage measurements into an image is heavy-duty math; the same sort of ultra-large-scale mathematics I was doing in physics in structural modeling, and things of that sort. I jumped in and I did the stupidest thing a consultant could possibly do. I said, "No chance in Hell.

We can't make it. These won't work." And I thought, "Man, that's the end of the gig. I'm in trouble here, guys." Working with a terrific partner, we put together a business plan to improve the technology and build advanced imaging equipment. And that became Aguru Images, for which I was the CTO and CEO, and then just CTO later when we found serious management grown-ups to manage it.

S. Donaldson: Real managers.

Miller: [Laughter] Yeah, exactly! Real managers. We built ultra-high-end imaging equipment that's been used extensively in the movie industry for capturing all the data needed to do advanced special effects. That company continues under Maybridge Imaging. It's a new company under a different legal form, with different ownership, but is building ultra-high-end optical scanners. The company doesn't have the scale to produce a mass-produced product for volume. So it's constantly about inventing the next frontier and selling people a concept and then building it for them.

S. Donaldson: Okay.

Miller: We're doing that now and, in fact, this afternoon I'm working on software for that. I'm doing that, not a full-time gig, and along comes the smart grid investment grants and the smart grid demonstration program—huge stimulus projects from the DoE [Department of Energy], multiple billions.

S. Donaldson: Right.

Miller: NRECA, National Rural Electric Cooperative Association, invited me over to help them win grants and demonstrations. Because of my experience at SAIC and elsewhere, I'd become a bit of an elephant hunter, you know, learning how to win big gigs. It's more than just having a technical vision.

S. Donaldson: Right.

Miller: It's putting the names on it, people who the customers are familiar with. It's a lot of detail, which you know very well. So the first question they asked me was a great one. They asked, "What do you know about co-ops [utility cooperatives]?" I hadn't done my homework. I said, "My gosh. I don't know anything about co-ops. They're a riddle."

S. Donaldson: We're back to the insurance question!

Miller: Yeah, we're back to the insurance question! So they said, "Well, stop a minute." They gave me a briefing called "Co-op 101," which teaches you all about co-ops. After that I said, "Can I not do my presentation? Can I actually think about this?" I thought about it for a little while, overnight, and I said, "This group can't lose because they have a history of doing research.

Seventy-five percent of all land in the United States is served by electric co-ops, so the DoE has to pay attention to them. Collectively we're the largest utility out there, provider of electricity. So there has to be a lot of money, there has to be a substantial body of research that has to go in to co-ops. We could be the best coop project because we deal with 900+ co-ops here at NRECA, and we put together a single project where the work is spread over a couple dozen co-ops. So we could get economic diversity, diversity in the kinds of projects we do, diversity in climate, okay."

S. Donaldson: Great qualifications.

Miller: So I looked at this and said, "Unless we do a bad job of writing it, this is a slam dunk." At the end, by the way, they asked if we had any letters of endorsement. Co-ops are in almost every Congressional district, at least half of the districts. We asked a few members of the House, the Senate, and governors, and everybody we didn't ask was offended for being left out. We got multiple letters of endorsement, including two from the state of Alaska, Sarah Palin and her successor.

S. Donaldson: So the Letters of Endorsement were longer than the proposal?

Miller: Yes, exactly! That was embarrassing because it looked like we were just trying to buy the bid.

S. Donaldson: Right, right.

Miller: But we didn't know how to tell a U.S. Senator, "No, we don't need your endorsement."

S. Donaldson: Yeah, probably not a good career move.

Miller: So I'm here running a very large research project in the smart grid and trying to knock down barriers.

S. Donaldson: Out of all of those positions, what did you enjoy most as you progressed?

Miller: Well, I learned that I'm a two-year guy. And by that, I mean, when a new problem comes up, the first two years are incredibly exciting. You have a blank sheet of paper. You can go in any direction. There's a high premium on innovation. There's the hard question of how far do you go? As you may recall, when they were building the atomic bomb, when they were three-quarters of the way through, Andrew Teller and others realized that they could build a fusion device rather than a fission device, and he wanted to stop work on the atomic bomb and build the "super," as he called it, because it was a fusion device and didn't need all this plutonium and uranium. Well, you know, there's always that question. Do you go for the super, or do you take a more certain but less advanced win? Where do you go? Those are the hardest, most exciting questions. Two years in, they're answered, then it's grinding out the project. I'm competent at that, but my passion, the part that just excites me, is the first two years. The problem is finding a way to make it interesting before everybody realizes I'm no longer the guy. I mean, they love me the first two years. The third year, they going to say, "What the hell do we have this guy for?"

S. Donaldson: We've got a couple of very interesting areas to probe here. One is your role here at NRECA.

Miller: Sure.

S. Donaldson: Also the Aguru Imaging that you did.

Miller: Sure.

S. Donaldson: In terms of the technology, could you give us a little bit more insight into both jobs?

Miller: Let's do Aguru first. It used to be that you took a picture on film. You don't do that anymore. You now capture the information digitally. You make images from them, but you can do more than that. A charge-coupled device, the core of every camera, is just a collection of voltmeters. They're photo-sensitive voltmeters. You have a 20-megapixel camera; you have 60 million voltmeter measurements, red, green, and blue, or 80 million if it's a CMYK camera [cyan (bluish-green), magenta, yellow and key (black)]. So think of it not as making pictures, but as very precisely spatially registered voltage meters, light meters. I know if I'm looking at a scene and I have something about the geometry of it, I can use those voltage measurements off the CCD [charge-coupled device] to do what's known as "optical metrology." That's measurement of things using optical means. Now, suppose you want to do special effects. What you want to do is you want to take an actor and put his face in the movie. They're asked in one scene to do something they couldn't possibly do.

S. Donaldson: Right.

Miller: Working on the movie G.I. Joe, one of the guys we built an image of was drilled into the head in a torture scene. Obviously, the actors weren't queuing up for that job! The guy's name was Screaming Man. Unfortunately, his one scene was cut. He was a great guy. But what you need is a human head that looks exactly like the actor. A generic human head is pretty easy. You make some shapes and you sprinkle pimple dust over it, and it looks like a real person. Everybody goes, "Ooh!" There's the detail. That's easy.

That kind of special effect is easy. The hard part is where there are live actors in the scene. Then the face has to be done digitally because it has to match a specific person, not just be a realistic one, and people are complicated. There's the shape of the face and if you're really going to be realistic, you have to go down to the level of the pores. There's the way they move. It's called the "rigging." You know, people's faces move different ways.

I saw a woman on TV. Her name is Greta Van Susteren. She only smiles on one side of her mouth. If the digital Greta smiles with both sides everybody would say, "That's wrong."

S. Donaldson: Right.

Miller: Jim Carrey, I don't know how you rig him. He can do anything. So there's the rigging, and then there's the other very complicated part, and that's the reflection. If you look at a person, you see some shininess off the surface of the skin. You see pink on the cheeks because you're looking straight on. And you're seeing into the fat and the blood and everything else, but on the sides you see tan because the light you're seeing is refracted through multiple layers, and you're no longer seeing the pink.

So if you simulate a person and they turn their head, the pink has to move, right? So you have to capture a staggering amount of information on the shapes of faces, on the way people's faces move, and on the reflection properties, so that for every little tiny polygon on a face, you have to say what it will look like from any angle under any light. That's a huge, huge amount of information. But once you've got it, if you have a giant render form, you can make a perfectly realistic person.

What we did is we went into the area of optical metrology and developed flat-bed scanners for looking at materials, like woods, leathers, vinyls, furs, any kind of flat thing. Then we developed a 12-foot-diameter flat sphere that the actor sat in the middle of. It had 946 lights, 93 computers, all synchronized. Using a technique developed by a terrific scientist at the University of Southern California, a fellow by the name of Paul Debevec who isdefinitely the best brain in the space of special effects and imaging. We had an actor sit in this camera and the lights swept from back to front, top to bottom, and swept over him in different ways while we captured the information on the cameras.

S. Donaldson: Okay.

Miller: We were able to derive these reflection models. This is now the standard approach, frankly, for developing digital characters in Hollywood. Unfortunately, there are competitors, who also work with USC, but that's the concept. The concept is this advanced optical metrology and reflectrometry.

S. Donaldson: Since we're on Hollywood, what are some of the movies that you guys have gotten involved in?

Miller: Oh, I'll only mention two. G.I. Joe was a great film because G.I. Joe was a $200 million, super special effects movie with incredible people, really interesting people, costumes, sets. And this was our first time. We were naïve. I'd never been on a movie set before. And we set up our camera inside a completely black tent and operated there. We operated our own camera because we hadn't trained anybody else in how to do it yet. We were special effects photographers. Let's say there's a huge hierarchy on a movie set. You've got the talent, you've got the directors, all of those guys. And way down at the bottom are the special effects photographers. They send guys over to you to capture the data, not the guys who do the special effects. They're heroes.

S. Donaldson: Right.

Miller: But they're not on set. They're doing their work with computers off somewhere else. But these guys are just capturing the data. So it was really fun for me, for the first time in my life, to be at the absolute bottom of the totem pole. I mean, it was phenomenal. We had a personal assistant who was supposed to help us out with things, and I realized, "Oh, that's really cool." In reality, he was supposed to make sure that we were ready to go when the director wanted us to be ready to go or when somebody needed us.

So it was fascinating. But what would happen is that the actors would come in and we would do the models. And some of them were, "Just take the picture. I want to get out of here. I've been around all kinds of movie stuff." Others were really cool, and there was a family day and one of the actresses on the set was Sienna Miller, who's pretty famous. She brought her mom over to see our camera, which was really cool. So we made a digital of Sienna's mom, which we haven't deployed anywhere, because you need a lot of software to use ours.

S. Donaldson: Oh, that's cool.

Miller: But she was really sweet. And another actor, who was a real athlete, climbed all over our dome and stood on the top like King Kong, which was just fun. It was an entertaining experience.

On the other side, the biggest movie ever made in India is called Endhiran. Endhiran is worldwide, and it stars superstar Rajinikanth, who is by far the biggest Indian actor. He was a total hit. He was fun. He came to Los Angeles, and enjoyed not being the most famous guy in the world. You know, he could go into a fast food restaurant and just sit there. It was fascinating. It impressed the heck out of me because what I didn't realize is that entertainment is one of the largest exports out of the United States. It's a huge cash export. And we totally dominate the business, not just because of the PR [public relations] and the actors and everything else, but also because we have a technology lead that is totally insurmountable. Nobody can do digital effects like the United States.

S. Donaldson: Were you able to do an Alfred Hitchcock and show up in the movies someplace?

Miller: No, I wish I could have. [Laughter]

S. Donaldson: So back to what you're doing here now, can you talk about the technologies?

Miller: The biggest project that this country has ever done is rebuilding the smart grid, rebuilding the electrical grid. In the 1980s, we made structural changes in the electrical grid. We deregulated and created competition. There's a plus side to that: without a doubt, some elements of competition have helped. But there are also things that fell through the cracks. And one of the problems we had is that we underinvested in transmission and distribution. We've gotten to the point now where the average transformer in the United States, the average transformer, is older than its design lifetime.

S. Donaldson: Right.

Miller: So how do we fix this? Well, the old metal that was the driver for the electrical utility industry was copper. But this isn't a copper problem. We can't deploy thousands or tens of thousands of miles of heavy new copper. Site issues, lots of new transformers and everything else, are all very expensive. But in the meantime, silicon technology has developed. We now have the ability to use the information that we can get from the grid through sensor technology to control it with much greater precision, to make better use of copper assets.

I talked a while ago to some students from the co-ops about this topic. They came here to learn about NRECA. What is the Cooperative Research Network? What is the smart grid? I did some work the night before talking with them and I said, "How can I impress some of these kids that this is a cool thing to do?" This is bigger than the Apollo program. It has more parts, it has a bigger budget, it has more people involved, and it's going to have a greater effect on the welfare and economy of our nation. This is the Apollo program of the 21st century, or at least the first half.

S. Donaldson: Interesting comparison.

Miller: I hope, for the people at the end of the century, we have it solved and that there's another cool problem to solve. But for 2011, the coolest problem there is right now is building the smart grid. Everybody thinks of it in terms of meters. "I'm going to give this person a meter, and they're going to walk in, and they're going to see an in-home display, and they're going to sit there every night, managing their energy." Well, I'll give you a clue here, CSI [Crime Scene Investigation] is a hell of a lot more interesting than anybody's in-home portal.

But there's another part of this smart grid that the average Joe doesn't know about—shouldn't know about—because they're not in the business. And that's the kind of sensor technology that tells us, with great precision, how much current is flowing on this line? What is the phase? What is the voltage? And that precision allows us to use more advanced controls to make better use of the copper.

I'll give you a little example. I've got an electrical wire that's swinging back and forth in a bad wind. Its carrying capacity is actually lower than if that cable were hanging there precisely still. The physics of it is pretty clear. They're just fields interacting with each other. But in the old days, we didn't know what the capacity of a line was going to be. What's the wind blowing? What's the temperature now, and everything else? We would rate every line at its lowest capacity, under the worst conditions. We're assuming 110 degrees and a hurricane. The actual capacity is higher. Now we can develop technologies like dynamic line rating that measure in real time the capacity of every line and allow us to use it effectively. We can do conservation voltage reduction. We can reduce voltage in small amounts, below the level that's damaging to transformers and motors, and get more capacity under extreme circumstances. Here's the problem, here's what we're doing: number 1, obtaining much greater knowledge of state; knowing exactly what's going on in every single part of the grid. That's what we're trying to achieve. Number 2, we're trying to develop controls that allow us to moderate the flows and turn devices on and off and react to those. In the middle is the coolest and hardest problem of all. That's taking industrial control systems that are kind of old and kind of limited and enabling them to use all of this information dynamically to provide sort of the brain between the state side and the action side, the corpus callosum, if you will, of electrical utility operations. The amount of information that we're going to get is orders of magnitude larger than traditional amounts. EPRI [Electric Power Research Institute] estimates the data is going to be 10,000 times the amount of data we're processing now. IBM estimates it's 100,000 times. So we take a system and you scale it up 100,000 times, and anybody who's ever built big systems knows you don't just turn the crank. You don't just turn up the accelerator when you're going up 100,000 times. You have to do things differently.

Now, that's a really hard problem, the biggest control problem ever made, ever. Okay? Nobody's ever built control systems like the ones that we're going to have 10 years from now. What makes it particularly difficult is that it's different than deploying sensor technology. I can add one sensor, two sensors, 100 sensors, no big deal. Increment. Little baby steps. I can do the same with controls. Big batteries for frequency control? Those are pretty hard, but you can still do them one at a time. How do you transition, though, in that back end, the brain that's driving all of this from something that's very static and operating in a small scale to something that is totally different? Not just in scale, but in architecture?

We have to swap out these systems in big chunks, taking into account the cloud, taking into account virtualization and security, overlay that with the most delicate and important systems we've got, and we are going to have to make use of cloud computing. So how do we make it work?

S. Donaldson: In addition to the technology, there are the people who will need to use the technology.

Miller: You bet.

S. Donaldson: Is the manpower there? Is the education directed that way to help support the largest transformation we've ever had?

Miller: [Laughter] We're getting there. You know, there's a saying in Africa, and remember DiData was an African firm, so I spent a lot of time in Africa. And there's an old joke about how to eat an elephant, and the answer is, "One bite at a time."

S. Donaldson: Right.

Miller: The paradigm that we have to institute here is not jumping to these new supermen, but being better a month from now, three months from now, six months from now. One step at a time.

Drucker's book on management, Management, I mean, great title. You've got to be there early if you're going to get the name Management for your textbook, right? As far as I'm concerned, every other book I've ever read is a riff on that applied to a different context. One of the points he made is that excellence, or quality, is not a state that you achieve but a metric by which you measure yourself. So that you're never good enough, you're never good enough, okay?

S. Donaldson: Right.

Miller: So what we're trying to do is to set out plans, technological, organizational, procedural, to achieve continuous improvement. That's the metaphor.

Stan Siegel: You and I come from similar backgrounds. I'm also a physicist.

Miller: Hey.

Siegel: So my question to you is, as part of your CTO role, do you get into discussions regarding where your company should move with respect to things like, "Let's do away with above-ground transmission lines?"

Miller: At NRECA we don't have a CTO title. I'm senior program manager. But the answer to your question is yes, we are absolutely in that dialogue with all of our co-ops. We spend an awful lot of time listening. I can theoretically talk about above-ground vs. underground, and then people come along and start to inform me of the reality on the ground. For example, Delta Montrose Electric Association would say, "We don't have soil, we have rock."

But the answer is yeah, we are very much looking at those issues, and physics factors into it a lot. One of the most important things we can do now is develop storage, grid-scale storage, batteries that have a megawatt hour-type capability because they help integrate renewables, but they also help frequency control because a lot of the renewables, for example, create frequency variations on the grid.

S. Donaldson: So for the uneducated, what are frequency variations and associated issues?

Miller: Frequency variation can be very, very damaging to end-use devices. Normally, we're 60.0 Hertz; that is sixty cycles per second. But if that goes too high or too low, it dramatically shortens the lifetime of all kinds of electronics, not just the low-voltage electronics like computers and stuff. But it also affects the performance of high-powered stuff, like large motors and capacitors. We like 60.0. We're committed to it.

What happens is if I build one windmill and I connect it [to the grid]? The windmill makes electricity because there's a shaft going around and blades driving it. And that shaft has magnets and coils, and as the coils pass the magnet, it makes electricity. The voltage goes up and down. It's higher and lower as each of the stators passes the inductor part. So it's creating a little chatter that's out there that's affecting me. Now, if I run that through a battery, it might snap back instantly to 60.0. Because the battery's absorbing it: "Yep. We're storing energy." And then when you pull it back out, it's 60.0. So we're looking at big batteries for energy storage.

But the physics comes in there because ultimately, every battery just consists of something that moves an ion from one place to another, and the question is, how small can those little ions be? If I'm talking about lithium, lithium's the third-lightest element in the periodic table: hydrogen, helium, lithium. You're getting down to the limits of the tiniest things you can move around. If I were talking about the old heavy, lead-acid batteries with their electrolytes that were up in the sulfur range, much lower performance.

So the physical limits are ultimately a factor in the engineering of all electrical systems. The challenge we have is this: when we're talking about Moore's law and computers, and the density of transistors kept getting higher and higher and higher, everybody calculated out that, "The ultimate density is this and then Moore's law is going to stop." Then, of course, we smashed through it because people found other operating principles. They found ideas like parallelism and stuff of that sort. The issue in what we're doing now on things like storage, is how are we going to bust through our physical limits to make our Moore's law on the cost of storage and the cost of photovoltaics go away?

S. Donaldson: Right, right.

Miller: So I cannot think of a better education ever than physics. I got a report yesterday I won't talk about that had an egregious mathematical error. I was able to find that mathematical error because, being trained in physics, you learn to do arithmetic pretty well. It just jumped out at me and I laughed my head off at it, but it completely undermines a major report that came out yesterday.

S. Donaldson: So, Stan, you and Craig can get together later on and . . .

Miller: We'll do the secret handshake!

S. Donaldson: And laugh over this math error you're showing me. So let's do this. Let's switch gears a little bit. And talk about what you do day-to-day. If there's one, what's a typical day look like?

Miller: I play Whack-a-Mole a lot. It's a terrific game. It's good for reflexes. It takes out all your violence. The project that I'm running right now is a big one, it's $68 million. It involves 23 cooperatives over 12 states and it involves the deployment of between 250,000 and 300,000 smart grid components. Without a doubt, the most complex thing I've ever tried to run. I've run big projects before, but 90% of the people were in the same room. And we had weekly meetings. I don't know how to do this one. This one's tough. It's broken into 85 subprojects. So I took an entirely different approach to management.

S. Donaldson: Okay.

Miller: I was actually in the airport in Milwaukee when there was a huge snowstorm in Washington, so I couldn't get home. I had to sit three nights in the airport hotel. It was early on in the project, so I said, "All right. I've got three days. I'm not even leaving the hotel. I'm living on bratwurst," that's what the bar served, "and I'm going to design this project." I sat down and I listed everything that has to be done on this project, just a complete list. It was about 170 things. I said, "This is how I do it." I then did a cluster analysis, saying, "The people who do this one could also do this one or this one." I did a cluster analysis of all the functionality. I defined a team for each one of those clusters, and I came up with 17 teams. It sounds like a lot, but there's a lot going on in this project. I came back here and we staffed the teams: who's the best person to lead this team? We eliminated a lot of committees. Committees talk about stuff. Teams do things.

S. Donaldson: Right.

Miller: So there was a team lead on every cluster. I sat down and I went over my list, and I asked each team to write their own charter, a description of how they were going to do their work. There are two reasons for that: number 1, it is incredibly stupid, it is the biggest error you can make in business to not have a capacity for self-doubt. I have analyzed this project, but there are a lot of smart people in this world. I wanted other smart people to write it themselves. They wrote their charters, and then I compared it to my list, and then we synthesized. I gave them a general description, I had a specific one, and then we synthesized.

Every team wrote their own instructions. Every team lead found and recruited the people for the team. They had people they trusted. They also all came to me and said, "Well, this is with that other team, isn't it?" I said, "Sure. Figure out how you're going to work with them." We spent an amazing amount of time on organization.

Also, we were going to buy about 300,000 things, right? How do you do that? Well, the first thing you do is a cluster analysis of all the things you're buying. Then you write a template RFP. You can buy them from different co-ops; there might be little differences, but they're general. You vet the crap out of that, and you talk to DoE and say, "Is this kosher?" The answer is, "Yeah." You put in place an evaluation process. You lay everything down. At the beginning of this year, when we were ready to start buying, we were a little criticized by DoE because we had only spent 2% of the hardware budget. Six months later, we'd spent 75%, and not a single procurement was difficult for us or expensive, and they were all in complete compliance with DoE. So I spent absolutely everything on organization.

What people here haven't figured out yet is that we are now in Whack-a-Mole mode, meaning the systems work, the processes are in place, everything runs smoothly. My job is just to sit here and wait for somebody to raise their hand to say, "Oh, we've got a problem! We've got a problem!" Then a person comes into my office and says, "What are we going to do about this?" So I scratch my beard and I think about it a while, and I say, "What team do you think would be best at that?" And they would say, "Well, that's a study issue." "Ahh. Good. Take it to the study team, okay?"

So all I am is a traffic director. And it's great. I'm also a pretty good spokesman for the project because part of this is to communicate what we're running. It's not just deploying stuff. It's teaching people about it. And I do that a lot. But right now the balance of this project is in total Whack-a-Mole mode. We've got the systems to do it.

S. Donaldson: What do you see as your biggest challenge?

Miller: Biggest challenge? Technology change. The smart grid now is the dotcom in the early first part of the decade. When we started this project, the cloud was not an issue. "We're not going to use the cloud because the cloud isn't secure; because we need immediate control over this; because the cloud isn't reliable, yah-dah-yah-dah-yah-dah." Now, we discover that these new systems that control the smart grid are staggeringly complex, 10^4, 10^5, larger. What do you do? Do you triple the size of your IT team? Do you send them all to school to learn new things? I don't know about that. So what we're seeing is that the big vendors, the people who build these systems, are increasingly offering from the cloud on a paid-per-drink basis. And I like that for a few reasons:

It gets it under really professional management;

The capital cost is modest; and

Improvements can be propagated across the entire industry very quickly.

I had not anticipated the pace at which we would be moving to the cloud. I anticipated that we would be moving to the cloud because IT is not a core competency of co-ops. Their core competency is maintaining the copper and a great customer relationship. They're good at IT. It's not what they get up every morning wanting to do. Technology change is the biggest challenge and the cloud is the biggest change for me.

S. Donaldson: What external organizations do you interface with? Do you have associations with universities?

Miller: Yeah. We have associations with universities, U.S. national laboratories. University relationships include North Carolina State University, which has something called the Freedom Center. The University of Tulsa is a leader in good cyber-security. Carnegie Mellon University does some good stuff, and I was just up at Carnegie Mellon two weeks ago talking to their doctoral students about advanced research, and we learned a lot from them. We have relationships with a lot of local universities, University of Tennessee, Missouri and others.

S. Donaldson: The co-op is spread out across the country so you've got associations across the country.

Miller: Yeah, absolutely. We have associations with national laboratories that are incredibly useful. Pacific Northwest National Lab has been invaluable in helping advance our understanding of good cyber-security. We have association with the regulatory agencies such as NERC [North American Electric Reliability Corporation] and reliability councils such as NIST [National Institute of Standards and Technology], because another monster issue for me is standards. And EPRI, of course. I hope somebody else has mentioned the name Annabelle Lee, one of the absolute leaders in the area of cyber-security, formerly the head of that function at NIST. We talk to a lot of people.

Let me mention NIST in particular. The greatest technological success in the U.S., in the world actually, in the last 20 years has been the internet and the way we make computer networks in general work. The foundation of that success is standards that allow people to concentrate on a particular function, not having to try to solve the whole problem, and to make things interoperable. Everybody buys a little wireless router from Radio Shack, takes it home, plugs it in and it works. And nontechnical people do that.

S. Donaldson: Right.

Miller: That's only because the engineering's so good. The foundation is the interoperability standards. On the copper side of the grid, we have excellent standards, IEEE [Institute of Electrical and Electronics Engineers] has for over a century pounded those out. The plugs fit [in the wall outlet].

We are way behind in the area of IT interoperability standards related to the grid. The most widely deployed standard is the one developed by NRECA called "MultiSpeak." I think it is the best interoperability standard, but I think it has a long way to go before it's good enough.

S. Donaldson: Where do you look for technical people to come in and work here and help you do what you need to do?

Miller: I have the world's simplest interview form and criteria, it's: Unintelligent? Yes or no. Prima Donna? Yes or no. Difficult to Work With? Yes or no. And that's it. I only work with the smartest people I can possibly find—literally, the smartest people, provided that they are not prima donnas. They recognize that everybody else on the team has something to contribute and they're not difficult to work with. They're not going around misbehaving and undermining people.

S. Donaldson: Okay.

Miller: Everybody interviews everybody I work with. If they get a negative grade on each of those three criteria, they're hired. There was a study done by Robert Glass, who was a systems analyst-type person, not computers systems, but human systems analyst. He worked for IBM, and then went to Carnegie Mellon. He looked at the productivity of software developers, and he had an objective criterion, and that was: how many lines of code that they wrote showed up in the final product? Utterly ambiguous, and a guy who gets a low grade can say, "Well, mine was important in this and that, and it led to that," or "He based his on mine." And Robert Glass would say, "Yes, thanks very much. How much of your code made it into the final product?" He found that the top 5% in IT produced 27 times as much as the bottom 5%, 27 times, okay? Similar metrics have been calculated for other industries, but none of them rivals IT or math.

So I figure, "Hmm. Why don't I just work with people in the top decile?" No management issues. No matter what you pay them, they're cheap. So I've consistently, through Aguru, GridPoint, and here, worked with largely the same group of people. We come together and we collaborate on interesting problems. I came into NRECA and I met other people who apparently, on their own, had come up with this strategy, and some of the very best brains I've ever met in the energy industry are already here. They are guys I work with all the time. Find super people and tell them you love them.

S. Donaldson: Okay. You've talked about some of the technologies that are important. Like cloud and cyber. Are there other transformative technologies you see?

Miller: Here's the one that could change everything. I was up at Carnegie Mellon two weeks ago, and we talked to all the graduate students, and they asked us, "What are the game-changing technologies?" And I showed a slide. It showed the flux capacitor from Back to the Future, you know, where you put the bananas in and all the energy comes out. And everybody laughed, and I said, "I'm serious." Absent that, which we have no idea how to do and it probably violates every law of physics, we're not talking game-changing in the grid because it is so massive. The investment is so large. And because the performance criteria are so high, you can't just throw something in and hope it lasts. How long does a meter in your house last? Forty years, fifty years. Transformers, 40 years. Because they're difficult to maintain, and they would be difficult to maintain if they ever failed. They don't and because people's lives depend on this, and welfare and the economy, we have incredibly high standards, we operate under the most difficult conditions, and the investment is trillions. No such thing as game-changing technology. That said, there are areas that are harder than others, and one of them is grid-connected storage, very large batteries. I already mentioned that.

S. Donaldson: Right.

Miller: The second is the sophistication of the control systems. That's a huge area. We're going to make massive things. But here's the third one: learning how to do power electronics in solid state. Right now a transformer essentially has a yoke with coils, a number of wires on one side and loops on one side and a number on the other, and the voltage changes the ratio. Well, there are problems with that. Those are heavy machines, and they can't continue to change voltage. They're always up by 10 or down by 10, right? Up step or down step. But if we want to do precise voltage control, what we'd prefer would be a solid-state switching transformer: choo-choo-choo-choo-choo-choo-choo. Those types of transformers exist. You can buy them. You can use them in your PC, no problem. Well, the PCs don't use anything that expensive because of the price.

S. Donaldson: Right.

Miller: But if you had high-performance electronics and you wanted digital voltage control, you could do it. But they can't handle the currents we handle. So the real breakthrough I think is going to be solid-state high-powered components, and that kind of work is going on at a number of laboratories. I've seen a solid-state transformer that appears to work perfectly. It's about the size of the office we're sitting in, and there is a very earnest graduate student from Korea explaining it to me. I said, "You know, it's really nice, but it's going to be hard getting it up a pole." He was so earnest, he didn't laugh and but proceeded to explain to me their 10-year strategy to minimize the size. [Laughter]

S. Donaldson: So they could get it up on the pole.

Miller: Yeah, exactly. If we can take solid state and move it into high-powered electronics. I don't mean kiddy-level power electronics, building-level; I mean grid-level. That's a phenomenal breakthrough.

Siegel: How much time do you spend with your physics background looking into things like what's rattling the physics world now regarding things being able to move faster than the speed of light?

Miller: Well, I posted one of the 80 alternate explanations to that, but that was just for fun. That wasn't part of my job, and mine didn't win. I was another defender of Einstein. The answer is, everything I do, everything I see is viewed through the lens of physics because in the end. For example, there's a group out there who want to grow algae. And algae is phenomenal. Algae is probably one of the only solutions to carbon dioxide. It absorbs CO_2 faster than anything else and it's incredibly valuable stuff if you use it right. You can feed animals with it, you can burn it, you can make straight-chain hydrocarbons out of it, great stuff. I can't tell you the number of people who have actually proposed to me growing algae under artificial light. What's the problem with that? Well, I burn energy to make light and, of course, it's not 100% efficient to make the electricity. Then I take the electricity and convert it to light, and it's not 100% efficient, and then I shine it onto algae, which don't absorb 100% of the light. What am I doing here guys? I'm using energy to make less energy. Doug Dannelly, a brilliant MIT engineer who works in the next office here and who is one of my pals and one of my team—I've been working with for a long time—keeps a list of proposals to violate the second law of thermodynamics. We have an entire collection of them. We've seen people actually shine lights on photocells, which is hilarious.

So the answer is: I see everything through the lens of what's possible in physics. The best thing about physics is that it encompasses the rules for operating the world, and that physics problems are genuinely hard. So when you're working on a hard problem in physics, and my area at the doctoral level was low-energy collisions which are very complicated because in high energy, you either hit the target and blast it to smithereens, or you miss it and you just go by too fast. Low energy, everything's about orbits and forming molecules and bond cession and DNA and stuff like that. So it's actually pretty complicated mathematically. I learned to think about a problem really hard and nothing but that problem for weeks. I don't know too many other disciplines that will let you think about something for weeks.

One of the problems that I've always had in my career is that when I get to something like that and I want I think about a problem for a long time, people are so tied into email now, but also meetings and memos in the old days, they couldn't quite understand why I would be sitting on the floor in my office—and I do my best thinking sitting on the floor. I don't know why. If the guy sits on the floor of his office for two weeks, is he goofing off? Is he dead? I don't know, but sometimes problems require that. For example, we've become convinced here that the way energy technology is being modeled for evaluation purposes is fundamentally messed up because everybody's developing their own little piecemeal model and they don't work off a common world view. We're starting construction on something called the "Open Modeling Framework," which manages our worldview and our grid and will have hard interfaces that technology modules can plug into so that we can do AB comparisons of this versus that. Right now we can't do it. I've got an analysis of this and an analysis of that battery. How do they work in the actual grid? So that's a whole different way of approaching it, but that took probably six weeks to think about and sketch out and the only education that I know that pushes you in that direction is physics.

Siegel: Craig, let me ask you this since you and I come from similar backgrounds, been there and done that. Are you viewed by your peers as a visionary, and when you stand up and say, in mixed company, "I think here's a good idea that we may want to invest in to push the frontiers of science." Do you get involved with that type of stuff?

Miller: Oh, totally, totally. And do I have the respect of my peers? The answer's, "Hell, yes." In fact, one of the problems is that people don't call "baloney" on me enough. One of the things that I've been reading in the last two years is why we believe things and how we learn. It's very clear that belief comes before the rationalization now, that we're making our decisions at a subconscious level and then making the facts to support it. We're far less rational than we were. We're better at rationalizing things.

So the thing that I'd been trying so hard to cultivate is a capacity for self-doubt. And while I will ultimately not achieve the level of doubt that I want, I try very hard to have everyone around me doubt because that's the only way to harden it. Charles Darwin—fantastic—I mean, anybody who's done science has to really, really read Darwin, not just The Origin of Species, but his books on pigeons, his books on worms, everything this man wrote because he was so meticulous, so relentless, so objective. He's so far beyond me. He's beyond "the me of my imagination" on its best night. Charles Darwin was phenomenal, but one of the things that Charles Darwin did is whenever he had a fact or an opinion or something appeared to him that disagreed with his model, he wrote it down immediately. He didn't stop. He said, "Wait. I have to write this down," because he observed that the things that contradict your worldview are very quickly forgotten.

They are now looking at PET scans in real time, proving that's true. I don't know, the ACH experiments, A-C-H, psychologists. He took a very simple test, and he drew a vertical line on a piece of paper, on a card, and then he held up another card that had three vertical lines on it, A, B, and C. And you were you supposed to say which one was the same length as the one on the first card. Very simple test, very simple. And he would do this 100 times or whatever. For the real test was there were five or six people in the room—actually, it was eight initially, but he got down to smaller numbers. Everybody except one person was in on the game, and they would name the wrong length of the line. What they found was that everybody went along with the prevailing opinion, or the majority went along with the prevailing opinion, more than half the time. Now, that's cool, but he did this back in the '50s and '60s.

Recently, they have actually done the same experiment but while people were having their brain scanned. They have determined that the people aren't lying to conform to the other people in the group, but that their worldview has actually changed. That the only parts of the brain that were lighting up were the perception part and not the part, the cerebellum, where they would be analyzing it, saying, "I need to conform." So we've demonstrated an absolute ability to fool ourselves. If I'm sitting here trying to drive research in a particular direction and potentially committing a lot of resources and even beyond our resources, leading other people to move in a particular direction, I have to doubt. I have to listen to everybody I can. I have to sit down and critique my own arguments and say, "Why do I believe that?" Not the facts that would indicate it's true, but why do I internally believe that and then attach my facts to it?

Gary Donaldson: They used that same experiment to explain the influence of culture on behavior.

Miller: You bet. Thank you. I was aware of that, yeah. Isn't that impressive?

G. Donaldson: I have a question about the science paradigms you mentioned. You stated several times the supremacy of physics. Do you see any convergence between the different disciplines in any way?

Miller: Oh my goodness. I would not go into physics if I were to go into college again, if I were an undergrad. And the answer is yes, there's a convergence, but the convergence is actually driven by technology. In my youth, biology consisted of coming up with a name for every animal, cladism, and really crude, nonmathematical stuff. Chemistry consisted of mixing things together, kind of turning your head so it doesn't blow up on you, and the number of chemistry experiments that were literally, you know, "Try A, B, and C, and see what happens." Both chemistry and biology, and we're just talking about the core of sciences now; the old natural science core is having phenomenal advances mostly because we have instrumentation and computational power that allows us to address them analytically.

Even though physics is the granddaddy of all sciences and the foundation of everything, I think all of the excitement right now is on these new areas, these other areas in chemistry and biology, because we've gotten these phenomenal new tools so we're making such rapid progress. Take the field of optical metrology, going back to Aguru Images. We can, from 6 feet away, tell you the depth of the actor's pores when we measure them. I mean that's the kind of thing that's possible now in the technology developed by a pretty small company of four guys hanging around together screwing around with cameras.

S. Donaldson: Sitting on the floor!

Miller: Sitting on the floor! Yeah, literally. To me, yes, there's a convergence because everything's becoming analytical. Lord Kelvin said you don't know anything until you can say it with numbers, and right now, biology and chemistry are saying it with numbers in a way that they never have before.

G. Donaldson: In terms of social behavior, psychological behavior and so forth, are you suggesting that it can all be reduced down to physical science?

Miller: No, no. Not by any means, yet. But, for example, in the arterial occipital lobe, if you look at the way we make decisions—it's happening at a level that we don't really understand. All of our decision-making models aren't there, so we know that there is an underlying physical component to this. And that the biology is ultimately physics, but so much of what we do is genetic. For example, there's a famous line of questioning in psychology where the hypothesis is that there are a brother and sister who love each other, and they decide to become sexually intimate, and they take the appropriate birth control. They have sex and they're both happy. Is this right or wrong? Well over 90% of the people will, even in that test case, will say it's wrong. Incest is wrong. And you say, "Why?" And the person says, "Well, you know, their child is going to have two heads and whatever." "Well, no, their child didn't have two heads." "Well, it's going to ruin their relationship." "It didn't ruin their relationship."

You go through all the logical reasons, and then it comes down to "just because." I fit into that category: "Oh, that's creepy." And the reason for "just because" is at a level of our biology that's deeper than we can access with our conscious thought. Something in our evolution has encoded that. If you go to Dawkins' concept of memes is one of the most abused things in science right now. People think of any sort of pop culture idea as a meme. Dawkins was proposing a very specific thing, and that is that an idea can act like a gene, a meme gene, and that a particular idea has a survival value, that it enhances tself as a meme, but it also survives in part because it enhances the genetic viability of the organism, of the subclass that holds it, such as religion, for example. Religion has proven to be perhaps the most powerful of human memes. People belong to religious communities; have the comfort of the community: the protection, the fulfillment, and everything else.

Memes as things that drive the evolution of society is a vastly larger concept than Lady Gaga as a meme. I've actually seen that as a reference. By the way, the other day we were listening to the table next to me of some young men who were discussing Barney [a children's television show produced in the United States], which made me feel very old that these were three guys from the Army. They all had the "high and tidy" haircut and the whole bit, and they were talking about Barney. They said, and I quote, "Barney really "jumped the shark" when they got into that bit about space and time travel." I had to write that down. You know, it's like, so "jump the shark" doesn't make my category or my cut of what's a real meme.

S. Donaldson: Right. We got into describing various technologies. How do you invest in technologies here? Are you part of that process? Is there a formal process?

Miller: The way we do it at NRECA is very good. We've broken the space into six areas: renewables, energy and energy storage, transmission technology, distribution technology, end-use efficiency, and smart grid. Each area has a senior program manager.

The other hat I wear is that I'm the senior program manager of things related to the smart grid, one of the six. We spend an awful lot of time walking through doors. We visit people. We visit co-ops. We're trying new things. We go to a lot of laboratories and a lot of conferences.

Then we get together with what we call an advisory group. This is a group of a dozen to 15 people that we think are the best in our area, among the co-ops. A member in this case means a member of the co-op, and they're members of NRECA. We go through a two-day session twice a year when we discuss the research. How did we do the old stuff, but what are the new opportunities? Then from that—we call it ideation—we come up with 8 or 10 research priorities.

Then we have the best meeting of the whole year. Everybody writes up their stuff, and then all the senior program managers, everybody else, all of the CRN gets together in a room for two days and we review all of the ideas. We refine them, we mark them up, we say, "Maybe next time. Tune it up a little bit." Or, "This one's a good one." We either use our own research budgets or we go out and we find partners, like EPRI or somebody else, or we syndicate it. We say, "Twenty co-ops, each throw in 50 grand and we've got a project here," or we go after grant or research funds. One of the decisions that comes out of that process is we say, "What are we going to do? What are the priorities? And how are we going to fund it?" Then we just do the research.

S. Donaldson: Are there any mergers or acquisitions associated with this organization? Do you bring in pieces or do you just grow organically with people?

Miller: Totally organic. We're not-for-profit. We are very well established. No mergers and acquisitions.

S. Donaldson: Let's switch gears here a little bit and talk about your vision of the future. What do you see evolving over the next five years? What do you see happening?

Miller: I don't even consider five years the future. I consider five years an engineering project.

S. Donaldson: Okay.

Miller: And that's the nature of the utility business. We don't deploy anything at scale that hasn't been tested, refined, tested again, beat over the head. We're careful. I'll tell you another thing that's leading to that is that silicon technology has a very short half-life, partly because we make improvements so quickly, and partly because we don't design it very well. If we know it's going to be obsolete in five years, why build it to last 50, right? So there's a time constant, a difference in the time constant between our two metals, between copper and silicon. The time constant of copper is 40 years; the time constant of silicon is five. And the question is how do you design a system that takes that into account? That's a challenge. So five years I don't even regard as the future. I can tell you technologies we're deploying now.

S. Donaldson: Okay.

Miller: The future beyond that in the grid is related to, in my opinion, silicon moving up to the power side, migration of almost all of our operations to the cloud. Ultimately a redefinition of the business model away from, in the co-ops or even in general utilities, to, "We maintain wires? Generators?" And we deal with the customers and it's sort of the evolution of the business to look more like a telecom business over time.

My real concern for the future is this: we have not yet evolved the social and societal systems to deal with the fact that the average person in the world is unemployed. We manufacture things so efficiently that we don't need everybody to grow our food. We don't need everybody to make all of our products, but the entire social system is based on the idea that people only get paid for growing things or making things. And that could potentially lead to a polarization of society, for example, Mexico. Wonderfully productive country, but large poor class, very small rich class, and a not huge middle class. I think a lot of travails we're going through right now are adapting American society to that new world. And that's a system that is way beyond my tent. I don't know how to do that.

G. Donaldson: Craig. I agree with you on that 100%. In your trending predictions, do you rely on anything such as the theory of inventive problem solving?

Miller: Funny you should mention it. The answer is yes. [Laughter]

G. Donaldson: How does that work for you?

Miller: I really can't say. I sort of factor everything in. I think it comes in on the self-doubt side. I can sit down and chart everything out, and you come back to ludicrous things like the six computers or however many computers that IBM was going to sell or whatever.

G. Donaldson: Right.

Miller: Behind the theory of inventive problem solving is why I believe in Moore's law even when physics says the opposite. I believe that when things get hard enough, you have to doubt the linear projections. That's why I'm not a Club of Rome guy. It's why the CO_2 problem, while insurmountable now in the ways we see it, I believe that we can, in fact, grow algae well enough and we'll figure out how [to solve the CO_2 problem]. There's going to be some brakes put on. So I tend to look at trends in improvement and innovation and cost trends, even when I can't look at a particular underlying technology that drives it.

S. Donaldson: Are there some key lessons learned that you'd like to pass on to people who have this technology bent?

Miller: Yeah. I'm over 60. Most CTOs aren't. Most people practicing avant-garde technology are not. I walk into rooms with 35-year-olds all the time, and I try to figure out what makes me different. I think what makes me different is I've grown up enough to know that what I'm good at is technology, vision, and arithmetic. I'm real good at arithmetic. And by that I mean pretty sophisticated math. I'm good at math, but "Unto thine own self be true. Thou canst not be false to any man." I'll never walk to anyone and say, "You know, I'm your stud manager." Once I realized that I didn't want to be the CEO, I was able to love what I'm good at. So I keep reinventing myself. I mean, I read this all the time. I still write code. I will never stop writing code.

If I don't write code, then I'm "full of baloney" when I tell people about something. I still solder circuit boards. It's because I've reached the point of knowing what I'm good at and what I love, and I don't ever want to be obsolete, so I study constantly.

S. Donaldson: Okay.

Miller: Biology is my current passion because I think the future's there. I understand why algae absorbs CO_2. I understand how to drive the efficiency in algae. I understand how to grow it really fast because I studied that area, and I got down to talking about the ferredoxin cycle and all of the other things that go on.

My dad had a philosophy. My dad grew up during the Depression, and he had to drop out of college because the family couldn't afford it. So the rest of his life, he felt he never had the education he wanted or should have had. So he taped to his mirror, "What have you learned today?" He put that on the mirror.

S. Donaldson: That's great.

Miller: And if he couldn't answer it, he went downstairs and got out a book until he had something to answer. So I think I learned that from him. But then the next thing is this: In the early stages of life, kids want material things. They want toys; they want this or that. I think people grow out of that and become experience-based: "I've done this, I've seen that, I've toured Paris, I've skydived, did that." Eventually, when the body starts to wear out, and mine's getting to that category, I think you've got to find something else. And I think some people find it in spiritual growth. You know, sitting cross-legged and chanting. I think the other alternative for a terminal state is intellectual fulfillment and just the joy of learning. How incredible it is to end up every day saying, "I did learn something."

S. Donaldson: That's right, that's right.

Miller: To me, if you're a good technologist, if you're a CTO out there and you get up and you say, "Damn, this job is cool," keep the job forever. Learn every day so that you're never irrelevant.

G. Donaldson: Craig, would you like it to actually be part of a curriculum in school?

Miller: I'd love it, yeah.

G. Donaldson: So that people learn to be lifelong learners, to be experiential learners.

Miller: I went to the University of Virginia—that's where I got my doctorate—and they don't have freshman, sophomores, juniors, and seniors there. That term is never, ever, ever used because Jefferson believed in lifelong learning. So you're first-year, second-year, third-year, fourth-year, and unfortunately, fifth-, sixth-, … but that's lifelong learning, man. It can make you happy.

G. Donaldson: That actually sounds like your father's quote, "What have you learned today?" I found that in helping organizations innovate and change how they conduct business that it's really helpful to approach it as a learning experience as opposed to being directed specifically on what to do. I think your father's statement is a very powerful one.

Miller: Well, it was a powerful one from a guy who was not an intellectual. He was just a regular schmoe who got hit by the Depression. My father would never state it in intellectual terms, but he gave me all these aphorisms. When they landed on the moon, when Neil Armstrong landed on the moon in '69, he said, "Craig, do you think the Apollo program's successful?" And I said, "Sure, they just landed a man on the moon." He said, "What are they going to do next?" And I thought, "Hmm, there is nothing after Apollo." So he said, "It's not a success because they don't know where they're going." He said, "Any plan that doesn't end in global conquest hasn't been thought through to conclusion." Okay, now, he's not saying global conquest.

S. Donaldson: Right.

Miller: But his aphorisms stick with you.

S. Donaldson: Right.

Miller: And so one of the things I've learned is always not, "What's the next step?" but, "If that step works, do I know what I'm doing after that? What's the second step and the third step?" And, of course, the haze and the uncertainty increases as you go out.

S. Donaldson: In fact, that was my next question, which is, what do you see next in your career?

Miller: I'm going to finish this project. It will take me three more years, which will lead me to 64 years old. I'm going to do one of two things. One of them is going to be about enabling innovation. I don't know if you guys have played with Arduinos. Arduino is a hobbyist-level, general-purpose, programmable circuit board, and a guy who can't design a new controller can sit down and write a version of C to make a little tiny computer do cool things. We all learned to build with erector sets when we were kids because mechanical was what we did, but you never made a real product out of an erector set, but you learned diagonal truss and cantilevers and all that stuff. Well, the future is electronics, and not just computers but things that act where the computer actually interacts. I want to start a company building innovation toys, like Lego MindStorm or the people who build the Arduino, or things like that. And that's one of the things I plan to do, and I plan to get started on that probably in a year because if this project is really as Whack-a-Mole as I think—by the way, there's some serious self-doubt about that conclusion. [Laughter]

S. Donaldson: The circle is complete [self-doubt].

Miller: But once we get into that, I want to work on enabling innovation because it's so much fun and so many American students are intimidated. They're afraid of it. They don't understand technology and they don't even understand mathematics. I've heard a local speaker, wonderful talk radio show, Diane Rehm, phenomenal lady, great show. I love it. Who doesn't love Diane? But she was on there once when somebody talked some very elementary statistics, very elementary, and she and the other guests all laughed, like, "Oh ho, mathematics. Ha, ha, ha," as if innumeracy is socially acceptable. I don't consider innumeracy any more socially acceptable than illiteracy.

S. Donaldson: Right.

Miller: But it's only because it's been mystified and made difficult. It doesn't have to be difficult. I have proven that I can teach all of trigonometry in two days. Literally, I've done this, because trigonometry is primordially simple. It's the unit circle and the Pythagorean Theorem. There are only two concepts in all of trigonometry. You can derive every single one of them from understanding the unit circle and the unit sphere and the Pythagorean Theorem. That's all it is, and you can derive all of trig in two days if you teach it right. So I want to work on that problem. I want to let people believe they can succeed in technology.

The second thing I want to do is write about one problem that is really bothering me. We're going through the 13th mass extinction, the fifth very large one. Species are dying off. There's something that bothers me about that. In every very single one of the predecessors most of the species in the planet died off. And as soon as it happened, there was an incredible flowering of biological innovation because the top-line predators were no longer there to eat the little ones. So every little goofy bad idea in biology had a niche because there wasn't anybody big around to eat them. The problem with this mass extinction is that's there only one top-line predator, and that's us. And we don't just predate; we alter the environment to suit our needs. The evolutionary difference between us and other animals is that overwhelmingly the species on the planet have evolved to fit their environment. We have evolved the most devious of all evolutionary tricks: we don't fit the environment. We fit the environment to us.

S. Donaldson: Right.

Miller: So I believe that this mass extinction is actually fundamentally different from all of the preceding ones; that this time we have the potential to do vastly more damage, that there may not be a flowering after us. And that the damage we do will not just be undone in the next phase. And so it's an imperative call. The book I want to write is about ecological damage and how we can't take it lightly.

I started on this book, and I was doing really well, and then I picked up E. O. Wilson's book on the subject because of course you have to read everybody who wrote on it. I read his book, and I said, "I will never say it a tenth as well as him." So the steam sort of came out of me. But not everybody reads E. O. Wilson. Maybe somebody will read my perspective, so I want to get back to it.

I'm honestly concerned about the environment because we right now control a greater percentage on a mass basis of the biosphere than any other single species. We talk about, "Oh, the dinosaurs lasted a hundred million years," but you can't look at any one dinosaur species lasting that long. Dinosaur species came and went, and when they were there, they did not control the biosphere beyond their own mass, whereas we do.

S. Donaldson: Right.

Miller: I think there has never been a species that so completely dominated the earth's biosphere since cyanobacteria. The atmosphere in the planet used to be a reducing atmosphere and when cyanobacteria evolved, through the trick of photosynthesis, they were able to explode in numbers such that nobody else had access to sunshine because they were the only animals or only organisms that were doing photosynthesis. So they had access to sources of energy that nobody else had. They were just living off of heat and chemical energy. They led to a massive change in the entire planet, and changed the atmosphere to an oxidizing atmosphere, and everything we know of starts there.

S. Donaldson: Right.

Miller: That's the only precedent for what I believe we are capable of. So a book on that subject will enable kids to innovate.

Jerry Krill

CTO, Johns Hopkins University Applied Physics Laboratory

Dr. Jerry Krill *is the CTO of the Johns Hopkins University (JHU) Applied Physics Laboratory (APL), located in Laurel, Maryland. He has been at APL since 1973 assuming the CTO position in November 2010. At the 50,000-foot level, APL encourages and fosters innovation. More than 70 percent of APL's nearly 5,000 staff members are scientists and engineers.*

Because of his role at the premier institution of JHU APL, his influence extends to the U.S. Department of Defense and the Defense Advanced Research Projects Agency as well as to other prominent institutions. Dr. Krill was APL's assistant director for programs since 2005. He oversaw APL's 600-plus programs and led its quality management initiative. He is also an inventor with patents and patents-pending as diverse as a plastic electric motor and a 3-D virtual reality display.

Before becoming assistant director, he led the Power Projection Systems Department for four years, also heading up the Precision Engagement and Infocentric Operations business areas. He spent the first quarter century of his career working in air defense and served as APL's system engineer in its technical leadership role in developing the Navy's Cooperative Engagement Capability.

Dr. Krill obtained his Bachelor and Master Degrees in Electrical Engineering from Michigan State University, Lansing in 1973 and 1974, and his Ph.D. in Electrical Engineering from the University of Maryland, College Park in 1978.

Stan Siegel: We are here to get some insights into how CTOs in various environments operate. We'd like to begin with your journey to the CTO position. How did you get to be the CTO?

Jerry Krill: This is a long story that spans my career progression since coming to the laboratory. Initially, I thought I was going to work at APL for 2 years and then go on to grad school. But I just kept becoming intrigued with new technical challenges and with working on areas that were national in their importance. Besides, APL allowed me to pursue my doctorate while working full time. So I have never left! And as I gained increasing responsibilities, I broadened my professional capabilities and gained increased exposure to technologies. I became a fairly good inventor and researcher before I got into systems engineering and the delivery of large-scale system prototypes. I have had the opportunity to serve in most of the laboratory's technical leadership roles in my 38 years here—from programmatic through technical. I worked in the research center while pursuing my PhD, working primarily on air and missile defense projects. From the '70s I had the chance to participate in the development of concepts for advanced air defense networking that were so visionary that I spent the next decade working to implement them. Some are only now being implemented. So, I would say that I was recently appointed CTO by the APL (Applied Physics Laboratory) Director, Ralph Semmel, based on my exposure to the breadth of APL's mission and corresponding technologies, my research and innovation experience, and my broad experience in delivering large-scale systems.

Siegel: So when did you actually decide in your career that you wanted to be CTO?

Krill: I never thought of it, actually. It was an offer made to me about a year ago. I had been the assistant director for programs, in charge of ensuring that all our programs delivered as promised and that our sponsors were satisfied. My approach was, based on my engineering and science experience, to make sure that our research and development work was rigorously performed. I introduced our labwide quality management system. And I participated in troubleshooting programmatic issues as well as sitting on PDRs [preliminary design reviews] and CDRs [critical design reviews] as necessary. When our director, Ralph Semmel, took over, he asked me to move over to this role. And I actually realized I relished the opportunity to "innovate our innovation." Also, I'm fortunate to be able to stand on the shoulders of my predecessor John Sommerer, who now leads our space department.

Siegel: So he essentially made you an offer you couldn't refuse. Is that correct?

Krill: Yes.

Siegel: Okay. Along this path, did you have mentors that helped you along the way?

Krill: Many. From the very beginning I would seek mentors. I would seek supervisors who were mentors for me and helped me grow in my assigned roles. I have had a broad spectrum of mentors. Some would mentor me in technical areas; some would teach me about how to best work with sponsors and military officers, from junior to very senior. I have always felt that I have something to learn from everyone. Mentoring has been important to me during my entire career.

Siegel: We read with interest your involvement in this 2003 task force regarding APL collaboration with the Whiting School of Engineering. And we have a couple of questions in that area. First, what made the team click? I noticed in the report there was the use of the phrase "cultural differences between one environment and the other."

Krill: Well, you probably know a little bit about that [as employed by JHU at that time].

[Mutual laughter]

Krill: Well, that study was an effort by the provost at the time to get APL better connected across multiple JHU divisions, and especially with the Whiting School of Engineering. Some improvements occurred, and some did not. The academic environment is different from the R&D environment of APL as a DoD UARC (University Affiliated Research Center). We have different criteria for delivering products, and we deliver different types of products. We're now reopening that dialogue in light of the expected need for broader collaboration in the coming decade. We're re-examining how we can be more flexible to increase our collaboration across the university.

Siegel: Okay. Now let's shift gears for a second to discuss your design for the award winning 3D virtual reality technology. I guess it was back in 2004. What were the key technologies involved with that particular effort?

Krill: You're asking interesting on-the-spot questions.

[Laughter]

Well, most of my inventions have been in response to learning about sponsor needs and trying to spur creative thinking at APL. And so, I sometimes lead by example. This was a situation where we were exploring command and control challenges, especially in terms of the fundamental sciences and disciplines. We realized that there were perhaps more issues than we were aware of, such as how a person could be better 'immersed' into a command

and control situation – how to better leverage human senses and experiences in dealing with the fog of war. So that was the motivation for the invention. I initially conceived the walkthrough display idea myself which was the basis for the award. We have staff here that are experts in optics, ocular science and mining large databases of imagery. So after the concept was formed we had a follow-on implementation effort with a team of experts to develop an approach involving an eyepiece and background imagery so that a person could literally walk through a display and could look at the situation from multiple aspects. It also could be used for tele-visiting. So you could actually—if the data's available, probably terabits—be in Chicago and I would be in Maryland, but I would see you as plainly as I'm seeing you now in a common, virtual room. We'd need extreme communications bandwidth so we'd be able to have high visual resolution to enable reading of body language and viewing detail. And so we could virtually visit and virtually experience together. In terms of military command and control, if I'm in CENTCOM (U.S. Central Command) in Florida, but there is a situation on the ground in Afghanistan, I could be virtually present. And we have some ideas on tactile aspects as well – the sense of touch– where you could shake hands remotely and have a sense of grabbing the hand. The key to this capability—and this is not so obvious in the invention—is extremely high-capacity communications between collaborating locations for the visual detail, especially if the background scene is changing and needs constant updating. Optical fiber lines can be used for stationary sites, but they are not always available, especially in military situations. So we've also been working over the last decade on free space optical communications within the atmosphere, especially to solve fundamental problems of transmission through atmospheric turbulence. If solved, one could communicate at 6 to 10 Gigahertz bandwidth per user per second, so that's like 10 HDTV movies every 10 seconds with compressed imagery. You need that kind of data rate if you're going to generate the kind of high resolution in the volume of a dynamically changing scene that you need for a 3D walkthrough display.

So, again, the motivation was for me to lead by having us explore a technical frontier; and to continue to encourage our staff to not just deliver quality products, but especially at the very beginning of a project, to think creatively about what could be possible. This is increasingly important.

Scott Donaldson: I would like to ask a follow-up question. Has that technology been adopted out in the general industry?

Krill: No, It is possible for established sites with in-place optical fiber, but it requires databases that cannot currently be built on the fly in dynamic environments. The technology would need to be developed with funding, and no one has picked that up. For the dynamic, open field version that might be needed for military purposes, the advanced optical communications are also needed since optical fiber would not generally be available.

S. Donaldson: Okay.

Krill: There is work going on—we're working for one sponsor on free space optical communications, and some records have been broken for data bandwidth and ranges for surface-to-air and air-to-air communications within the atmosphere. There needs to be more data capacity infrastructure before we can generate and update the kinds of data that this 3D walk-through capability could leverage in areas without optical fiber. We're really not there yet. Some of these things take 10 to 15 years to advance an infrastructure like this.

S. Donaldson: Is the computing technology available for it?

Krill: Yes, that is available.

S. Donaldson: So that piece is solved.

Krill: There is pre-existing IP (intellectual property) developed at APL that we're using in some programs for our sponsors. For example, we are using LIDAR (Light Detection and Ranging) technology, which gives you exquisite 3D image data—with as much resolution as your eye can manage—but does not generate high resolution 3D imagery beyond what you are presently looking at.

Siegel: No peripheral vision is what you are saying?

Krill: Or it fades to the lower resolution of peripheral vision so that you will experience it in a natural way. You can take a database that would normally take many blade servers to process, and you can run it on a laptop because the algorithm parses the imagery for you, by tracking your viewing behavior. So computing is not really the issue.

Gary Donaldson: You had mentioned several times now the role of creativity in both your career path and in the technologies you've helped developed and so forth. Could you address that with a little bit more detail about how you do that?

Krill: Well, it's interesting. We have been developing an innovation framework from which we can assess our innovation environment. I'm leading that effort as CTO.

The framework is essentially drawn as a pyramid. At the bottom of the pyramid is the label "national challenges and opportunities." We ask ourselves,

"What are the national challenges or technological opportunities that exist that we need to, and can as an organization, tackle because of our mission and role with our sponsors?" That's where we need to really understand what the Fleet needs, what the Air Force needs, for example—truly understand. We need to be really well connected, not just with our sponsors but also with the operational users to understand the challenges—also with industry and labs to make sure we can together come up with practical solutions.

S. Donaldson: Right.

Krill: The next layer of the pyramid is the needed expertise and capabilities. "Do our people have the requisite credentials, and do we have the requisite facilities? Have we anticipated the technologies that we're going to need?" So that is the next layer of the foundation. The third layer is, essentially, "What other ideas are out there potentially relevant to the selected challenges?" The literature on innovation maintains that new ideas are born from the nexus of old ideas and people willing to connect not-obviously-related ideas. So, APL, and probably every organization, needs to 'get more connected'— always more—in the sense of being truly aware of what is going on technologically in the world. This goes beyond the generally excellent global awareness in fields of research specialty that our experts pursue. This involves broader awareness of activities that, on the surface, may not seem relevant to an application.

Siegel: Well, that's quite a cultural shift then.

Krill: Yes.

Siegel: For this organization, isn't it?

Krill: Yes—for any organization, I suspect. So that's the third layer. Now we get to the fourth layer up the pyramid, the creativity layer. We need people to get together and collaborate, both internally and externally, to come up with ideas to solve the national challenge problems. The ideas may not initially be very good. You want to get a high yield of initial, immature ideas, from which you can harvest the better ones for further development. From the idea-generation layer evolves a good idea and the ability to take a good idea and mature it well enough that it could qualify for IRAD (Internal Research and Development) or seedling funding.

Let me backtrack for a moment. Down at the expertise and facilities layer, the ability to collect scientific and engineering data is very important. You can have lots of conjectures and hypotheses. But APL has been built on the ability to collect information, instrumented information, to translate a need into technical requirements. And that's a key part of our capability.

So, let's go back up to the idea layer. Now you've got a good idea, and you've developed it somewhat. If it is good enough to gain sponsor or internal research or exploratory development funds, we can further investigate the idea and, hopefully, establish its feasibility. Finally, if worthy of further funding from sponsors, we can develop an implementation of the idea at least at the prototype level. That's the point when the creative idea is implemented; that you have produced an innovation for a customer. We're systematically assessing ourselves in the context of the framework, "What does this framework tell us about what we have implemented to increase our environment and effectiveness of innovation?"

S. Donaldson: It sounds like a seven-layer protocol for innovation.

Krill: In a sense, yes, it's like that with fewer layers.

Siegel: Okay. Could we shift gears here now for a minute and talk about your day-to-day job?

Krill: Okay.

Siegel: And to drill down a little, what are your responsibilities and to whom do you report?

Krill: I report to the APL director. We have a basic management practices document that describes the roles and responsibilities of the executives at APL. And we've redefined the role of CTO so that it includes the position of assistant director for S&T.

Siegel: So you—what I hear you telling me then is that you have a job description. And that's been recently reformulated, is that correct?

Krill: Yes.

Siegel: So I guess you're still feeling your way around regarding whether what you're doing is in line with your evolving job description. Is that correct?

Krill: I believe I'm moving forward because I have a strategy for each area of my responsibility.

Siegel: Okay.

Krill: For example, part of my responsibility is to ensure an adequate technology base, and in response, we are reorganizing our research center. It's going to be about 400 staff, twice the size of the present center, and will include our fabrication groups for the first time. As for identifying national challenges and opportunities, another responsibility, the director and the assistant director for strategy have developed a new strategic process. We collectively develop a tiered set of Vision-Strategy–and Execution Priorities

(VSEs). Technical strategies that are defined from that process form a primary basis for our business area IRAD proposals for the coming year.

Siegel: How does what you just described link up with the systems engineering institute that you guys are working on? What's the connection there?

Krill: Okay. One of my responsibilities is to connect to S&T stakeholders, and obviously Hopkins, as our parent university, is a big stakeholder for us. I'm the primary technical point-of-contact to the other Hopkins divisions. I work mostly with the dean of the Whiting School of Engineering (WSE). APL plays a leadership role for the WSE EP (Engineering for Professionals) part-time graduate program. I'm responsible for making sure that APL executes its responsibility to that program. A former APL executive is now the WSE associate dean for EP. The idea of the systems institute was conceived by APL's Ron Luman, the chair of EPP's Systems Engineering in concert with the dean, as I understand the history.

Siegel: So you do interact with Ron, is that correct?

Krill: In fact, Ron is right next door to my office. He's also the APL assistant director for strategy.

Siegel: Okay.

Krill: On a day-to-day basis, we're [Ron and I] very linked in our APL responsibilities. But in terms of Homewood (Homewood is the main campus for Krieger School of Arts and Sciences, Whiting School of Engineering, Carey Business School, and School of Education), I deal with broader Hopkins issues related to research and technology, and Ron's primary focus is on systems engineering for EPP.

Siegel: Okay, so you told us who you report to; so who specifically reports to you?

Krill: I had a number of staff reporting to me, but as of July, they are transferred to the new research department, called the Research and Exploratory Development Department (REDD). My administrative assistant Natalie (who also works with Ron) and the head of the new department report to me now.

Siegel: Okay. Getting quantitative here; how do you measure success at the CTO position?

Krill: Well, we have a number of metrics we are developing. I said one of my jobs is to ensure the technology base. At the highest level, research breakthroughs and technology transitions are the two most important factors. And they're basically measurable. You can argue with the level of a breakthrough, but a breakthrough that's an enabler or a game changer for our sponsors is what we're looking for. "How many can we have? How many of our technologies can we transition to a sponsor need? And how quickly can we do that?"

So, we also will be more methodical tracking our science and technology work with potential for breakthroughs. As a UARC we are allowed to compete for science and technology work.

Siegel: Right. I was going to ask you about that.

Krill: Yeah, the good news is that our ability to compete ensures we remain competitive at the world-class level in S&T. But there's no assured block of R&D funding for us. We will monitor how much work we have in each of those S&T categories, and decide if the distribution is adequate to maintain our technology base for new challenges.

Siegel: Okay. So it looks like Ralph, since you report to him, he keeps the scorecard on you. Is that correct?

Krill: Yes.

Siegel: Okay. Is there a CIO position at APL? And if there is, how do you interact with that person?

Krill: Yes, there is. Our CIO is responsible for the laboratory's unclassified IT infrastructure. He is also the head of our IT Services Department and is engaged with the cyber defense of our information. We have totally separate classified IT systems under government oversight and not under the purview of our CIO. But for our unclassified networks, the CIO is responsible. Now, for APL to guard data entrusted to us requires us to be proactive in security technology introduction and security monitoring. So his department works directly with our experts supporting our cyber business area to ensure the latest available information assurance capabilities in our IT infrastructure.

Siegel: Okay. So, picking up on that, I guess you would view this CIO as your peer, and who are your other peers that you interact with?

Krill: He's a peer, but I don't really work with him on a daily basis.

Siegel: Okay.

Krill: Our CIO ensures an infrastructure capability. Other peers are Ron Luman, who is the assistant director for strategy. Strategy is one of the director's primary areas of focus. My previous position, assistant director of programs, is now held by Tim Galpin. I work with him regularly because of our responsibility overlap in science & technology programs. I make sure we have the appropriate types and number of S&T programs, and Tim ensures that we deliver the S&T products to the sponsors. S&T programs tend to have higher technical risk, so we must work closely together. Another peer is Ruth Nimmo, our assistant director for operations. We work together, for example, to ensure technical facilities that are really critical, especially to S&T.

Siegel: So do you periodically meet with these peers?

Krill: All the time. Almost daily. We set up weekly appointments as a default, just in case we aren't able to keep up each other's activities. We work as a team.

Siegel: All right, so that's the internal situation. What about the external organizations that you interact or collaborate with? Who are they?

Krill: This is still being developed because, as we've talked about, I believe APL leaders and staff need to engage externally more broadly to gain greater awareness of global S&T developments. So let's start at the global level and work our way in if that's okay.

We all recognize that, based on sheer numbers, the world plays a major role relative to the US in S&T developments. In time we could be technologically surprised more and more if we don't become more broadly connected. We are focusing on fundamental and applied research. We've just named Bharat Doshi, who is a world-renowned researcher and worked for many years at Bell Labs, to be our manager for global S&T outreach. It will be his job to get us connected strategically with technologically active parts of the world. For fundamental and applied research, there are few international restrictions other than protection of intellectual property. We are exploring potential strategic relationships with universities who are already well connected—"connecting with the connectors."

Domestically, we're working to get more connected as well. There's a new forum of CTOs for some of the larger FFRDCs and UARCs, and we're meeting every six months.

Siegel: When was that set up?

Krill: It just happened this spring. It was first held at MIT Lincoln Laboratory. It's an interesting mix of organizations. We compare notes. "What are we each doing as CTOs? What is our span of control? What innovation activities are we engaged in? Who are we talking to? What are our problems? How should we work together?" Things like that.

S. Donaldson: Is the plan there to have it hosted at the different participant locations?

Krill: Yes, it's at MITRE this fall. I think it's going to be on the West Coast, for the meeting after that. That's what I understand.

I'm also connecting to the CTOs of the for-profit US government contractors. We can talk about our IRADs and what we think is important based on our respective perspectives.

Siegel: Let me ask one more question regarding your day-to-day job and then we'll move on to APL itself. And that is, what key CTO lessons learned would you like to pass on?

Krill: I would say that—and this may be my career-long lesson—there is a dynamic tension, that needs to be carefully cultivated, between creative free-thinking and the discipline of technological development for product delivery. Helping our leaders and our staff understand which of these is important when, and how they work together seems to be the key in my experience.

G. Donaldson: How do you make that work? What have you found that works?

Krill: Well, it's an interesting question. About three years ago, I introduced our first comprehensive quality management system. We're ISO-certified, which is interesting for a laboratory. We worked to develop processes that did not stifle the creativity at the front end, but assured that engineering disciplines were handled, especially at the later phases of a development. However, as for any initial build, adjustments are needed. It was determined that the system of processes needs simplification and greater flexibility. Our assistant director for programs, who is also the chief quality officer, is leading the simplification effort.

And so, I am now working the other side of the innovation-discipline tension—how to make sure that our people feel motivated and supported in creating ideas and taking technical risks that could eventually lead to prototypes through disciplined engineering. As I said, you have to work across the spectrum of technology development from creative ideas through disciplined engineering and rigorous research, and that's something I learned with my systems engineering experience. When I started at APL, I had the chance to help create the system concept called the cooperative engagement capability (CEC). Years later I was responsible as the lead APL systems engineer to provide the technical leadership for the Navy delivery of CEC to the fleet. If you have experienced something from idea stage through implementation you begin to understand the context—and tensions—between innovation and discipline.

Siegel: Now let's shift gears and talk about APL. At the 50,000-foot level, in your opinion, what makes APL different from other R&D laboratories?

Krill: That's a big question. [Laughter.] There are a lot of great R&D laboratories, many with similarities to us. And because of some capability overlaps we often collaborate in our work for mutual sponsors. I would say that one thing that makes APL fairly unique is that we are currently working in significant science and development roles in almost every national security mission at our single site. Some labs are involved in single or perhaps a few missions; so one will focus on undersea warfare; one will focus primarily on air defense. APL works across the spectrum of mission areas such as cyber, space, homeland protection, and missile defense, among others. Because of that, and because our staff are mostly all at the same site, we have an opportunity for our staff to collaborate to find cross-mission/cross-technology domain solutions to problems that are increasingly complex.

Siegel: Okay. So that explains now why you and the systems institute really have collaborative goals here. And you guys really *do* systems engineering then in the broader sense. Isn't that correct?

Krill: Yes. I was part of the team that developed an articulation of what is unique about APL and Johns Hopkins systems engineering. Our 'research' in systems engineering is ultimately about what new techniques and methods we need to develop to deliver some particular first-of-a-kind system. The approach required for a particular system then becomes integral with our methodology. In contrast, some organizations consider systems engineering as a technical discipline and they perform research of the systems engineering process itself. As you probably know, the other Hopkins schools, including medicine, are increasingly interested in the systems approach as key to future capabilities.

Siegel: Good; it's nice to be ahead of the pack.

Krill: Some of our engineers used to say to some medical researchers, "You could use some systems thinking."

Siegel: Now they're coming to you.

[Laughter]

Krill: Now they're coming to us.

Siegel: Well, that's what really turned me on about the systems institute. That is really very insightful. Now, what do you see as important issues confronting your customers not only today but also in the future?

Krill: Today I believe this country has an asymmetry issue in national security. On one hand the US military is so powerful that potential adversaries look for ways to use cheap technology to go against us in novel, surprising ways– as in the case of improvised explosive devices (IEDs). We need more and more innovative approaches to maintain an effective capability against potential surprises. In a time of reduced military spending how can this country repurpose the assets we already have and modify them, or integrate them, in new ways to develop clever, innovative, new capabilities? How can one take missiles that are designed for one mission and use them for some other mission? How can you modify combat systems to be more resilient in cyber environments while performing their conventional missions? So those are the challenges that are in the near term, but they also set the stage for the far term.

Let me now move from the near term to 10 to 20 years from now. One can read what the futurists think. But each CTO must consider what could happen relative to their organization's mission. One can review future intelligence estimates. One can also get connected to universities and research centers across the globe to gauge what is coming out of the laboratories. We can ask, "Well, what is this university or that university working on?"

We are placing some bets in our research to prepare for the future. For example, we believe that 'applied neuroscience' is going to be increasingly important in several ways. APL is leading the development of a prosthetic forearm and hand. It's got more than 20 degrees of freedom, comparable in flexibility to a human arm and hand. The most remarkable thing is the neural interface. A demo occurred recently with a monkey with a cortical interface. The monkey learned to feed itself a banana with an artificial arm just by thinking. There are already commercial products where you can think and a computer performs some application. Where will this technology lead? And how might this technology might be used in less positive ways? So we're thinking in the far term, and that's an example.

Siegel: Thank you for that insight about the context of your work within APL. And now let's talk, although you've touched upon it already, about the technologies. You've already indicated that this neuroscience thing is going to be on the forefront here, but what other technologies do you view as important to APL and why?

Krill: Okay, well, we're rethinking this question as part of our new strategic process. We just appointed the head of our new research and exploratory development department (REDD), Jim Schatz, the former head of NSA [National Security Agency] research. Jim is well experienced with thinking about the future. He and his team are in the process of re-examining the S&T strategy of the new RED Department. Some present technologies of interest are likely going to remain on our list as strategic, but we are not yet sure what other technologies will be identified as strategically important.

One technology that will likely remain strategically important to us is 'functional materials'. Coating materials, for example, may move toward more complex functions, more like animal skin. Functionally, they might sense, perceive, even swarm a response to a penetration or stimulus. This probably relies on nano-technology.

Neuroscience, combined with autonomy, could result in systems that are able to go where humans can't, or where we don't want to afford humans to go. Some of us think that is going to be an opportunity. The autonomy/robotics community needs to decide what portion of autonomy—versus reachback communications for human control—we should apply for given applications. You can't tie up a whole crew to remotely control a vehicle—it's not particularly scalable to a lot of vehicles. We need to have systems that can 'think' for themselves at some level. We have experience with that at APL. Consider our New Horizons spacecraft that is on its way to Pluto—we spent a *lot* of effort on autonomy because it can't 'phone home' during the short time it goes by the dwarf planet after nine years of travel. It takes hours for the speed of light to get the message back to us, and a human response would arrive too late. The spacecraft has to act on its own if anything is amiss.

So we believe that autonomous operations are going to be important for this country. It may also play a substantial role in the future of spaceflight. If we can't afford sending humans, we can send autonomous systems. And using something like the 3D walk-through display we talked about before, a scientist could perhaps sit back in the lab and experience a planet's surface as if they were actually there. This could save a lot of money. So, yes, we think that's going to be important.

We have initiatives in biomechanics and biotechnologies as well. Perhaps a system that uses human genome information in identifying and resolving genetic diseases in a new generation of individualized healthcare systems technology might provide a basis for more affordable healthcare. Perhaps with this approach and with more direct networking from medical research to medical practice, medical care prices could become more modest, in line, while continuing to advance medical technology.

Siegel: Oh, well, given the size of that list and how fast technology advances, how do you keep up with technology? Networking? Conferences? How do you do it?

Krill: Well, one thing that's nice about APL is that we have 3300+ technical staff that I can talk with, and I have a lot of personal connections from my 38 years here. I go to conferences, as I determine the need, to get up to speed at some base level, or present a paper, or to network. For example, I went to an orbital mechanics conference once, just to be somewhat knowledgeable in that domain. I read a lot. Besides our staff, it's really helpful for me to maintain relationships with my fellow CTOs and with other leaders who have their own connections, such as universities—again, 'connecting to the connectors'.

Siegel: But how do you do that? There's only 24 hours in a day.

Krill: We have a strategy that we're putting together. We can't talk to everyone, but we can decide on what strategic relationships we want to have to broaden our research awareness, and then we filter back what we think we as a lab need to focus on based on what we're hearing.

S. Donaldson: That's a great idea.

Krill: We're building our network of contacts and will monitor our connections and findings.

Now that we have our new RED department head, I expect to have more personal time to connect to others.

Siegel: So let's get personal here for a minute. What technologies do you personally keep an eye on?

Krill: Well, I have my personal favorites. To make sure I understand your question—there are the technologies that I keep my eye on for the lab and the country, the strategic technologies. But I still do have my own personal interests in inventing and writing papers, often as pathfinders, but sometimes for fun. I sometimes test the waters before I make a case for an APL technical initiative. For example, about 10 years ago I thought free space optical communications was going to be important. I asked, "What are the technologies? What's missing?" Today APL is considered by some as an organization well equipped to build an end-to-end free space optics communications network prototype operating in the atmosphere at long range and with high data rates. We're testing that right now. But the present prototype relies on a gimbaled telescope for connectivity to each node. Placing a large number of gimbals on each ship or aircraft, one for each other neighboring node in the network, is impractical. So several of us invented, and have a patent-pending for, a phased-array laser aperture. If you think of an Aegis radar with a microwave phased-array antenna that can electronically steer a radar beam in different directions almost instantly, our invention allows one to electronically steer a laser beam. So now you can build multifunction sensors and communications at laser frequencies like we can for microwave frequencies. One could have optical communications that you can burst to different users in different directions in milliseconds using a single thin laser aperture, without having to physically point it. I focus on critical technologies that, if we can find a viable approach, could be game changers.

We also recently presented a paper on swarming sensor networks. Consider small sensor nodes sprinkled around an area being monitored. These pebbles contain very rudimentary sensors and signaling electronics and could be disguised as pebbles of about a centimeter in diameter. If an intruder goes past a "pebble" and is detected by the pebble's sensor, the pebble will 'sing' a single, very low power microwave tone—micro-watts. If any other pebbles nearby receive the tone, those pebbles are cued to lower their detection thresholds to make it more likely that they will also detect the intruder. Miles away a monitor terminal receives the microwave tones of the transmitting pebbles and tracks the intruder with a high gain antenna. You can scale the field of these 'swarming' pebbles from a couple square miles to hundreds of square miles with no change to the system.

S. Donaldson: You must be a hard man to buy for at Christmas.

[Laughter]

Krill: Books! Online books.

S. Donaldson: There you go, there you go.

Siegel: To drill down a little bit here, with everyone on the move today, how are you addressing mobile computing?

Krill: Well, I have worked on projects at APL for many years requiring real-time computing on mobile vehicles such as ships and aircraft. Any system I've worked on, it's always been about real-time, mobile networked computing. We are involved with distributed computing among mobile systems. I have the technical background on that at the system engineering level. CEC has distributed computing among ships and aircraft in a network.

Siegel: Well, I guess that's driven by the way your career progressed and so it's ingrained into your thinking.

Krill: A technical concern is that these distributed computer networks often must be provided with extremely reliable data and to do that requires high reliability communications, which can be difficult to maintain. In the future we must rely on less certain communications connectivity and less assured data, both in recognition of the evolving cyber threat and the high cost of such exquisite communications. That is a technical challenge requiring novel design approaches, such as autonomy.

Siegel: Let me ask a quasi-technological question here, and that is how is social networking like Facebook, YouTube, Twitter impacting your research? Or is it impacting it at all?

Krill: Do you mean the technical or the personal?

Siegel: Both.

Krill: Okay, so let's start with the technical. We are researching the use of social networking towards determining whether one can gauge the mood of a people or neighborhood. As we know from Iraq and Afghanistan, this can be important. Perhaps one can listen to the Twitter traffic of a particular country and assess the mood of the people regardless of what its government is saying. Theoretically you might use that to help the troops on the ground to anticipate what they might encounter.

G. Donaldson: I have a question about that. How do you know they're representative of the population you're talking about or just a small subgroup?

Krill: That is part of the research. One could compare Twitter results with polling results as a calibration. Whether it works for different cultures also needs to be explored.

Now, when it comes to APL we are working to encourage our staff to become better connected through conferences and participation with professional societies.

Siegel: How difficult was it to engineer that—no pun intended—that cultural change?

Krill: You know, by the time I took this job, changes were already in the wind. They just needed a nudge. We're experimenting with virtual connectivity for our staff. We recently launched an experiment that we're calling "Ignition Grants." Our Ignition Grants initiative is an APL social experiment using an internal website known as 'Cooler,'- where staff can connect online as if they're talking around the water cooler. We essentially said, "Give us your ideas, technical and nontechnical, post them, let people comment on them, improve them as people comment on them, and once every four months, we will have the staff vote on the best ideas. The ideas winning the most votes will receive seedling grants to develop the ideas further." And, we have to admit that some of us thought, "We might not get good ideas out of it, but at least we'll get people talking." However, we are getting some *really* good ideas. So we're building on this experiment.

S. Donaldson: That's fascinating. So how large are the grants?

Krill: Ten to twenty thousand dollars. It's a few weeks' worth of work, but we're now asking: "Okay, so they've got a good idea and developed the idea but ran out of funds" Perhaps it's still not mature enough to win an IRAD. We need some sort of transition funding. We need to nurture promising ideas to get them to the next level, and we're working on that.

S. Donaldson: I'll take that concept back to our CEO.

Krill: Really?

S. Donaldson: Yeah. I think it's a great idea. To reach out, to get to the technical community we have different ways to do that, but this is an excellent mechanism.

Siegel: All he's saying here is it's just a generalization of the water cooler idea.

Krill: And you know what? Part of that idea was conceived by some young people in our research center. The key was that APL management was willing to risk trying out the idea.

Siegel: All right. Let me ask one more question about technology before we move on to technology investments. Are there any big projects that are now taking place?

Krill: There are big projects in our IRAD and big projects in the sponsored work.

Siegel: For example?

Krill: Well, in the sponsored world, when we build a spacecraft, that's a big deal. We're presently building twin spacecraft that are going to orbit within the Earth's radiation belts called Radiation Belt Storm Probes. The radiation belts present a very severe electronic environment for satellites flying through them, and so with RBSP we can better understand that environment and how it affects communications. But it requires spacecraft with a very robust electronics design to withstand the radiation.

Our space department also is part of a proposed NASA mission called 'TiME (Titan Mare Explorer)'. The project is to develop the concept of a large-scale primary mission to Titan, a moon of Saturn, for which we're going to have a robotic boat, an interplanetary navy, operating on the moon's methane sea. It will be the first alien sea explorer.

S. Donaldson: We'll see what the Army has to say about that.

[Laughter]

Krill: Ground vehicles were not part of the winning proposal to my knowledge.

S. Donaldson: There you go.

Krill: So that's one that's pretty much out of the box in terms of creative thinking.

Siegel: Thank you for giving us some good insight into the technology areas. Now let's shift gears and spend a few minutes talking about technology investments. How does APL invest in technology, and what is your role as the CTO in that technology investment?

Krill: We have a new process, essentially invented by our director and assistant director for strategy, based on some key literature. We are in our first year, and it seems to be going well so far. Our new strategic approach is for technology investments to be more integrated. We have an integrated investment planning strategy team, or IST. It consists of me; the assistant director (AD) for strategy; the AD for operations; the AD for programs; and our CFO. Starting at the lab level, and then with every business area, we develop or refine a set of vision, strategy, and execution priorities, we call them the 'VSEs'.

At the highest level the VSE articulates APL's vision for the future along with multiyear strategic objectives and the next year's execution priorities to move the strategy forward. They are developed via combinations of discussions with sponsors and stakeholders, projection of technologies, and recommended improvements to facilities to position us better for an uncertain future.

We have a technical portion of the VSEs at the lab level and we have technical aspects in the VSEs for our business areas (BAs), which are analogous to mission areas. Each business area proposes for the next year, the concept development work and the IRADs at the strategic level to the IST. This also includes the capital for technical facilities that are needed to carry out their strategies. This IST reviews the proposals, relative to the VSEs, for impact and technical advancement. There are several other criteria as well: strategic alignment, probability of success, and making sure they're technically risky enough—that they're not going to be too easy.

The IST then proposes an allocation of funds, both capital funds and technology investments, based on the proposals. In addition to that, the BAs collaborate to propose cross-mission, 'big-bet' IRADs to address key mission areas and they also propose 'challenges-after-next'—beyond the sponsors' time horizons.

Siegel: So what specifically as CTO, though, is your role in those processes?

Krill: I'm primarily lead on the technical aspects of the evaluation. The AD for strategy ensures that the strategic alignment is in place. The AD for programs makes sure that the proposals are well aligned with sponsor needs. The AD for operations makes sure the facilities are affordable yet effective. I'm the one who ensures that the technical impact, technical feasibility, and the technical risk are consistent.

Siegel: When you do that, how much power do you have in influencing the outcomes of what you just talked about?

Krill: Well, we're still forming as a group, and obviously everybody has opinions about all the aspects, but for this first round I felt satisfied. First of all, I listen to what the others are saying. If someone says, "You know, that's a really key thing. This is why I think it's important," I take that on board. Or if there's a question, we'll go back to a business area and say, "Why did you do it this way and not that way?" I feel satisfied that we have taken ourselves to a new level of innovation seeking, risk taking and impact potential with the plans that we've put together for fiscal 2012. The debate solidifies the technology strategy.

Siegel: Well, since you mentioned fiscal, how does your role save money for APL?

Krill: There are two ways of looking at that. I will break your question into two parts. First, "How does my role help ensure adequate investments and program funding even as we save money?" Obviously efficiency's important.

In my view the trick in these uncertain times of government funding is not to hunker down into a defensive posture to be the cheapest supplier if that is at the expense of the quality of our contributions and culture. We need to have such compelling economic and practical ideas that a sponsor, even with their limited funds, feels compelled to come to us as a value-added organization. We want to help the sponsors figure out what can be done with more limited resources.

Now I'll get the second part your question as I am interpreting it, "How can we make the investments and leverage them in the most effective way?" For example, let's not keep working on an IRAD when we could probably take the idea or technology to a sponsor and get funding to free up our internal money for other purposes.

Let's make sure that our researchers do not feel 'entitled' to their IRADs, but that they propose very impactful ideas to leverage every IRAD penny. Let's make sure that our staff feels motivated to gain funding as soon as possible for the earliest positive impact for our sponsors. That way we'll be ready with timely responses to newly emerging national problems. And as the inevitable and unpredictable drops in program funding may occur in these uncertain times, we need to make sure that the breadth of skills of our staff is sufficient to enable them to move over to new tasks if those they are working on go away.

Now another thing that we're doing is that I'm heading a new executive forum within APL called the "Management Forum." Our executive level line managers form this forum. The forum is developing new tools to ensure that our staff's areas of expertise are discoverable and can be leveraged from across the Lab.

S. Donaldson: What's the size of the IRAD budget? Or your investment budget?

Krill: Our total IRAD plus concept development plus proposal funding is about 5% of our revenue – not huge. Now, as for capital investments, we're heavily facilitized because, for example, we build spacecraft and prototypes. This investment category is comparable to the percentage of IRAD, etc. In addition, we have significant direct work in S&T. If you add the internal and external S&T funding, I believe we're in pretty good shape.

Siegel: I would like to switch gears now and discuss your vision of the future. Are you involved in developing strategies to move APL into new research?

Krill: Yes. The big bets we're placing are essentially to examine emerging areas that could affect not only all of our current missions but could cause new missions to emerge. For example, if autonomy concepts pan out, they could change the technical approaches in some of our business areas. If the neuroscience research bears fruit, this would be a game-changer in which human brains are intimately linked with computing systems.

Siegel: Okay. So now let's get down to the business level. How do you evaluate your competition?

Krill: Well, let's talk about who our competition is. In science and technology, we're all in competition with our ideas—academia, industry, and laboratories. APL does not manufacture and is not-for-profit, so the primary competition that I personally feel is the competition of ideas. To be of value, we have to develop good ideas that our sponsors need, our lab counterparts respect, and industry values as something they can produce.

Our fundamental approach is to provide critical contributions to critical challenges. "Are we providing valuable contributions to the most difficult national technical challenges?" It's a complex question with a different answer for each different mission area.

I would say we have a collegial competition for ideas among the UARCs and FFRDCs and a productive dialog in ideas with our sponsors and industry.

Siegel: Nice response. Now, what do you see as your biggest challenge?

Krill: The biggest challenge for me is to help APL generate great ideas, and to do that we must preserve and nurture the 'small flames' of promising new, immature ideas lest they flicker out before they have had a chance to be considered and improved. Innovative ideas are our legacy and our future.

Siegel: Okay. You already mentioned the recent reformulation of your job description. Picking up on that, how do you see the CTO role changing over time?

Krill: Well, it's been an abrupt change in the last year.

[Laughter.]

Let me just say again that there are basically four different things that I'm responsible for: our tech base, our gaining insight into national challenges and opportunities, our global connections for emerging technologies, and increasing our innovative spirit. Those are the four responsibilities I'm measured on and they are based on principles that will not change much over time.

We're only now launching this newly defined CTO role. I would say that the sum of these four responsibilities is to ensure that we are so flexible that we are capable of sprouting a role in a new mission, if needed. For example, we didn't even have a substantial role in cyber or special operations missions a decade ago.

We need to be so flexible and adaptive that we can change the course of things we are doing. We've got to reduce our momentum when needed, so we can merge and split our efforts and organization as needed.

Siegel: That's an interesting expression: "reduce your momentum."

Krill: When we reduce our organizational momentum, we can gain technical agility.

G. Donaldson: Have you formulated your strategy in how you're going to do that?

Krill: Well, we have been building towards that. We used to be organized only as departments as recently as a decade ago, with each department a monolith unto itself. They really didn't interact with each other much. Then, ten years ago under our previous director, we developed the concept of 'business areas' as a program approach allowing us to be more agile to follow sponsors' needs and national challenges. So that was our first step.

The latest step is that we are in the process of having the biggest reorganization that this lab has seen in decades. We're organizing into 'sectors', with 2 to 3 missions, or business areas, in each sector. The purpose is to allow our business areas to be more synergistically aligned within sectors for collaboration and cross-mission initiative as well as to facilitate moving technical staff among the tasks of these BAs for which the requisite technical expertise is similar.

So we're systematically reconstructing ourselves to make it easier to be agile, but we're also working on the culture so the staff are more comfortable with proposing new ideas and are invited to think in an agile way.

G. Donaldson: May I ask, how do you support that part?

Krill: The culture?

G. Donaldson: Yes.

Krill: Well, with initiatives, such as the Ignition Grants, to encourage and foster new ideas until they can be evaluated; inviting people to propose regardless of where they are within the Lab's organizational structure. We're working at the grassroots level.

G. Donaldson: And how are you putting in, fostering the collaboration to do that so it's just not solo folks coming up with ideas but people wanting to put together ideas?

Krill: This Ignition Grants initiative is essentially a 'crowd-sourcing' approach, where our staff are invited to build on each other's ideas. And in the very first round, the winners, who reported their results during a colloquium, said that they are now working together with people and capabilities they didn't know existed prior to the Grants. Communities are forming around topics. So, we think the virtual connection exhibited by the Ignition Grants is important—especially with the new generation of staff—and it's actually providing enough of a 'buzz' that people even of my generation are getting involved, which is very interesting. Many people seem to have reinvented themselves.

Siegel: To wrap up here, I'd like to ask you two personal questions. First, what's next in your career?

Krill: That's a good question. I love what I'm doing here. I love the career I have had. It's been a wonderful ride. I'd like to continue it. I'm not sure I'm one of those people who can just retire. My hobby is technology—inventing -research—so to the extent that I can support this organization or the country and have fun doing it, that's pretty much as far as I've thought.

Siegel: One final question. What keeps you up at night?

Krill: The totality of the things we've talked about, "Can we get our level of idea-forming, innovation and flexibility, and at the same time research break-throughs and transitions, up to speed fast enough for the coming technology turbulence—both on the world stage and in terms of national security fund-ing—that's coming?" But I have to say I am more often awake with the ex-citement of the technical possibilities and opportunities.

Siegel: We really appreciate you taking the time to talk with us today. Thank you.

Wesley Kaplow

Polar Star Consulting

Dr. Wesley Kaplow is the CTO of Polar Star Consulting, a small company (approximately one dozen people) located in the Washington, DC, area. The company provides information technology solutions to the United States government where it distinguishes itself by eliminating network and information systems constraints to accommodate new applications critical to government operations.

Dr. Kaplow has developed solutions for a broad range of requirements, from special facilities-based regional and nationwide networks to the latest in Ethernet technologies and network operations services. He is experienced in understanding the customer's mission, creation and analysis of customer requirements, system engineering, vendor selections, complex program management and implementation processes, and mission critical operations support.

Prior to his current position, he spent ten years as the CTO of Qwest Government Services (Qwest is now CenturyLink, which is the third largest telecommunications company in the United States; Qwest began doing business as CenturyLink in April 2011). In that position he provided the technical vision and leadership for that organization and their customers, among other things. Prior to Qwest, he spent ten years as a member of the technical staff at Lucent Technologies/Bell Labs.

Gary Donaldson: We want to get a sense of your journey to the role of CTO. What was the path you've gone down in terms of your educational background and employment history? Would you like to start with your education, or did it start before that?

Kaplow: No, I don't think it started before that. My high school experience may have had some impact. Much of the CTO role is an influencing role and it's a communication role, and some of the elements and experience of my high school years gave me an appreciation for teaching and for being able to communicate, laying out expectations and providing the kind of coaching required to get the best out of students. I went to Fordham Preparatory School in the Bronx, which is a private school run by the Jesuits, so it gave me a very interesting perspective on life and many of the kinds of teaching techniques, cajoling, and methods they used there had some impact.

G. Donaldson: So their method of teaching helped draw out and build knowledge for you?

Kaplow: Well, I think it may have—I don't know if it's unique there, but it was my experience. Having a great love and appreciation for communication, engaging people and providing them direction seemed special. I thought it was important and I actually used it when I went back to finish my doctorate at RPI [Rensselaer Polytechnic Institute]. At Rensselaer, I taught for a couple of semesters. There was no requirement for me to do it, but it was an opportunity for me to use those teaching skills. I had a successful couple of semesters teaching, and I probably would have taught longer, but as my advisor, Bolek Szymanski said "You can teach longer and stay here longer or you can finish and graduate."

G. Donaldson: So that experience helped shape your interest in the influencing role and communication role of the CTO, and you saw how you could apply those skills as you grew your career. Where did you go to school?

Kaplow: For my undergraduate, I went to NYU [New York University] and I majored in physics and in history. I realized that physics, although I enjoyed it quite a bit, was not necessarily the long-term path, but it did give me the opportunity to work in the High Energy physics department. I supported some experiments, mostly on the technology side for data acquisition and analysis. I realized that physics wasn't really going to be my true love, but I enjoyed it immensely and had some great professors. I was on campus there for four years and then I moved to the computer science department at the Courant Institute of Mathematical Sciences, which was sort of a natural progression from the kind of computer work I was doing in the physics department. It's probably a little bit better known for math, but it is a very, very good computer science department and had some great teachers. So I did a master's degree in computer science and started on my doctorate. At the same time, the whole "going to school forever" thing started to wear thin. I took a job over at Bell Laboratories in 1987. So I just got my master's degree in 1985, I started working on my doctoral requirements at NYU, and then once I started working, that was way too much of a workload to be successful. I sort of puttered around trying to complete my PhD, but that didn't really work.

G. Donaldson: What did you do at Bell?

Kaplow: I originally started as a member of the technical staff. They had a relatively flat staffing environment, and most people went in as Members of the Technical Staff and then worked there for their entire careers and came out Members of the Technical Staff. Bell Labs had developed a series of microprocessors and I started out doing performance analysis work in the microprocessor division in Holmdel, New Jersey. That went reasonably well. AT&T [the larger company] had gone through and continued to go through significant upheavals during that time. The microprocessor activity eventually wound down and we started doing other performance analysis work related to transaction systems and those sorts of things, and that was interesting to a point. And then I got a call from Ed Hummel, whom I worked with and is still at Bell Laboratories. He was getting his PhD when I was in the physics department at NYU, and he called me up and said something like, "We have a project. We're going to build this fantastic supercomputer gizmo for an avionics application," and he'd love to have me come and work on it. So from there, I transitioned from a performance analysis environment to systems engineering role with some development work associated with it. That environment was good, as was the previous experience of essentially digging into whatever problem presented itself. One day it could be how could we improve the performance of some network interface that we designed. The next one could be, "Go figure out why the network interface we designed doesn't work correctly." The next day could be, "Go talk to customers and represent what the performance of the system could be." Then the next, "Go write some benchmark system applications to show how it works." So it was a very wide range of things and got me exposure, in developing reasonably concise information where I could convey a message. I worked with multiple companies that were targeting their applications through this environment.

G. Donaldson: And from there you moved on to Qwest, is that correct?

Kaplow: Not quite. At Bell Labs, we went off on a slightly different tack in terms of the work that we were doing and started looking at the operation of telecommunications equipment and services.

G. Donaldson: Okay.

Kaplow: It also was really my first nontrivial introduction to the government. Even though we previously were building this thing for the Advanced

Tactical Fighter (ATF) program, it sort of stood on its own. The work that I started doing was in telecommunications systems and systems analysis and its impact on the government. The Internet Protocol was still a very small piece of the telecommunications picture but growing rapidly. The types of things that the government was doing were impacted by the changes in the methods of communications and the protocols that were being used, and it got me into really thinking about what the future looks like and what those impacts and trends would be.

That work got me into writing a pretty lengthy report that had some traction within certain areas of the government that had a different perspective on things. You're not really building things; it was more along the lines of, "What's the state of affairs today? What are we projecting that state of affairs to be in 5 or 10 years, and what do we need to do to meet our goals as a government in that particular mission? When do we need to start thinking about what we have to build to meet that program's needs?"

G. Donaldson: More strategic.

Kaplow: Right, a little more strategic. So you can focus intently on what's there, but they really didn't want to know that. They wanted to know over time what things would look like and how the telecommunications landscape across the world would go. "Wow, we spent 100 years developing the wired phone system we have in the US and some small country just got the old cellular wireless system from Argentina. A third-world country has gone from nowhere to pretty much, I wouldn't call it "state of the art," but not that far behind, like that [snapping fingers]. And so those jumpstart kinds of things start impacting us. Of course, in retrospect you start putting these thoughts into place that, "Wow, I must be thinking about these things as I do my job," but at the time that had no impact.

G. Donaldson: So you had to marry legacy systems with strategic thinking about where things were evolving?

Kaplow: That's right. And it was everything. So here I am thinking about, "Wait a second. This country just bought a new 5ESS switch [a telephone electronic switching system sold by Alcatel-Lucent] or DMS250 switch [sold by then Nortel] or a new wireless system just got plopped down," and over here, my local telephone switch, when I lived in Greenwich Village was still a mechanical switch. I mean, it was fine because that was a cost-optimized solution with respect to rate-of-return and the regulated environment rules. You could see the rapidity that things could change outside of what you would consider to be the high-tech zone. I think that you see that right now and how quickly you can build a factory to build phenomenal devices in China and other countries almost on a dime. And it didn't take that huge an infrastructure to start and it's transportable.

G. Donaldson: Right.

Kaplow: So while that was happening, we lost that program [ATF] in 1992. My mother always wanted me to be a doctor, but the medical thing wasn't going to happen. She was on me every single day about how come I haven't finished my degree. I thought about it and I said, "I've never really gone away to college." I mean, I went to NYU; I lived on campus, if you can call it that at the time, and I lived in the Village [Greenwich Village]. I said, "You know, I've never really gone away to school. I've never been at a school that had a real football team." So I said, "I want to go somewhere where I can get a campus feel, because there's only really one chance to go." This is sort of the second chance; I'm going back after a number of years out of really doing anything terribly academic. So I decided to go back. I was able to set up an arrangement where I got partial support from AT&T. I went to Rensselaer and I lived up there for four years, and I still worked part-time. The experience gave me a different perspective. It was more of a campus life. I was able to expand my set of friends and it gave me the opportunity to both complete my degree and also to teach.

G. Donaldson: Being connected to people is an important theme that seems to emerge from what you've shared so far, the importance of relationships and how to maintain them.

Kaplow: Yes. However, I'm plagued with a poor memory, unfortunately. But I build good relationships with people I work with on a constant basis. It's difficult to continue that and keep that larger social circle going. As a personal critique, I probably need to network more and I think that would help. Part of the challenge is to stay reasonably current across a broad set of technologies and not to be completely inward-focused against a particular customer or the particular problem set of the moment. That's a challenge that happens all the time. It's easy to get comfortable staring, you know, navel gazing at your problem. For me, it takes definitive effort to keep looking outside. To help, I try to write about my observations periodically in my blog.

I was up at RPI for four years and then completed my degree when we moved back to New Jersey to get closer to Bell Labs. Bell Labs was formative in the sense that I was able to apply my previous experiences, pedagogy and teaching. It took a heck of a lot of work, as Stan knows from teaching classes. I mean, preparing material is a very difficult thing to do. I was able to apply a lot of the lessons learned that worked for me.

G. Donaldson: What are the lessons? Can you give an example of one of the lessons that you carried forward?

Kaplow: There's an informality that works and there's an informality that doesn't work. You can't be their buddy because then they don't respect the fact that there's an obligation forward other than their grade. I treated it very seriously. I used to joke around, but had to keep the relationships professional. I had a friend, whom I have not kept in great contact with, Pete Floriani, who was getting his PhD basically at the same time. We joked about when we graduated, we would go teach in our cap and gown because we thought that would be appropriate. So I think that you want to be approachable but you want to set that expectation that there's something of importance happening. And I think that that was key lesson.

G. Donaldson: Is that something that's carried over into your CTO role?

Kaplow: I think so. I laid out very clear expectations about how the grading was going to go and what the assignments meant. One of the lessons I learned is that you've got to be very careful during the examination process. You have somebody who knows 99% of the information, but they know 80% of the questions that you've asked, and that somebody gets a crappy grade because that one question, which, on a five-question test, is worth 20% of the points. That person is sitting there going, "Oh my God, I'm getting a crappy grade. I know all this material and I'm just freezing on something, and I'm screwed." What I would do is a couple of things, which were quirky, that came from my high school experience. I'd put extra points on the exam, so that there was always a little bit of escape valve associated with freezing or if that question was the one thing they just couldn't quite grasp even though they knew 90% to 99% of the information. I also did something that would probably make the dean go crazy. As they handed in their exams I would scan them. If I didn't like what I saw, I sent them back to their desk.

G. Donaldson: So these experiences that you had in school, they've carried over into your role as you've progressed in technology, in managing teams and customers.

Kaplow: Certainly in managing teams. I've had only three major jobs, which is almost unheard of today. I spent about 10 years at Bell Labs, almost 10 years at Qwest, and in October it will be three years at Polar Star. A lot of activity is basically communicating information to customers, and a lot of that comes in a presentation format. It comes in a proposal response. There were a lot of times where I had to hand my team's "exam" back to them—that is, the work they were doing in putting a proposal together.

G. Donaldson: Right.

Kaplow: A proposal to a customer, especially if it's a new customer, is your first work product that they see. And so it was very important to me to apply thoughtfulness in relating information. It is important to understand what the relationship is with the customer and understanding what we are trying to accomplish with them from a technical perspective. It is also important to work with the team to make them understand the relationship they need to have with the customer. That it is important that their work product communicate effectively. That it is important to relate to the customer their preparedness, their grasp of our technical capabilities, things that we could do, and things that we could stretch.

Stan Siegel: Wes, what was the factor that moved you over to Qwest?

Kaplow: It was a very, very difficult decision. I had been promoted that summer to a DMTS [Distinguished Member of the Technical Staff] position, which represented probably about 8% to 10% of the entire technical staff. And, essentially, from a non-management role at the time at Bell Labs, that was where you went. I still keep in touch with the guys that I used to work with at Lucent Government Services; now a subsidiary of Alcatel-Lucent. So it was a very difficult thing to even contemplate. I had never done anything terribly entrepreneurial. So I went from college and graduate school and went to work at Bell Labs and worked on some start-up type of projects within the umbrella of a huge company in pretty much a position that required sort of an HR [human resources] violation to get fired. So, that certainly was not what happened. I was working on a study project, a systems engineering task related to a government program, and an opportunity came up. It was an opportunity to do something significantly different for the government than had been done before. As part of the study program, I was introduced to Dean Wandry, who was at Qwest, about the opportunity. He was working with several of our customers, who are my customers today, or who have been customers. The government floated an RFI [request for information] and Qwest had no way to respond to it. One of the salespeople [at Bell Labs] was John McGowan. He saw this as a great opportunity, that there was something special that was going to happen. And John could have a pretty infectious attitude—like, "Oh my God! You should see what they're doing! It's sliced bread." So I looked, and I said, "This looks pretty interesting." And we arranged to help Qwest respond to the RFI. I had a difficult decision to make. George Johnston [also at Bell Labs], John McGowan, and I got together, probably instigated mostly by John, and said, "If Qwest is going to go after this big, potentially huge government contract they have to think outside of the box. They're a startup company; they're building a network. There's a lot of opportunity here. There are artificial pricing umbrellas in the marketplace. We should put together a little business proposition and we should pitch it to Qwest management. We shouldn't just help them respond to the RFP [request for proposal]. Maybe they should start a government division to respond to the RFP and then go from there."

Siegel: So when you made that transition, when did the idea occur to you that eventually you wanted to become a CTO?

Kaplow: It's was a natural progression. Essentially, there were three of us. We had a sales person, an operations person, and I was the engineer—systems engineer kind of troublemaking person. So it happened. We responded to the RFP, and we won. Actually, we flew up around Thanksgiving of 1997, flew out to Denver, met with Qwest leadership and presented our business case. They said, "We're going to hire you," and the most difficult thing I had to do professionally, aside from dealing with people who need to "leave the program," because I had to fire them, was to call my boss [at Bell Labs] and tell him I was leaving. I started the first business day in 1998, and that was it. I was the technical response proposal person. I did what normal proposal people do: I helped drive the process; outline the initial story-boards; collaborated on their content; I reviewed it with the team; and was the primary author on the technical side of the proposal. And that effort represents many, many hundreds of millions of dollars to my old company [Qwest is now CenturyLink].

G. Donaldson: Does your interest in teaching carry over into helping developing storyboards?

Kaplow: Yes, part of teaching is telling a story, taking your students on a journey that does not leave them asking "So what." At Bell Labs, we had proposals that we had done and I just don't remember the process being very successful. It didn't leave a lasting impression on me. Some people are good at languages, and some people are good at mathematics. For some reason, the storyboard process seemed to be a natural thing for me.

G. Donaldson: Okay.

Kaplow: Declarative request [in an RFP], declarative response. "We want a Washington Nationals baseball hat," and I said, "Well, let's figure it out. Do we have baseball hats? Let's go get baseball hats. Have you made baseball hats before? Yes, we've made lots of baseball hats." So it's lots of very declarative things that are said, that yes, we can do it; how we would do it; why should you reasonably expect us to be able to fulfill on our delivery; and any additional benefits of our product. It seemed very logical to me.

So to answer Stan's question: we started the group and the natural issue is, well, what have you done lately? I mean, in a sales environment, technical or not, that's it. At that time, I don't think we called it "sales engineering," but that became the technical part of the sales team for Qwest in the government marketplace. And the team eventually grew and grew and at some point grew to some reasonable size, maybe 10 or 20 people. I had a director of engineering title or something like that, and my boss James Payne said, "That doesn't really express to our customers what we're really trying to do. So, we'll call you the CTO". Inwardly you are representing customer needs back into the corporation. Outwardly, you're reflecting that environment to the customers that we're trying to make a sale to. To be really successful in selling anything, you have to know what you're doing. And so that led me to interacting with the people internally and externally who could help make a difference in providing an understanding and influencing our products both from technical and process perspectives.

S. Donaldson: Was the nature of the job to produce a series of products, and produce a network?

Kaplow: Yes to both. In principle, we were responsible for building and the caretaking of a network infrastructure. However, we are also looking for new customers for commercial telecommunication services, potentially tailored for government needs.

S. Donaldson: Okay.

Kaplow: And so there are a lot of components to that. It allowed me to be in a position where I had to find the right people. I had to find the real technologists associated with optical transport technology and our commercial networking products and what was changing there. I had to reach out and find people.

G. Donaldson: How did you know where to look?

Kaplow: Initially, Qwest wasn't really all that big. Qwest started to grow and bought LCI and then US West. One of the first things when I got there was—we, naively, because we didn't know completely what we were doing—went after a large contract at the time with TRW [now Northrop Grumman], for the Treasury communications system. John McGowan helped us. He latched on and said, "I need to find the people who really understand what's going on because those are the people that excite customers in making that connection between desire and capability, and they tend to feed off each other." So we latched right on to the people who were building, designing, operating network infrastructure at Qwest. Those are the people to help write the proposal for that contract.

G. Donaldson: So did John help mentor you in that skill?

Kaplow: I don't know if "mentor" is really the right word, I think it was more by example. Nobody sat down and said, "Wes, what you really need to do is …" I think it's more by example. He knew his infectious love for the job reflected itself both to get people to help him internally, as well as reflected out to customers. Ultimately, and what I've learned over time, is that people buy things and do things with people they know and trust.

S. Donaldson: Right.

Kaplow: And that trust relationship can be because we have a better technical idea, but the customer has to know that you care. And, I think that was something from my teaching experience, they had to know that it was an important relationship and there was care. And I think it's the same kind of thing.

Siegel: With all that tremendous success you had in what you just described at Qwest, what motivated you to make the transition to Polar Star?

Kaplow: I was at Qwest for almost 11 years, from January 1998 to October 2008. I had helped build a good organization, and it had matured well and it was successful. I had a great team. A couple things started to occur. I became very identified with Qwest. In other words, my name is Wes; the middle letters of Qwest are "Wes." Somebody said, "Hey! You can't have Qwest without Wes". So that was one thing maybe in the back of my mind. I was so identified, emotionally engaged in the company, and that emotional engagement is a benefit because it makes you … it just has a certain drive there and people around you see that you love what you're doing. It has a downside in that you're driving your emotions into a large corporate culture.

Another part of it is there were some people that had matured in the organization. They had started early at Qwest. Maybe not quite as early as I did, and they had gone off and started going into other positions. Dave Peed runs Ciena Government and Ken Folderauer runs tw telecom, very successfully. And so they had sort of graduated into a different environment and at some point they were looking at me and saying, first of all, that they would hire me and, second of all, they said, "You know you've been there a long time. It's time to do something else." So there was a little bit of a peer pressure thing. I also started in what was essentially a startup mode, in an organization with three people and that evolved over time to three, four hundred people. I had various roles and bigger and smaller responsibility and pretty much found out what I wasn't good at. And that's a good thing, by the way, a very good thing to find out. I said, "Well, you know, we won the big contract with GSA Networx. This was a huge thing and getting some customers on that was a big corporate objective. What is going through my mind was, "This is my day every day. I'm going to be here to try to help people get these proposals out, deal with what I can deal with, and deal with HR situations that are just not what I wanted to do. Doing performance reviews every year is just not the love of anybody's life. I said, "You know what? I think I accomplished a lot here." I left a good legacy. I left good people in place. I left them in a strong position. They had a great year after I left. It wasn't like I was going to jeopardize their business. "I'm leaving very well respected, and it's time to do something a little bit different in my life. I think I can go make an impact somewhere else." And that was sort of the totality of it.

S. Donaldson: So how did you meet up with your current business partners, for example Bert Crinks?

Kaplow: What happened when I was still at Qwest was that we got a request from the government to do a major upgrade of their infrastructure. We had to do a significant technical evaluation. I had to go off and help our program team to make sure that we got the right people. We used a lot of resources from the corporate part of Qwest, the CTO's office at Qwest. I built a good relationship at the time with Balan Nair, who was the CTO and then Pieter Poll. I helped get those resources to respond to the RFIs and the RFQs [request for quotations]; set up vendor meetings; do the vendor evaluations; do the analysis required for us to make a recommendation to the government; and spent a lot of money. Now, in that process, Mark Stine, who was in my organization at Qwest, said, "Hey, you know, Bert Crinks is over there [at the customer]. He might be interested in coming over to program manage this thing." I had an opening for the program manager. At that time, all the program stuff reported to me. So I called him up and spoke to him, and he said, "Yeah, this sounds like a wonderful thing. I'm going to come in and I'll run this program."

And he did a fabulous job. So he worked for me briefly and then we reorganized and he worked directly for the senior vice president. He's not the typical corporate guy and didn't enjoy the performance reviews, this and that. He accomplished what he wanted to accomplish on the project and said, "You know what? I'm going to go back to work as a SETA [systems engineering and technical assistance] contractor to support the customer." And he left in very good, very good circumstances; no hard feelings at all.

So around that time, around the summer of 2008, as we talked about, I was thinking that there's something else to do." I saw Bert in the parking lot and I said, "Bert, what's going on? I'm thinking maybe it's time for me to kind of reach out and do something else. I've got friends who are yapping in my ear, telling me I'll look stale if I stay where I am."

S. Donaldson: Right.

Kaplow: Salespeople [Dave and Ken] can convince you of anything. Bert said, "That's interesting. We should talk. We're starting a small company." And sometime around the August-September timeframe, I made the decision. So he worked for me, and now we're essentially partners working together.

Siegel: So you co-created the company with him and others?

Kaplow: No, my partners started the company in 2007. At least on paper, we had some clients. The other major partner is Elaina Mangione. She had a business doing technical accounting for government contractors. She brought some of her clients in.

Siegel: Right.

Kaplow: She sold part of her business. So, technically, the company was there. Then John Sherrard, who's the other partner, joined. I was employee four. But really, in stride, things really probably didn't start until 2009 or so.

G. Donaldson: Are you a partner in this business?

Kaplow: Yes, I am. I don't think I would have left [Qwest] if that wasn't the case.

G. Donaldson: In your career path toward becoming a CTO, what have you found that captures your imagination and curiosity the most?

Kaplow: So there's technology for technology's sake, right? This is the one-hand-clapping problem. But what really intrigues me is how to manage the technical business process. How do you work with people and organizations to get them to use new technology? How do you help the technical business process move forward to help the client manage the change required to in-corporate technology or change the business processes that they're using to deploy technology or provide services? So that's where a lot of the teaching role and the mentoring skills come into play. In a lot of cases it's sort of a force-of-wills thing, especially in the position I'm in now, because I'm not a government employee. I support government managers, who are trying to ef-fect change within a large government organization. But ultimately, I can jump up and down 'til the cows come home, but the government makes the deci-sion. It's their company, so to speak. It takes a lot of effort to play that role. For example, let's say I have a vision of a service or technology that I believe is important for the organization to provide or employ. At the same time, within the organization there are other contractors that have different roles and other customer personnel who may have a different view. It is difficult to try to get those competing visions to line up so we can be successful. At least right now, with what we're doing, it is the exciting part of the job and it's also very frustrating. Every time the ship moves about a degree or the piston goes off top dead center; it's a major victory.

G. Donaldson: Well, it's a shift from leaving a large company where you had a large staff, about 300, to now where you have, what, about a dozen or so folks working with you?

Kaplow: Yeah, we have about a dozen.

G. Donaldson: What has been involved in that shift? How has the shift changed your role as a CTO?

Kaplow: There are some similarities in the roles at both companies. I'm still the technical vision person. For example, at Qwest that meant talking at conferences and interacting with our customers at that level. For those examples, the role doesn't change as much. In the current role, I'm sort of a CTO for hire. I take my skills and I help our customers. To inwardly focus when you've got a group of 12 people, there are not many big technical decisions. Google Apps has been the biggest decision, and I think it sort of made it on its own.

S. Donaldson: So in your current role then, as you go in as a CTO for hire, so to speak, do you have a technical counterpart? Is it usually another CTO? Is it the CIO? Is it both?

Kaplow: For my government contract work, my government point of contact is the CTO for the organization. My relationship with him is to help provide the kind of analysis and direction along with other people and help him make that his own, of which he does a good job. He's only been in the position three months or so. Without having a counterpart, it just doesn't work all that well.

S. Donaldson: Does he have counterparts for a whole contractor team? Are there multiple contractors involved, so there's like a technology community that's helping advise him?

Kaplow: In this particular contract, we are part of the technical advisory team. There are other contractors, but for the prime contract, we're a major part. We have probably over half the technical slots. We're advising them on everything from hosting and cloud infrastructure to network transport technology to all sorts of services-related kinds of things. I'm the designated enterprise architect. My major role is to help define a series of technology roadmaps. This is an interesting problem because I've never quite done that before. I've done a lot of take one thing and explore it. But this particular organization does everything from provide raw telecommunications transport capability to desktop services, and that set of capabilities turns out to be rich and complicated.

S. Donaldson: How do you lay out the technology roadmaps? Is there a process for technology road mapping?

Kaplow: We looked at some examples of what some other organizations in the government had done. How do you know how to organize services, capabilities, and technologies? There's some art involved. I just came from a presentation to the assistant deputy CIO for an organization. I was there to explain, "There's a little art to this. There are lots of reasonably correct answers." And that's probably true in a lot of cases in life.

We just started saying, "We've got things that we can pick up and break and we're going to make those things for the user, for example workstations and phones. We've got moving data around in networks, so we call that distribution." And then we said, "Well, we've got security things and controlling access to information. Well, that sounds like access." And then we were a little conflicted on what to call the compute and storage environment. We said, "You know, let's call it cloud." And then somebody says, "What's cloud?" And then you're in this whole philosophical argument, so we said, we call it "data," and that seemed kind of silly. We said, "Okay, it's hosting." So we called it "hosting." Then, there are all the things that people use, email, document sharing services, video chat and voice communications; we called that integrated communications. Finally, consolidated management is where we placed the operations and management systems. After that we assigned individual subject matter experts to those different areas and they started looking at the areas and they said, "Well, where would this go?" "It goes there." And we haven't really found anything from a technology perspective that doesn't fit.

Now, we're reorganizing the budget against the evolving roadmap. Actually, we're changing the way that money is looked at, decomposing projects into their roadmap areas. This helps identify overlap, technologies required, and the funding elements needed to achieve the vision.

G. Donaldson: Did you provide that picture for them? Or did you facilitate the discussion?

Kaplow: I helped facilitate those discussions. And so that's a walkthrough process. It's hard to do. It's not like solving a math problem. What we're really doing is defining services. So, the discussions became the elements of a services CONOPS [concept of operations] and an enterprise operations model.

G. Donaldson: In the process of helping them with the technology road-map, did you teach them how to do one for themselves? Did you codify what you were doing for them?

Kaplow: First of all, we had to do it for ourselves, right? And we're doing this in partnership in some sense with the government. So we said, "Well, what do we need to do? We need a vision." We said, "What should things look like in 2015 or 2017? Somebody better say what that vision is." Some people said, "I'd really like to have everything right there in front of me. To-day I've got to go here, and I've gotta go there, and I've gotta use this computer, that computer, and I've got this system and that system, and it's a little bit of a mess. Maybe we can coalesce those elements," so that consolidation became part of the vision for nearly every aspect of the roadmap.

Along with that vision, we said, "You should have goals. What are the goals here? Improved operations? Reduced costs? Speed to execution? What operating system should we have, and how often should we refresh it, and when do we make decisions on do we stay with Windows, or do we look for something different?" The discussion became a lot of internal wrestling with that whole group to develop a vision of what things should look like and why.

The documentation of the process is incorporated into the work itself.

G. Donaldson: Okay.

Kaplow: Now, the way the agency is structured, there's a CIO and different divisions that have CTOs and associate CIOs associated with them. The CIO has a vision of what she wants for the agency. She needs a mechanism to get them to execute, so her office provides high-level planning guidance and policies. We started talking to them [CIO's office] about our organization's roadmap and how we see the environment. "We have multiple systems and we're going to try to get the number down, and we have a vision for this hosting environment" and everything else. It had a lot of resonance with the CIO. The CIO organization, at least where I am, doesn't really have an engineering team. They have a good set of people, mostly focused on policy. They're smart, they go out and interact with communities and vendors, and they understand more of the art of the possible. They're not the group to engineer the changes between the art of where we are and the art of the possible. We use them for guidance and ask, "What would you accept in a system?" Ultimately, they're the ones that have to accept it. And now they're calling on us, based on our road mapping experiences and vision, to ask, "We have this community problem and we're trying to figure out how to do something. Can you apply some of this stuff that you've been doing in your organization?" Our roadmaps approach is being incorporated to capture the CIO's direction and our technology and services plans.

S. Donaldson: Is the roadmap done in the context of a larger lifecycle development? Agile? Engineering "V"?

Kaplow: The organization I support builds systems to support critical government missions—and these are systems that once deployed can't be repaired in the field. So, if you get that wrong, it's a problem, right? These are areas where hard, detailed systems engineering is critical—you have to get it right the first time. Overall, in our case, the mission is not to provide IT services on somebody's desktop. It's hard to get people to realize that providing desktop services is an administrative support function. It's a necessary evil to figure out and decide what you need to buy and help get it built—the actual mission.

Most of the services that we are roadmapping don't require the same type of systems engineering detail. In these cases, we use the roadmap as the guide and our approach is to employ a more agile development process.

S. Donaldson: Gary's come up with a phrase that describes this situation: "Technology is the enabler. It's not the mission."

Kaplow: Right. The mission isn't email!—Although, some would argue!

S. Donaldson: In the commercial world, it's make money. Here it's mission accomplished.

Kaplow: Right, exactly.

G. Donaldson: What do you do in developing the roadmap? Can give an example?

Kaplow: It's a coaching thing. I help lay out a first vision and help people iterate. So part of the process is bringing along the customer.

G. Donaldson: And how do you do that?

Kaplow: That's an interaction thing. Organizations tend to start being inwardly focused. I try to foster discussion across the larger organization, as well as within the organization. For example, I recommended that we needed to have regular CTO roundtable meetings, which are forums where we're presenting the roadmap, ideas, services, and technology presentations in the context of an interactive classroom. Depending on the goal of the meeting, we may have vendors, other contractors, and government people across the division, from operations or from the CIO's office participate. The forum becomes a continuing education process in socializing the roadmap.

Stan: What is your role in that forum? Do you facilitate that discussion?

Kaplow: I tend to be the protagonist of discussion. I find that asking simple questions is the most powerful thing. Simple questions are the things that motivate the thought process, but sometimes the question is just one word: "Why?"

G. Donaldson: Right.

Kaplow: And a lot of times you get, "Because that's not the way we do it." Well, that's not particularly satisfying. So I lead that kind of discussion and sometimes, without trying to be overly argumentative, I start a little bit of discussion. Someone once told me I can argue with myself and lose, right?

[Laughter]

So, I try to start the discussion. "You may think it's A, but I say, 'How about B? I think B.' " And then they defend A. And I'm like, "Yeah, A is the right answer."

It's almost like a protagonistic/antagonistic kind of thing. I call it "constructive non-complacency." You're not happy with the answer, but there's two ways to go about it: (1) you can beat somebody over the head with it, or (2) you can try to shepherd the discussion by asking and by demonstration. I don't ask anybody to do anything that I wouldn't try to attempt to start myself. I have no problem when somebody takes it and makes it their own. I don't worry about the fact that maybe the idea came from me.

G. Donaldson: I get the impression from how you do your work that you're actually a psychological CTO.

Kaplow: I think there are classes of CTOs. It's hard to say, but you could be a CTO who's really focused on a very specific piece of technology and you're essentially the guru associated with that company's product in that environment because you invented or created something – a genius with a thousand helpers.

G. Donaldson: I want to go back to a point you had raised earlier. You said that you helped people change the way they see money.

Kaplow: It can be difficult when you have a fully depreciated infrastructure. Your are not investing in it and it's generating revenue or providing the needed service—you're nuts to change it. If I'm going to put another dollar in, I lose a dollar.

S. Donaldson: Right.

Kaplow: But, you know, that's a finance view. Over time I've gotten more appreciation for that.

S. Donaldson: So, with that in mind, I imagine your clients are wrestling with this whole issue of the cloud. There's a huge infrastructure in place; there's a lot of equipment out there; things are aging; things are changing. So, from a technology viewpoint, can you give some insight into what you might see as the trend in the cloud computing, how it may be being adopted in the government sector?

Kaplow: Sure, it's an active part of what we're right in the middle of right now. We're creating a private cloud infrastructure for our agency; for a portion of their requirements.

S. Donaldson: Do you see people going to the private cloud as the first step in general?

Kaplow: We have a unique situation. Most of the interesting things that we do are classified. The information is classified. There's not a whole lot of opportunity right now to use a commercial service for that.

S. Donaldson: You've mentioned that inside the government, there's some opinion out there that you need to put a private cloud in. Is that what you're saying?

Kaplow: The goal is to produce information that's used as part of a decision-making process in defending the country. When I first started the job, I said, "There are two things that we do: we're either protecting our country or we're helping the people protecting our country. And if you're not doing that, if what you're doing is wasting money, you're not being effective and you're not doing the mission."

Our biggest problem, actually, is that everybody is buying different hardware and to some extent software. The killer is that all these things have to go through a certification and accreditation process. This is a difficult, documentation-heavy, frightening-to-people-like-me process. Every time you do that, it takes time, money, and resources.

S. Donaldson: Right.

Kaplow: So the goal from the CIO is you've got to virtualize stuff so that you're buying less of the stuff you're buying. That's a baseline step in some ways, and virtualization is not the same thing as the cloud.

S. Donaldson: Right.

Kaplow: You have to create a cloud environment where people will say, "I trust you to run my application and I'm not going to operate the infrastructure anymore. Some operations group is going to do it." So it becomes a service, and you have to think about it as a service model.

So the easiest thing to do is look around and see what you've got and say, "I can create this service model. I can build a processing and storage infrastructure. I can overlay an operations software and support environment." Then we build an infrastructure where customers feel cozy about placing their requirements.

When people go to the cloud, they need to understand what that environment looks like. Amazon, Microsoft, and Google can all tell you what they have. It's an understandable environment and set of services that you can target your applications to and start understanding performance in that environment and what you need to do.

Now what's really intriguing is that we're not the only ones that have a compute environment that we're creating that's cloud-like and sits in this classified kind of space. Other organizations do as well within the government and should meet our security needs, so why don't we use theirs [a different agency or a different agency-sponsored environment]?

S. Donaldson: Right.

Kaplow: Then the CIO and leadership are telling you that you don't have to make everything yourself.

S. Donaldson: What about cyber security? How does that technology play a role?

Kaplow: So that's part of this closed environment where there's a defined set of users. A lot of security attention is paid to only letting authorized users get on the system. That's the number-one criteria, right? So only cleared people have access to systems that have classified information. So you try to harden the ability to use them. Most of these systems are already in a physical facility that's locked. So information is encrypted as it's transmitted, all that good stuff. Using other people's infrastructure is then the question of trust.

G. Donaldson: What about going mobile? How's that influencing what you're doing?

Kaplow: It is a very difficult problem. It's a problem technically and it's also a problem culturally. However, the CIO's vision is that at some point I get a device and I'm in a classified space tethered to that environment. It knows where it is so it allows access to classified information. So think about a Google Chromebook, right? The Chromebook's got a browser. It doesn't really retain any information – everything is in the cloud. Now when I take this device and I walk out of the building's secure area, this "something book", knows it's no longer there. Now it won't provide the same access to information – but it functions on a different security level, allowing me to get to my unclassified environment. Oh, by the way, it's on the roadmap.

S. Donaldson: So how do you create your own systems?

Kaplow: We do requirements analysis and then we define the system. We do all these system reviews, and everything else. They still want a project framework, but they want a project framework that allows you to be more flexible where you don't necessarily have all the pieces together as you run through that process.

G. Donaldson: Would that be similar to agile development?

Kaplow: Yes, either spiral development or agile development. There are lots of different ways of talking about development.

G. Donaldson: So part of your trusted advisor role is to help them work through that?

Kaplow: Yeah, absolutely. We have a common view and I help push that. That's beginning to be reasonably successful, but like anything else, it takes time and effort and skill.

G. Donaldson: How do you get that common view between you and the customer?

Kaplow: The customer comes at it from the perspective that not everything that you do is something that requires engineering every time.

S. Donaldson: What about internally?

Kaplow: The operations guy came to me and said, "These fricking printers are killing us. We've got the toner to stock and everything else; it takes up space and power. I mean, this is a green initiative for heaven's sake." That gets a lot of traction. We came to the collective idea of: "Let's have one set of printers and, from a security perspective, that set enables users to print lower-security classified material to higher-security classified material. And by the way, we have scanners and faxes, so why don't we just have scanners? So we get involved in then developing a proof of concept and say, "Hey, there's a better way of doing this."

As the rent-a-CTO, I look at what we've developed today, I've got a computer for this and a computer for that and a phone for this and a phone for that and a thing for this and a thing for that. And I say, "Well, is that really what we want?" "No, we probably want to have the minimum number of things on the desk."

S. Donaldson: Right.

Kaplow: Then you're dealing with it from a user's perspective, which is, "Where's the printer? I just printed something." "Well, it's that printer down there; it's this one." "Is that the unclassified printer, is it the high-side printer, is it the color, or the black-and-white?" "Oh, it's out of toner. Which one should I use? Well, is that a Xerox printer and that one's an HP. We don't want this … oh my goodness." I mean, think about the concept and just look at it from a complexity perspective to evolve a common understanding of what works.

G. Donaldson: So when you develop a common view, part of it is the roadmap that you develop over time. Is that accurate?

Kaplow: Yeah.

G. Donaldson: Is part of the interaction helping to expose people to other ways of how things can be done?

Kaplow: Yes. You know, it means giving someone a strong vision and saying, "I want one of those," is not a bad thing.

S. Donaldson: They will know what they want when they see it.

Kaplow: For them to see the solution makes it a little bit easier. But one of the things you have to be really careful about is in giving them options; you're lighting all these fuses.

G. Donaldson: Right.

Kaplow: And we all know that things are screwed up. It's how we are actually going to do something.

G. Donaldson: How do you deal with that then?

Kaplow: I think you have to be a little bit careful. You pick the things that matter. Other things may just wither on the vine. Architecture documents are written and nobody reads them; they don't care; they didn't affect anything, and this time we said, "In support of management, we're going to do these architect documents and roadmap and make them count." They hired us to affect that kind of change. So we said, "Well, we're going to do these roadmaps and we're going to define services," and of course, we didn't say this up front, as some of this has evolved over time. "We're going to have this concept of operations and an execution model, and then we're going to try to start looking at these things with regard to the projects and budgets that we have, and then we're going to start aligning our budgets to that, and then the program managers and the directors have to own this and say, "You see that milestone over there on the roadmap? It allows the ability for me to have a security device to allow me print a document from unclassified system or a classified system and have it show up on the same printer. Make it happen."

G. Donaldson: Right.

Kaplow: Securely. That's there.

G. Donaldson: Once it gets tied to budget and the budget process, then it's enabled.

Jeff Tolnar

CTO and CIO, BPL Global

Jeff Tolnar has over 20 years experience in the utility, networking and communications arena including leadership roles within Fortune 50 companies and start-up environments.

Mr. Tolnar is presently the Chief Information and Technology Officer for BPL Global® (BPLG). BPLG is a smart grid technology company dedicated to leading the transformation of energy efficiency and reliability. The company provides solutions to electric utilities enabling an intelligent grid to more efficiently manage demand, integrate distributed energy resources, improve service reliability, and optimize cost and capital productivity. He was one of the originating members of the company and is responsible for leading all technical aspects of BPLG for its regions throughout the world. These responsibilities include: R&D, applications development, system integration, vendor selection, network design, and corporate information technology. Under Jeff's technical leadership, BPLG has won numerous industry awards in the smart grid sector including Going Green East top award winner, Venture Summit 100, and Going Green Global 200. The company has stayed true to its course and in six years has grown from an idea to a company doing business with more than 125 utility customers on 5 continents.

Prior to joining BPL Global Jeff held Senior Executive positions at American Electric Power, Sprint, and was co-Founder of Amperion.

Scott Donaldson: The first area that we want to spend some time on is your journey to the position of Chief Technology Officer. Could you give us background on how your professional career led you to where you are today?

Jeff Tolnar: Yeah, it's interesting; well, maybe it's just interesting to me. I've always had a technological bent. I am an Electrical Engineer with an MBA, so even from an educational perspective; I have the technology side and the business side. I started off with Sprint back when it was United Telecom, passed through power engineering, transmission engineering, and project management. When I had an opportunity to go into sales, I met with a director and he said, "Now, Jeff, at some point in your career, you're going to have to make a decision whether you want to be in technology or in marketing and sales." I took the sales job. That went well, and I enjoyed it for a few years. Then I was asked to go to corporate and head national product management of all network and data products for Sprint back at United Telecom. I did that for a few years and then I went into general management where I ran a two-state region within Sprint. I grew that business quite a bit. And then I got another call from the same guys I used to work for in the network organization, they asked me if I was ready to come home. I decided it was a good opportunity, that it was time to go back to network, so I ran network administration and operations. In that position I was responsible for operating procedures, national process, and engineering standards. From there I went to running network operations centers. We rolled out broadband local networks, which was part of the Sprint PCS launch nationwide. It was a very interesting deployment, very fast-paced.

S. Donaldson: You have a lot of experience with real technical dirt under your fingernails, getting it done, being out in the field, but also understanding how they work back at corporate.

Tolnar: Yes. I think that's key. From Sprint I went to American Electric Power (AEP), where I had a significant corporate development responsibility. I formed a company, sat on some boards of directors, got more strategically oriented, but also started looking at cross-corps technologies. Then I left the Fortune 50 world and joined start-up land with a company called Amperion, where I was head of sales, marketing, regulatory, and business development. I was back in sales. Then I joined BPL Global as one of the first three employees here as chief technology officer, head cook, and bottle washer. At the beginning you wear every hat that you can imagine.

S. Donaldson: Right.

Tolnar: So I've really taken a circuitous path into and out of technology.

S. Donaldson: So along the way, did you have some people who were your mentors, who taught you lessons that would help guide you on this path?

Tolnar: I would say that some of the best mentors I've had have been on the personal and professional growth side; more so than strictly on technological aspects. I remember our senior VP at Sprint, Will Prout, really helped guide me on how to manage large organizations, how to stick to my own thoughts and visions: "If you know you're right, then go for it and stick to it." When I was contemplating a career change and fretting over it, I asked another manager, "Should I make a move or not make a move?" He said two things that have really stayed with me. One is, "It's never a good time for a change." And two is, "Don't flatter yourself. You can always be replaced." I've always held true to that because the world does change fast and technology changes faster, so I try to stay humble, I try to learn, and I try to manage the group as best as I can. And you know, the results are the results. That's the bottom line.

S. Donaldson: So when you were at Sprint, did they provide you with any formal leadership training? Any technology training? Did they have programs for that?

Tolnar: We had such training at Sprint and AEP, but once I left Fortune 50 the formal training disappeared. Both Sprint and AEP had mostly leadership training. I was a part of that at Sprint, the same at AEP, where they trained us to be managers, negotiators, and business leaders. There was less training on the technology side, although if there was a new technology and I needed to take a course because we wanted to jump into it, they were always open to providing me the opportunity.

S. Donaldson: You described that you had various responsibilities throughout your career at Sprint. I would imagine there were a lot of deployment or delivery teams. What made those teams click? What do you think helped those teams think through how to get the delivery done or make sure that they answered the mail, those sorts of things?

Tolnar: It's having a clear definition of roles and responsibilities. Every person knew their role. We had very regular communication. I'm a very strong believer in treating people as equals regardless of position. We all have a job to do. My job is different. It's not more or less important than somebody else's. I want open and honest communication whether it's good news or bad news. If it's good news, we'll celebrate it. If it's bad news, we sort it out and try to get it fixed. No matter what job I've had, that's how it has been, that's what worked.

S. Donaldson: Let's switch gears a little bit and talk about what you do today. You have a position description. Could you talk about it a little?

Tolnar: Sure. I might have to read it. I haven't looked at it in three years. Actually, last night was the first time I've looked at it since 2008. My position has three primary aspects to it: technology strategy; organizational planning, strategically oriented from a technology perspective; and technology leadership, which is more tactical. Depending on the day of the week and the week in the month, I flow in and out of very high-level strategic discussions with potential investors, business partners, and other technology firms. Sometimes I get into product development scrums and root-cause analysis of what's going on as part of the quality assurance process. At the tactical level, we analyze specific details of how a product matches the original customer or market requirements. If they do not match, then it is flagged as a defect, prioritized, and returned to the development team for correction. The team also looks at the original use cases and how the product performs post coding to ensure that the operational intent is met as well as specific features or functions.

So what I do varies from day to day. I try to stay out of the weeds, because we've got very good people to do that. But there are some times where, as a leader, you just have to sit in the room and ask some high level questions, focus the team, and show that it's important just by being there.

S. Donaldson: Right.

Tolnar: Even though others understand the details better than I do, sometimes when I ask questions from outside the forest, it guides the decision-making process and guides the analysis a little bit.

S. Donaldson: You help coach them along.

Tolnar: Absolutely.

S. Donaldson: So inside the company, who do you report to?

Tolnar: I report to the CEO.

S. Donaldson: Okay. Who reports to you?

Tolnar: I've got the vice president of software development, the vice president of hardware development, the vice president of quality and process, the head of program management, and the head of solutions architecture. Those are the five primary roles. I also have the head of IT, there's a CIO part of my responsibility.

S. Donaldson: Maybe you could spend just a minute on that, on the CIO piece. One of the questions we were going to ask was, "Who is the CIO? And how does that relationship work?" But since it's you, why don't you tell us a little bit about what that responsibility encompasses.

Tolnar: I get along quite well with him. We see things in very much the same way.

S. Donaldson: Well that's good.

Tolnar: Our product sets are so IT-intensive and so tightly coupled with IT infrastructure that it made sense to combine the CIO and CTO role, where product development is a major part with the IT infrastructure, at least from a customer-facing perspective. And because we're still a rather small company, the corporate-facing part of IT is a relatively small part of CIO responsibilities. It's nowhere near as extensive as a typical Fortune 50 organization might have. It made perfect sense to combine the CTO/CIO role because of the tight coupling between the products that we offer and the predominance of a tightly coupled software offering with the IT infrastructure in which it operates.

S. Donaldson: On a day-to-day basis, how much time do you split between your management responsibilities, your administrative responsibilities, and your technical responsibilities? What's a day-in-the-life look like?

Tolnar: You know, I think that depends on the day, too. If I had to put it on a month-to-month basis rather than a day-to-day basis, I spend probably two weeks out of the month meeting with partners and investors or with other members of the executive team. These meetings are typically face to face so I'm traveling somewhere most weeks, sometimes internationally, but mostly one- or two-day trips in the US. I spend another week or so meeting with, overseeing, managing, and dealing with tactical issues with my team. Since my teams are geographically dispersed, this amounts to travel time in order to get some amount of face time with each respective group. The fourth week would be just a scattershot of about everything you can imagine that might come up: customer issues, technical symposiums, dealing with the odd issues that might come our way. Then, in rare cases these days, maybe a day or two a month I spend doing things that I consider more an individual contributor basis: working on a white paper or working on intellectual property evaluations. You know, just things that I'd like to spend more time on than a day a month, but we have a company that we have to run, too.

S. Donaldson: Right. You have described what the formal position was. And that's what they sold you when you came into the position. Has the position been much different than what you originally envisioned when you started out?

Tolnar: What's interesting is that when I started, I was one of only three guys in the company. So the hat I wore was chief technology officer, but I really had marketing responsibilities, regulatory review, corporate development, product development, and operational responsibilities. It was a very broad mix. What's happened over the past five years is that it's evolved more toward a traditional CTO role; although I still have quite a lot of oversight and responsibility and interaction with the business teams. So I think that early on when it's just three guys jetting around trying to get business, you're doing things differently because you must. Then when we scaled to a small company with some form of sustainable revenue, the silos start to build a little bit about core responsibilities. We are at the point now that we are going from small business to medium-sized. With a more scalable business you have to further differentiate yourself from other responsibilities.

S. Donaldson: I would imagine that process and procedures become more of the culture as you start to expand so that you *can* expand, right?

Tolnar: You have to. The only way you grow from small to midsized and larger is through repeatable efficient process. When we began BPL Global, our vision had always been to grow both organically and through acquisition. Either method of growth requires integration of people, processes, systems, and culture. When we began in 2005, it was three of us. Since that time, we have grown organically each year but we also expanded through the acquisition of five companies. Some worked out better than others, but all are now fully integrated into the whole from a people and cultural perspective. We do and will continue to unify process and systems. As I mentioned before, that's a part of taking this company to the next level through repeatable and scalable processes and by using systems as tools to support those efforts.

S. Donaldson: So when you carry out your job day to day, how do you measure success when you go home? Do you say, "Hey, it was a good day, a good month?" How do you measure the success of your job?

Tolnar: Day-to-day tactically, it's, "Did we take a step forward today?" There are days when you take a step back, and those are days that I feel less well about how things went. Then the following day, if you take two steps forward, you're still a step ahead. One of the challenges in running an engineering or technology organization is technologists and engineers in general are very tactically oriented. As a leader of an organization like that, what I have to do is try to lift them out of that every now and then and say, "Okay, guys, I know we're having problems now, but are we better off than we were six months ago? Have we made improvements?" "Yes." "Okay." There are many times when the challenges you face are multiyear fixes, and you have to be able to step out of the mix and say, "Are we edging the ball forward, closer to the goal line, even though we know the goal line's two years out?" And it's hard to keep engineers down that path, because they want things solved now; they want to fix things that are broken.

S. Donaldson: So do you have near-term goals, "near-term" being the next year or two, and then more strategic goals five years out? What are the time horizons here?

Tolnar: We're tracked from an MBO (management by objective) perspective every six months, so each person has a half-years' worth of MBOs. For me personally, I'm tracked on company performance. So my MBOs are very simple. They're all financially oriented. The team that I manage has a combination of financial objectives, revenue, EBITDA (Earnings Before Interest, Taxes, Depreciation, and Amortization), cash operations, operating cash flow, and then 40% of their MBOs are based upon specific tactical types of deliverables: product releases twice per year, business development support, integration with partners, and those types of things. But for me, it's if the company's successful, I'm successful.

S. Donaldson: Could you spend a little time on how you interact with your peers? Who are your peers in the company? And how do you interact with them? What's the management team? How does it work?

Tolnar: As CTO, I'm responsible for the technology. We have a head of North American operations who runs sales and operations for a region and there are heads of operations in the other regions that we operate in, the European Union and China (for Asia), respectively. In addition, we've got a chief marketing officer who handles product marketing management and marketing communications, a SVP of business development and a chief financial officer. Then, underneath those roles there are members of the senior team who are responsible for the larger business development and corporate development areas.

S. Donaldson: Right. So for a small but emerging company, it sounds like you have quite a reach. It sounds like the company's reach extends around the world; hence, it's a reflected in your name, BPL Global. What locations in the world are you in?

Tolnar: Our primary hubs are North America, Europe, and China, where China is Asia for us. We have satellite offices in Kuwait City for the Middle East and also a small representative office in London for the UK.

S. Donaldson: We talked a little bit about your internal interactions with the management team. Can you talk a little bit about how decisions are made and what that relationship is as you try to move this company forward?

Tolnar: I'll start with the more tactical technology-related decisions. If it involves how or when something is built, that is really within the technology realm. If it will affect a product feature that the customer will see, then the technology team interacts with our marketing and sales teams. If it's strictly under the hood technical details, then it's the architecture group, the respective development area, whether that's hardware, software, or firmware, and then we will interact and make some decisions. Then normally we'll make the broader team aware, but for the most part they're not interested. The CFO gets involved with anything that deals with incremental spending above and beyond budget. I involve the CFO to make sure that he is on board. I interact with the CEO just about every day, so when I want to bounce an idea around, I typically will bounce it off of the CEO. From a strategic aspect, if it's more of a market or product issue, I'll bounce the idea off of the CMO. If there's a broader decision set, like what direction we should take a product in, such as, "Should we integrate a standalone application into the core?" that discussion involves all aspects of the company. That question will involve a call that includes marketing, sales, corporate development from a partnership perspective, the CEO from a strategic perspective, and finance from a "how much will it cost?" perspective. So it could involve everybody.

S. Donaldson: What organizations and what people do you interact with externally day-to-day?

Tolnar: The partners in our peer group, whether it's a technology partner, hardware partner, or software partner, plus I have a fair amount of interaction with educational institutions. As the smart grid starts to emerge as an enormous space worldwide, most of the higher educational institutions have or are starting to specialize in smart grid and our technology space. We have regular interaction with places like Carnegie Mellon, Pittsburgh, and Ohio State. I want to branch out beyond that. With respect to industry groups, we have some interaction with them but mostly follow the lead. We simply don't have the time or resources to get deeply engaged with industry standards bodies. Those can be all consuming and we've got a company to run. We have a tremendous amount of interaction with customers and the technologists within the customer base. That's where most of our new product ideas come from.

S. Donaldson: What are examples of some of the partners that you deal with?

Tolnar: Examples would be smart metering companies, they're in our space, but in an adjacent space. Other partners could include Siemens, SAIC, and Schneider Electric. They're in adjacent space with very little overlap. What we always try to do is make a build-buy-partner decision. If we've got a sustainable differentiation in intellectual property, we will typically build. If not, and we see it could become a crowded space or already is a crowded space, then we typically make a partner decision. If we feel that through an acquisition we can gain a differentiated, sustainable intellectual property position, then we'll buy if the price is right. Otherwise, we partner. A company our size—it's typically build or partner.

S. Donaldson: Okay. So let's talk about the company a little bit now. Talk about what your marketplace is and what your products and services are for the marketplace.

Tolnar: We make energy-efficiency and -reliability solutions for electric utilities. That's the elevator pitch. What that means is we help electric utilities operate their businesses more effectively, more efficiently, and deal with the broadly changing environmental issues such as distributed energy resources, renewables, imbalance of supply and demand, aging asset base, challenges with reliability, and regulatory constraints. We bundle all of those issues into energy-efficiency and -reliability product solutions.

S. Donaldson: So do those solutions include both hardware solutions and software solutions? Some combination?

Tolnar: Yeah, it's interesting. Early on we thought, "We want to be in software." Hardware drives to commodity rather quickly and there is heavy hardware competition in our space. But what we learned over the years is that in an emerging sector like the smart grid, integrated solutions are really the key to making the market happen, at least for us. An example, a parallel, would be if I write software for Scott and I hand you a disk of software, if you don't have a computer, there's nothing you can do with that disk of software. So what we have to do is bundle, very similar to what Apple does when they bundle their solution sets. The proper combination of software, hardware and services make the value proposition.

S. Donaldson: Okay.

Tolnar: Eventually the market will mature to the point where software and hardware will bifurcate and then we'll make a decision about which aspects we stay in or move out of. But for right now it's a deeply integrated solution set for enterprise software that goes in the operation center of the utility; hardware, the sensor and control devices that go at the edge of the network; and firmware that sits upon those devices. When talking about the edge of the electric network, I am referring to the points at which consumers of electricity reside. The consumers can be residences, businesses, commercial and industrial facilities. The network edge had traditionally been at the electricity meter but now it is pushing even deeper into the premises with intelligent monitoring and management devices in the building and home.

And I want to make a distinction between the software and the firmware aspects, because one of the aspects our company believes strongly about is that intelligence is moving further and further toward the edge. So the firmware aspect is as important as the centralized software aspect because you'll have islands of intelligence, islands of control over time. The hardware component will be memory and processing, and relays and control points. The magic will be around how does that firmware interact with this central control system? That's what we do.

S. Donaldson: So can you give an example of a major project you might have now where you deploy an integrated solution?

Tolnar: That would be with our customer, FirstEnergy, and one of our leading products is for demand management and direct load control. It involves all aspects of what I've discussed. I'll talk about the market challenge and then how we solve the market challenge. I remember sitting in our boardroom about five years ago and was told flat-out, "There will be no market for demand management because that's the utilities' revenue stream." The vision that we had was to stick with our demand management offering as it stood, I felt strongly about that, and demand management is now our largest-selling product.

With that said, the way demand management had occurred in the past—and just really in the recent past, the past 10 years or so—is that a command signal would be sent out from a central aggregator saying, "I need 100 megawatts" in a given geographic area—maybe it's the northeastern United States—and that approximately 100 megawatts or so would be turned off or curtailed. The transmission operators and generators would have their needs met. The challenge was the local operators, the electric utilities that were delivering the energy; they really saw no benefit to that. In fact, they were the ones that were harmed by that approach. If I'm an electric utility that just spent hundreds of millions of dollars upgrading substations; I have plenty of capacity in southern New Jersey. However, in northern and central New Jersey, I may not have had the capital to upgrade those substations. The old approach would have said, "I'm going to treat a megawatt as a megawatt, no matter where it resides." So the command goes out: turn the load off; generator and transmission providers are happy, the independent systems operators are happy, their obligations have been complied with, but the electric utility responsible for delivering energy has a problem. In southern New Jersey, where they just spent a lot of money upgrading substations, their meters aren't spinning. That's revenue erosion. In central and northern New Jersey, they did get some benefit, maybe, by the load-reduction event, where they may have been at capacity at certain substations. We took a different approach and made the decision to tightly couple demand management directly with the operational aspects of the electric utility.

We've deployed a number of innovative ideas in the past four years. For example, we have direct load controllers tied into centralized air conditioning, water heaters, and pool pumps. Those load controllers have smart firmware on them. They also have a metering chip that measures and verifies that a load was turned on. When it turns on, it pushes a signal to the central system saying, "Hey, I've got 3 kilowatts available or being consumed." The central system then monitors every device within its purview in real time and it knows precisely how much energy is available in which operational area. In the example that I used before, if the electric utility was asked for 100 megawatts, they would want to turn off 100 megawatts in northern and central New Jersey, and let southern New Jersey run. That way, they optimize their revenue stream yet minimize their operational impact. That's done through a combination of central software that's monitoring tens of thousands, hundreds of thousands of control points in real time, each of which is feeding multiple telemetry points through a communications backbone. Then the firmware that sits on each of the edge control devices knows what to do when it sees a control message: "What's my state change?" and "Is my compressor on or is it off?" "Has my temperature risen by half a degree, or is it still stable from its prior state?" The firmware sends asynchronous control messages to the central software so that we can manage a very dispersed resource in real time and have a very precise and predictable solution back for the utility.

S. Donaldson: Who competes with you in that space?

Tolnar: We have distinct competitors for each of the solutions sets that we offer. For our transformer monitoring solution GE is our strongest competitor, the grid management product has a number of large competitors that offer a distribution management system. Our differentiation is in the integrated approach that we take to balance reliability, distributed energy and demand management. The primary competitor that we see regularly for the demand management solution we talked about earlier is Comverge. They have a slightly different business model, though. They're predominantly an energy aggregator. They traditionally have treated the market in the former way that I described, where they sign up load as a resource, and turn it off to meet an obligation to the independent systems operator, the ISO.

S. Donaldson: You're doing that but you're maximizing the potential revenue for the utility.

Tolnar: That's right, to increase the operational value for the utility.

S. Donaldson: And that's what is unique.

Tolnar: Exactly. Let's take that example a step further. If the utility doesn't get a call from the ISO to shed, to turn off load, let's say I've got one circuit that has problems. One circuit is on overload conditions. What do I do about it? Right now, I would simply monitor the circuit through a SCADA system. Maybe I would do some switching in the substation. Maybe I can't. Or maybe I hope it doesn't change, hope it doesn't fail. Well, hope's not a method, so what we allow the utility to do is ratchet down the demand on precisely that circuit, so that we can keep it within its operating parameters, and then as soon as the daily peak declines in the early evening, we release that load back. Demand goes back to where it should be, so we've maximized the revenue, minimized the operating risk. That's what our system does.

S. Donaldson: You mentioned substations too. My understanding is that you also have hardware associated with substation automation. Could you describe that?

Tolnar: Sure. I talked about demand management. It's a marriage of enterprise software, firmware, and hardware. On the other side of the spectrum from a substation perspective, we've got transformer monitoring and substation automation. Our transformer monitoring product line is a market leader. We measure the gasses created in the insulation oil of transformers. It's called dissolved gas analysis. This is an established science that had always been done in a laboratory setting under very controlled environments. We've taken the laboratory to the field. Our systems measure eight different gas molecules within the insulating oil. The gasses are created when a transformer has problems within its enclosure like extreme heating or micro-arcs that can be caused by insulation breakdown or poor connections. The combination of these gasses enables our software to notify the Utility if there is an imminent problem within the transformer that may lead to its failure. Our transformer monitors are deployed all over the world in more than 120 Electric Utilities so the science is proven and the solution is valuable. The substation automation (SA) solution expands our solution set within the electric substation and allows our utility customers to monitor and control various device types and models of substation equipment. The SA solution is capable of real time data aggregation and control and our system consists of both software and hardware. Over the years, there have been, especially in North America, a combination of many different vendors, makes, models, and versions of intelligent electrical devices in the substation, whether they're protective relays, switches, transformers. Everything you can imagine in a substation may be there. Some may be 20 years old, prior versions, some may be brand new. Our hardware platform is not magic. The firmware, though, that sits within that hardware platform takes all of those different and disparate protocols, different versions and types, combines them onto a common backplane, onto a common protocol, and then spits out a common language, whether it's IP, DNP 3 over IP, IEC 61850, or any of the industry standards. The value proposition to the utility is that it doesn't have to replace $10 million worth of substation assets. We put in an aggregation system that's technology-agnostic. We make them all look the same, all communicate in a similar fashion so that the downstream communication system, the enterprise software, now can treat them either from a monitoring or a control perspective.

S. Donaldson: So there's a wide range of skill sets that are needed to do all this. When you go looking for personnel, how do you recruit your people? What skills and experience do you look for?

Tolnar: We are structured by centers of excellence. Our Portland office is predominantly hardware and substation. Our Columbus office is predominantly enterprise software and distribution products. Our Paris/Le Mans office is predominantly communication oriented and also understands the EU and EU certifications. Depending on where the market is evolving and where the product line is going drives where we'll hire. In Columbus, our distribution products are taking off as fast as we can keep pace. What I look for in Columbus is, starting at the very top, a very innovative vice president of software development. I want somebody who knows not just how to solve problems today, he would get a C− or B+ for being able to do that. If you solve problems, that's one thing. I want you to prevent problems. So I found a very innovative, very forward-looking yet tactically strong individual. Working for that person, we've got various levels of developers. Those developers are based on what areas we need development in, whether it's Core Java, J2EE, driver adapter developers, firmware, or embedded system designers. Hiring is based on need; it's based on where the product goes. Then, from a hardware perspective, we use the same approach in the Portland office. We need engineers who can design printed circuit boards, mechanical engineers, thermal engineers, and software engineers for the substation product lines. We've also got chemical engineering needs for our dissolved-gas analysis based transformer monitoring product offering. We've got a very broad mix, and depending on where the product mix goes, that's where we hire.

S. Donaldson: How much of your development is done internally? If not internally, where do you get dev resources?

Tolnar: Development resources come from a variety of sources. Since our solutions involve software and hardware we have different resource needs for each respective area.

The software team, primarily based in Columbus, Ohio, is divided into four categories—platform, product, project, and integration. The platform and product work is very tightly held intellectual property (IP) and is done in house with BPL Global employees or dedicated contractors. Work in this category is typically bundled into two major releases and is driven by our product roadmap. Project work or integration work can be selectively farmed out to on-shore or off-shore firms depending upon if there is a clearly defined and well documented scope of work and little or no risk to BPLG IP. The deliverables in these categories are customer specific and may have a variety of release dates and timeframes. These interim projects or integration efforts are bundled as feasible and issued in maintenance releases that typically go out every three months.

As we scale the software engineering organization we will need to grow more of an outsource model but that also infers that we have well documented APIs, superb product documentation, and clear lines of delineation in the code so that we can efficiently outsource but also protect our IP.

Hardware development is accomplished by our hardware engineering team in Portland, Oregon. That team consists of mechanical, electrical, chemical, and embedded systems engineers. They focus on design, prototyping, and documentation associated with the hardware aspects of our product line. Once the product is designed, built, tested, and certified it is released to production. At that point it is outsourced to scale-oriented contract manufacturing firms that mine cost out of the bill of materials and build process. Some of the more intricate final assembly and test is completed in our Portland facility as well.

The final aspect of the build process and resource discussion involves the integration of the enterprise software and hardware components that I've described. This effort is accomplished by seasoned program managers who are internal resources in each of the respective offices.

Gary Donaldson: Jeff, you mentioned earlier that your systems engineers have trouble seeing the strategic view of things.

Tolnar: Right.

G. Donaldson: When you interview personnel, do you ever bring up that issue regarding whether the engineers can see the bigger picture?

Tolnar: It's a very good question. The answer is not really, and here's why. They need to get into the weeds to create code and solve problems. What concerns me about an engineer getting too caught in the weeds, especially when you're doing fault and problem isolation and trying to fix big issues, is that they tend to get down. They get less efficient. We can help them to manage through that, so really what we're looking for is excellence in development. I want people who can do the job exceptionally well. We're not counting lines of code developed. We want our engineers to efficiently deliver code that meets the requirements of the customer. That's the primary role, and I need them to do it in a fantastic way. Now, that's what we interview for, but things never go perfectly. That's when I need managers who are able to separate and identify that, "Hey, Stan is really struggling today. He's been fighting, chasing the same ghost in software for a week and a half. He's getting very frustrated and burning long hours." So the best way to lift him out of the weeds, from a management perspective, and help him see, "Hey, are we further along than where we were. We're making progress. Stick with this." That's why you also need to have a very good tactical manager who can dive in and say, "Have you thought of this? Have you thought of this? Have you thought of this?"

G. Donaldson: Do you ever get involved with mentoring these engineers?

Tolnar: Sure, absolutely, mostly from a business perspective. There's not a lot—I can help them with from a coding perspective—I haven't done coding for probably 25 years, but certainly from a "How do you survive in a high-pressure environment?" I'm pretty good at that.

S. Donaldson: What are the programming languages, the databases? What specific skill sets are you're looking for?

Tolnar: I wish it weren't as broad. Our core code enterprise software is done in Java. We have some J2EE for our portals. We use C and its derivatives, from an embedded systems perspective. We do some .NET, and that was through an acquisition. Then when you get into the deeper foundational aspects, from a data warehouse perspective, PostgreSQL, and from an enterprise service bus perspective, we ship with Active MQ. But we also have to have deep knowledge of the more traditional middleware products like TIBCO and IBM's WebSphere MQ. Our goal is not to be a middleware provider, but rather to use best of breed and integrate what the customers may already have in place. However, there may be some customers that do not want to integrate a new application to their enterprise service bus or data warehouse and that's why we ship with those components out of the box. Our goal is to enable immediate and turnkey solutions for the operations groups within the utility. The flexibility of the system also inherently offers the capability of integration to legacy systems as determined by the customer IT shops.

S. Donaldson: It sounds like those types of skill sets aren't exotic technologies in the sense that there are a lot of people who have those skills.

Tolnar: That's right.

S. Donaldson: You can get those skills. So what's the magic sauce here? Is it design work? The product? The technology roadmap of where you're going with things? Is it your vision of what the marketplace is and how you want to attack that? What's the special sauce in that?

Tolnar: The special sauce is really in the interactivity of the different applications. It's how everything glues together. That's the magic. That's the part that our competition, even though they may be public and have more capital resources than we do, are still struggling to do what we do with one product, let alone the six that we have to offer. We made architectural decisions five years ago. Four of us sat around a table at a restaurant and decided how we were going to design this system. And the decisions have really held true: service-oriented architecture for extensibility, flexibility, and ease of development. The architecture would be wrapped around an enterprise service bus of some kind, but we would not be the bus owner. Plenty of people do that. We decided we would go Java so that it would be platform-independent; Linux, UNIX, Windows wouldn't matter. So a number of the architectural decisions we made early on were very important. We also decided that processing would be done in the application. Services would house anything that could be reusable by multiple applications. Another design principle we decided on very early was that we would not be a silo developer of product. That everything we develop must support another application, so the demand management offering that we created supported substation automation. Substation automation supports demand management. When we roll out our iDER (integrated distributed energy resource) offering, it supports and utilizes demand management software; load is a resource. That further supports substation automation. The goal is that every application is a value multiplier. They are all decoupled yet tightly integrated. Which seems like an oxymoron, but it's not. The goal is to make a very sticky solution that can scale and is platform-independent, is technology-agnostic, and is standards-based.

S. Donaldson: What do you see as transformative technologies? Do you see such technologies on the horizon or are they already here, like cloud? How does that impact what your thinking is? How does that impact the industry?

Tolnar: Cloud certainly is important for us. It gives us the ability to ratchet up and down IT resources. It gives us the ability to offer smart grid as a service; so we can serve many with one. Another technology we're looking closely at right now is IT pods. I can't speak much about those projects right now but it is a strategic area of focus. In general, I see the industry moving intelligence more toward the edge. Power flows are changing. They used to be central to edge. Now we've got more and more distributed resources, where the power flows and protection schemes and delivery mechanisms are all changing. So the islands of intelligence have to go with that. That gives us an opportunity because we're built on a distributed model anyway. I think there's a strong parallel between where information delivery went in the '70s and '80s from a mainframe through desktop to laptop, where intelligence and information became distributed, yet integrated. Communications went in the '80s and '90s from a central office with dumb phones to smart phones that have more processing intelligence than any computer had 15 years ago, again distributed. Energy's moving that way, where we'll have islands of intelligence that need to be independently operated, so we've got to be prepared from a software and control perspective.

S. Donaldson: So you talk about the iPhone which brings to mind that the industry in general has gone mobile. Everyone wants to be mobile and connected.

Tolnar: Right.

S. Donaldson: So how does mobility play into the thinking down the road?

Tolnar: You know, when you think about it, the parallels are very strong with information and communications. Mobility's been around for an awful long time. As a world, we know how to deal with mobility. The electric infrastructure, however, has not had to deal with mobility. You can't deliver energy through the air—well, you can, it's called lightning or arcing. What you need then is some form of distributed energy that's created locally by some mechanism. It will also be stored, because if you're going to create it, that means I have to store it. So then you've got supply, storage, and demand at the very edge of the network. What will happen 5, 10, 20 years from now when emerging technologies make solar much more efficient, storage much more cost-effective? Demand will continue to rise, there's absolutely no doubt about that. So those islands of supply, storage, and demand are going to have to be coupled, but they will also be mobile and must be addressed by our company and the market. We've seen this type of movement to edge intelligence before, so the methods of secure interconnection, identification, and tracking can be applied to the energy industry.

S. Donaldson: Okay.

Tolnar: Now I would personally be hard-pressed to allow somebody to discharge the batteries that I've spent time charging in my car. But what might be ahead when there are 10 million of those EVs out there and we can push the charging cycle into the evening and actually, if I'm on vacation for a week, I guess I don't care if you're using my batteries, so maybe I'm willing to take a couple of dollars to discharge the batteries. So mobility is going to be tightly coupled to energy delivery.

S. Donaldson: Are you taking a look at such things as the storage of energy through air compression? Ice? Those sorts of things that make up the notion of distributed energy resources?

Tolnar: We recently completed the integration with a thermal energy management system called Ice Energy. It's part of our integrated distributed energy resource offering. There are many more to come.

S. Donaldson: And how you integrate that back into the static grid, this one-way grid, if you will?

Tolnar: I think the key is threefold. One is awareness of the situation. We have to be able to monitor what's happening. And when I say "we," I mean the industry in general, the utilities. I have to know where my assets are and I have to know where the users of my assets are. The assets are my central energy, its distributed storage, its distributed energy, and its load under management. Those are all assets that I could use. The users are then the demand on the system. So I'm monitoring at certain points along the grid.

S. Donaldson: Okay.

Tolnar: The distributed energy resources now are monitored. What do I do with those? I manage those. So now I know that I've got 100 megawatts of storage in a given area. I've got 30 megawatts of thermal energy through ice that I froze that evening and it is ready to melt as needed so I don't have to use an air conditioning compressor. Then I've got a certain amount of distributed resources through distributed generation sources. That may be solar, it may be wind, it may be backup generation, and it may be some other form of biomass. Now ... we can't control the sun. We can't control the wind—yet. But what we can do through tight coupling of the other resources is make a more predictable supply and demand curve, because the goal is predictability. Central generation is not going to go away anytime soon. What we have to do is make its life last a heck of a lot longer. We do that through predictivity and granular management of distributed resources so that central generation no longer has to cover the entire peak energy demand. We cover peak and maybe much more than peak through distributed resources and the balance with central generation.

S. Donaldson: When you develop your products and the software, hardware, and firmware, is most of that homegrown, outsourced, or some combination of both? Do you use overseas? How does that happen?

Tolnar: The applications are all developed by our company. That's our secret sauce. How we do that is also our secret sauce. We do have APIs (application program interfaces) that we can offer to outside parties. If they want to connect onto the bus and have their telemetry consumed by our applications, or have our telemetry consumed by their applications, we can write a system adapter. Our differentiation is in the applications and how the other services on our core interoperate with the applications. Now, as far as who does the development, anything that even smells of intellectual property is done in-house, on-shore. We keep it very tightly held. If it is something like a driver or an adapter to a third-party system, those are things that we can farm out. Quality assurance testing and other testing that we can farm out, we'll offshore, on-shore, wherever we can get the most cost effective best performance.

S. Donaldson: Okay. Well, with all these technologies, and they're changing as we speak, what do you do organizationally and personally to try to keep up with the technology blur that's taken place?

Tolnar: I read a fair amount but not enough. If there's something that's interesting, I'll jump on the web, look around, and see what others are doing. I talk to a lot of people. I learn by listening, by discussing. I like to learn what other people are doing. And what I've been very good at throughout my career is saying, "Hmm, maybe there's a different way to do that." Or saying, "Well, I see the A and the D." And then what I'm fairly good at is figuring out how to get B and C from an innovation perspective. So I learn by listening, learn by talking to others, and read some, but not as much as I'd like to.

S. Donaldson: You're constantly interfacing with your customer base, and they're all over the world; that's going to drive part of it. Are there professional societies, professional groups that you get to? Like regional CTO councils, those sorts of things?

Tolnar: Right now I'm strictly focused on industry groups, NIST (National Institute of Standards and Technology), CIGRE (International Council on Large Electric Systems), IEEE (Institute of Electrical and Electronics Engineers), and on industry based symposiums like DistribuTECH, etc. So I'm staying close to home, if you will. What I want to do more of is get more involved in broad CTO gatherings outside of the energy field. I am a part of Tech Columbus and Tech Pittsburgh organizations where I get to talk to some folks in different fields when possible. There just doesn't seem to be time.

S. Donaldson: Thanks. So let's switch gears a little bit and talk about technology investments, mergers and acquisitions. Do you play a role in that?

Tolnar: Yeah, absolutely. I am part of the decision team. My role on that decision team is to evaluate the strategic alignment of the technology of that company with the business and operational and product needs of our company. Then I'll look at things like, "Is their patent viable? Is their technology real or slideware? Has it been put together with duct tape and rubber bands?" I'll crawl under the hood a little bit.

If it has an odd smell to it, I'll bring our architects and our senior developers to dive in a little bit deeper. So it's the technology aspects of the M&A. It also comes down to financial feasibility, shareholder value, all of those other things, because then you consider your fiduciary responsibility, the company hat goes on.

S. Donaldson: How much do you do in terms of patents?

Tolnar: I'll need to split that one up between hardware and software. Inour hardware area where we have a number of patents for our transformer monitoring solution both filed and approved. With software it's a bit different in that you really can't clearly file for software patents and some countries simply do not allow them. What we've done in the software arena involves method and process patents focusing on key product areas and functionality. We make sure to file copyrights for each application and functional module then keep them updated as we iterate them.

S. Donaldson: Right. Since you're an emerging company, you've done some fundraising over the years as you've gotten investors to come in. How do you participate in those activities?

Tolnar: Wehave acquired five companies. So I have a fair amount of experience and have helped integrate those acquisitions. From an investor's perspective, I'm with our CEO and CFO in nearly every investor meeting, because really, when you look at what our company does, our value proposition is technology. It's what we do; it's our core; it's how we differentiate ourselves. So I'm in just about every investor meeting, investor call, and do a number of due diligence calls.

S. Donaldson: How do you, how does the CTO organization, how do day-to-day activities save money for the company, increase the efficiency of the company, and get more done with less? How does that work?

Tolnar: I think I look at it from two perspectives. Internally, what I want to drive my team to do is develop products that are more efficient. Let's do it once. Let's do it right. Let's make sure that we align the product development process right from the beginning. We need to make sure we have well-understood product requirements, that we design to those requirements, that we develop to the design, that the design and development are in line with the overall architectural vision, that we test for each of the requirements. That's how we can be more efficient and how we can be cost-effective and save money for the company. Are we perfect at that? No, absolutely not. We can always get better. And we need to get better. From a company perspective, many of the things that I do help the operations team from a product delivery perspective. My team will help do a faster root-cause analysis if there's a problem. So we help from a customer service perspective, operational delivery perspective. It does distract us from core development work, but it's what our company needs.

S. Donaldson: Understood. Do you have budget lines set up for development? Do you also figure out ways to come under budget so you can use the scarce resources that you've got to do something else with?

Tolnar: Absolutely. There are a number of things we track. The budget is the highest level, so for a development organization, the largest cost item is staffing, whether it's full-time employees or contract employees, it's staffing. So one of the things we're always trying to manage is our average cost per head for full-time equivalents. There are a few things we're doing now that once you reach a certain critical mass of development expertise; you can start being more creative about how you balance the remainder of the staff. You've got senior-level engineering positions. If you continue to solely staff senior-level engineering positions, you'll have fewer people doing a lot of work at a high cost. So then we have a lower level of engineering positions that report to them. And we've created a new position of more junior engineers, right out of college. When you balance the three levels, my average cost of FTE has gone down about 20%. Then there's a fourth position that we've created and we're experimenting with it. It's more of an engineering assistant. It's for the students who have an engineering aptitude and are pursuing their engineering degree. We'll bring them in as an engineering assistant part-time. They will help with some of the more rote tasks that the senior people would normally have to do. I would much rather have somebody paid $15 an hour or $10 an hour for uploading, changing firmware on a device than paying somebody five times as much to do that same task. So those are just some of the creative things we're doing to try to keep costs down it also provides a career path for our engineers.

S. Donaldson: Has the promise of cloud helped you reduce testing costs or deployment costs? We read a lot about that. What's the reality of it?

Tolnar: You know, what's interesting is engineers like to get a new toy. The cloud is the new toy, so what they have to realize—and one thing that we realized going in—is that the cloud typically is not just a fixed cost for operation, but it has variable cost based on usage. So the ability to quickly turn up resources, ratchet resources, modify those resources, becomes a very interesting, intriguing toy for engineers. They tend to separate mentally from the cost of those toys, so what we have to be very careful of is the overall cost. The cloud can absolutely save us money, no doubt about it, but it has to be managed much more closely because more people have access to it and the variable costs can get high fast. One of the things we're looking at is how to more effectively use the cloud? What are the highest cost components of CPU versus memory versus storage? How do you balance those aspects on a cloud? We're looking at those things now. But the cloud, absolutely, has helped us.

Stan Siegel: Jeff, how do you explain to the CEO in plain English those variables so that he can give direction to the rest of the company regarding what it makes sense to do with respect to the cloud technology?

Tolnar: It's actually fairly simple. Our technology requires a certain amount of resources. The resources that are needed for a large deployment cost $250,000: $300,000 in upfront cost, plus one individual to manage those resources, plus about a 15% annual cost for three years. Then we have to replace some of those initial resources. So the three-year cost of expenditure for that deployment is $750,000 to $800,000. If I use the cloud, it's closer to $200,000 per year, so my three-year all-in costs are lower, plus my cash out-of-pocket expenditures are lower in year 1, and then in year 2, I can apply those costs directly to my operations and maintenance agreement. So, to directly answer your question, Stan, I don't talk about the technology at all. I talk about the financials.

Siegel: I see. So you resonate with the CEO by saying, "Here's the bottom line."

Tolnar: You got it.

S. Donaldson: That's where the MBA comes in. You can talk to the business folks. Let's switch gears again here and talk about the future. Let's take a look at what issues you see confronting the industry that you're in and maybe a little bit about how you're positioning, from a technology viewpoint, the corporation to be well-positioned to address those technologies going forward.

Tolnar: We talked about some of those technologies already. The energy delivery mechanisms are shifting more to the edge. Now what that means to an electric utility is that the way that I designed my network over the past 100 years is going to change; it has to change. They know that. They're exceptionally good at what they do. They're good at delivering energy. Their world is changing in the next 20 years. Most large geographic regions in the world are pushing more and more renewables. Renewables are at the edge of the network, typically. So distributed energy resources (DER) and the impact that has on power flows, delivery, and safety are a major concern for the utilities. That's why we've created our iDER product, which meets those needs. Managing distributed energy resources is an emerging issue and an emerging technology. We believe we're still at the visionary forefront of that issue. There have been many billions of dollars invested in storage technologies and more efficient photovoltaic systems. As those efficiencies continue to grow, economic efficiencies and operational efficiencies, you'll see more and more solar, you'll see more and more storage coupled to solar. So what happens is the iDER issue we talked about becomes more and more significant because now as a homeowner, as a business owner, I can afford to put a PV (photo voltaic) system with storage on my site, on my house. I don't even have to tell the utility. But how do I manage it? How do I gain value from it? It's a resource the utility may need. If regulations change and all of a sudden there's a market for it, I may be able to cost-justify that storage PV system readily. I don't see a lot of micro-wind on top of a building or on a house. I see PV becoming very efficient in the next 10, 15, 20 years, to the point where it is affordable when coupled with storage. You want to tightly couple that with demand. Because there's the balance we talked about of supply, storage, and demand; when you optimize that balance, that's when you become most efficient. Central generation could last for an incredibly long period of time as more and more intelligence shifts to the edge. I think as more nanotechnologies become developed, materials sciences evolve, things of that nature start to become more and more prevalent within the equipment manufactured for the energy industry—that will also help from an economic perspective and an operational efficiency perspective.

S. Donaldson: Okay. How do you see the CTO role changing as you move to the future?

Tolnar: I think over the next two to three years it will become less tactical. What's interesting is that in the first two years, it was really innovative. It was create an idea, evolve that idea, sell the concept of that idea, people buy the concept of that idea, and then you build the idea, you deliver upon it. Now that's gotten to a point where it's replicable. More people have bought and more people have bought and more people have bought. So the past two years have been about execution, efficient execution. I think the next two to three years will be more about outreach, being the strategic visionary again, being the technology evangelist to the investment community, to the market, to the customers, to the industry segment at large. I think it will be less internally focused than it has been and more externally focused. Over time it will continue to be more so, more strategic and less tactical.

S. Donaldson: Okay. So with that in mind, what do you see as your biggest challenge?

Tolnar: The biggest challenge is implementation of process so that it can be replicable. It's implementation of standard methods of delivery companywide. Whether it's creation of a product or delivery of a product to a customer, we have to get to a point where it's almost assembly line–based. That's when we become very, very efficient. It becomes mechanized. That's when I can become more strategic. It takes time because it's a change in people, it's a change in methods, it's a change in procedures, it's documentation, it's how you do what you do, it's how you check what you did. All aspects have to change. But that's how we get to the next stage. That's the biggest risk. And, frankly, that's where most companies fail, when they try to go from early stage to midrange. They fall into the trough because they can't scale it.

S. Donaldson: I guess the other part of the trick is not to have too much of process and procedure or that becomes the product as opposed to what it is you're trying to build.

Tolnar: Right, exactly. You can't be stifling either.

S. Donaldson: I've got one last question for you. What keeps you up at night?

Tolnar: What keeps me up at night? I usually don't go to bed until really late, so [laughter] … it's the tactical issues. I don't really fret over long-term strategic things. It's typically a personnel issue or delivery-oriented. We've got something due on Saturday or five somethings due on Saturday. Are the right people doing the right thing in the right way? If they are, I sleep just fine.

S. Donaldson: You've got some big customers right now as I understand it, and you don't want to fumble that because that can impact you tremendously down the road.

Tolnar: Yes, I think the key for me is, are the right people doing the right things in the right way? If I can look at myself in the mirror and say "yes" to all three of those things, I sleep just perfectly. If we may not have the right person or that person isn't doing the right thing or not doing it the right way, that's when it's a challenge because you tend to have to bring somebody extra in or somebody different in, and that causes a cascading effect in other parts of the operation. So, yeah, if I can look at myself and say, "Are we doing the right thing in the right way with the right people?" That's the best we can do.

Marty Garrison

National Public Radio

Marty Garrison is the Vice President of Technology Operations and Broadcast Engineering for NPR.

As the technology leader, Garrison oversees the Information Services, Broadcast Engineering, and Distribution divisions as well as the Public Radio Satellite System. His primary responsibility is to ensure the integrity of NPR's daily technical operations, including information operations, software development, and telecommunications services; as well as production and distribution operations and systems.

Prior to coming to NPR in 2010, Garrison was the vice president of technology and operations at Thomson Reuters. In this position he was responsible for the professional division's data centers and strategies, server platforms, networks, database technology, SAP enterprise infrastructure and voice systems.

For over 10 years Garrison served as the senior vice president of global technical operations at Turner Broadcasting System where he was responsible for all aspects of the technological infrastructure for TBS, Time Warner Corporate, and CNN. He was instrumental in all broadcast and technology infrastructure for numerous buildings worldwide including the Time Warner Center in New York City.

Garrison holds a Bachelor of Science in Earth Sciences from the University of California, Santa Cruz.

Gary Donaldson: Let's begin the discussion with your journey to where you are now, your career, your pathway that you've done, and highlights along the way.

Marty Garrison: I'll start a little bit before my university education. I graduated high school and did not go to a university for five years. I was a climbing guide in Yosemite Valley, where I took people up big cliffs for a living. I also taught at Sonoma State where I had an outdoor program. I landed the teaching position at 21 years old. I was fairly accomplished, climbed all around the world, and when I was in the Himalayas, right around 4-1/2 years, I said, "I'd better get professional, or I'm going to have worn-out hands when I'm 40." So I went back to University of California at Santa Cruz [UCSC] where I studied earth science with a concentration in geochemistry. I graduated out of the Earth Sciences Department as the undergraduate of the year. Fortunately for me, one student per year was offered a job at an oil company. UCSC had a partnership with Standard Oil Company of Ohio. So my first professional job was an assistant geologist at Standard Oil of Ohio, which was purchased by British Petroleum soon after I arrived.

After one year, I saw an opportunity to apply my UCSC computer experience in both geophysics and geochemistry. I was working in a research department at Standard Oil with about 80 PhD-level geologists, who were doing everything by pen and paper. They were paleontologists, sedimentologists, and geochemists. My boss saw an opportunity to leverage my computer skills. In 1983, if you could do word processing, at least in an oil company, you were pretty impressive on a computer to folks who had never used one. So in 1984, I switched my career from doing pure geology to doing pure IT. The company offered to train me in a variety of technologies at a professional level, and I jumped at the opportunity. I thought that it would vastly expand my career opportunities and options.

I was no longer going to be tied to oil or geology. I did geology because I like rocks, and I like rocks because I like to climb rocks. I didn't have a big tie to geology, honestly. At that point I think I was 27 years old and I was getting probably a million dollars to computerize this organization. I worked very closely with the Standard Oil corporate headquarters for computers, which was in Dallas. They trained me and they helped with any buying decisions that I didn't make on my own. In about four or five years I was an Oracle database administrator of version 1 of Oracle. I was a VMS systems administrator on many computers when they were the state-of-the-art. I had a Cray to play with when Cray was *the* supercomputer. Big oil at that point was flush with money, so it was a phenomenal opportunity.

If you look at my career, I came up through the ranks, so at this point, except for security, there isn't a job, at least in the IT field, that I haven't done. And that's a great advantage. The only thing in IT that I didn't actually hold a position in was a security analyst. I was never a security specialist because we didn't really have security specialists when I was still in the ranks. We didn't have the troubles and risks that we have now.

So that experience lasted about four or five years. In the late '80s I was in the Bay Area when I left Standard Oil. I went to a company called Ingres, which was *the competitor* to Oracle in the relational database at that time. I started as a senior systems administrator. I built their first help desk, in 1989, before there were help desks.

Scott Donaldson: What was a help desk back then?

Garrison: It was three people. I had also learned UNIX, so I became a team lead; I began moving up the ranks. I became the manager of the systems administrators, but I was still hands on.

In '92 I was still with Ingres. I was still fairly young and I loved to travel and at that point, before the World Wide Web, there was Usenet, which was essentially a newsgroups platform, that caught my attention. I applied and interviewed for several cool jobs. One job was with Intel in Albuquerque, New Mexico. One job was with the University of South Pacific in Fiji, and one job was internal to Ingres and that one was in London. I chose London and stayed with the company. The job was a great opportunity. So between '92 and '94 I built a small data center in London. And I built one in Dublin, Ireland. Small by today's standards—not small by NPR standards—but small in comparison to data centers that I've managed. It was a phenomenal opportunity to learn the infrastructure and the business in a foreign country. We were in Ireland because of tax benefits to the labor there. So you learned how to get things done in a different country.

After 2½ years of working in the UK with Ingres, I got a great opportunity to return to the states and work for a former boss at Turner Broadcasting System Inc. in Atlanta, GA, and I took it.

When I arrived at Turner, I was responsible for their data centers and infrastructure. Turner was not the global company that it is now. It was still emerging. Turner was not the global company that it is now. It was still emerging. We had data centers in Hong Kong; we had a data center in London; we had little machine rooms in Rio at that point: one in Buenos Aires and also in Mexico City. My job began to grow at Turner.

While I was still in Atlanta, they were having a terrible time with their help desk, their server, their client services, and client server. I built Turner's first help desk, which was much larger than Ingres's. We had no standards. We did not have an e-mail system; we had five e-mail systems. We didn't have a network; we had five networks. It was your classic example of: if a business unit can't get service from corporate, they'll do it themselves. It'll happen every time.

We started bringing all that under control. I did a worldwide e-mail rollout in 1995, cc:Mail, and consolidated all these AppleTalks, all these networks. In those days, a worldwide e-mail rollout was somebody with a floppy coming and touching every single PC at Turner Broadcasting. We had thousands of people, all over the world. That had been a failed project by a colleague of mine, who was replaced, and they came to me to go dig it up and fix it. That became my reputation; I was a fixer, "We've got a problem. Fix it." So I completed that rollout. By this time I had a fairly large portion of the infrastructure reporting to me and the CIO came to me and said, "I've got a problem in London. The vice president there is failing. He doesn't have a customer service attitude. He's lost the business leaders support. London is a classic example of a failed organization. Would you like to go fix it?" And I said, "Sure."

I went back to the UK for three years, where I reported jointly to the CIO of corporate and to the head of Turner International, who was in London, and was my boss. He consolidated IT outside the US and I had everything outside the US, development, and infrastructure.

In 1999, it was late '98 through mid-'99, you were still doing a lot of touching computers because SMS [Systems Management Service], Microsoft's product, wasn't fully baked yet. No matter what they say, it wasn't fully baked. So, if you did a worldwide e-mail rollout today, you just push it. Frankly, you'd just do a web page and have somebody click a link. We were still into a lot of manual labor at that point. But because I controlled everything, I just broke it up into regions. I said to my head of Europe, "You're responsible for e-mail. And you have this much money, I don't care how you do it, and this is your time." And I did the same thing with Asia, did the same thing with South America; just broke it up into manageable parts. Do your easiest first. I see so many people fail at projects because they think, "We'll do the hardest thing first and get it out of the way." Well, they've got to learn how to do it first, and so they fail. Do your easiest first and do it step by step.

I got that done; it was pretty straightforward. It wasn't really that complicated. It turned the organization around. There had been some mismanagement and too many consultants. They were just burning cash with consultants. I'm not a big fan of consultants, so I got rid of them and got the budget in order.

Right around now we're at about late '99, and you're seeing a transformation in the television world from analog to digital. My ex-boss is now the CTO of CNN, and has been put back in place as the CIO of Turner. How are we going to take an organization into the broadcast engineering world, which is a completely different world from IT? It's very analogous to audio engineering at NPR, only it's video and audio.

My focus was to transform an organization. The technology was the easiest part. How are we going to transform that organization to be able to move from loading a tape on a tape card to understanding that you are now a systems administrator of a video server? It requires a completely different skill set.

I recruited IT skills out of Atlanta from Georgia Tech. It was just a stream of phenomenal employees. Where did you get broadcast engineering? At a local station in Iowa because he's a jack-of-all-trades; he's done everything. So he has a completely different mindset. Or at DeVry Technical, where they just have a different mindset.

It was the hardest challenge I've done in my career. One question I get asked of me whenever I interview, "What's your biggest challenge?" And that was transforming that organization. I had to transform that organization very quickly, and, frankly, I didn't understand the technology at all. I had never been in television other than supporting the corporate infrastructure. And so I had to gain the credibility and respect from the leaders of that organization.

G. Donaldson: How did you do that?

Garrison: I listened. I listened to them; I partnered; I learned their technology quickly. I showed up in the middle of the night for the graveyard shift and I bought them lunches and talked to them. I listened to their frustrations, and there were a lot of them because they were managed by the same people who built WTBS in 1972. They had just retired and all this flood of frustration about how hard it was to change and how, even though Turner at this point was a global multibillion-dollar company, in many respects, it was still managed like it was Ted in his pajamas. So I listened to them.

Here is a great example. One of the biggest things I did that went the furthest was when I went to broadcast engineering and straightened out their situation. They did not have phones, they did not have computers, they did not have a desk. They had a workbench and a tool belt. And these are the people that you're expecting in the next six to nine months to manage your video server.

I went to corporate. I said, "We've got to get them space. We've got to get them cubes. We've got to get them a phone. We've got to get them a computer." They said, "Okay." And we spent about a million and a half dollars, and these guys were over the moon. I mean, to have a phone—before they had one phone and a workbench that they all had to share. That's how they were treated. So they weren't treated professionally, and so first you just had to treat them right.

So those actions were to gain the credibility and respect, but we still had an organization that we had to change and transform, and not everybody was going to make that change. So every single person had to reapply for their job and be interviewed.

I did a couple of things. One, I reorganized. It's very difficult to find television engineers, just like it's difficult to find audio engineers, so I built a structure so that I could grow my own. I built what's called a farm team. In order to be a good broadcast engineer, you have to have about three years of experience in television broadcast engineering, and guys coming out of DeVry didn't have it. I built a team of about 26 people. For the first 3 years you're going to pull cable, you're going to do all the low-level stuff, you're going to be part of a team, and then I'm going to promote out of that. So I changed the structure.

Thirteen people didn't make it out of those interviews, and they didn't make it because they didn't want to make it, because they had been mounting tapes for 26 years and making $80,000 by this time just by getting a 3% raise year after year, and they didn't want to learn anything new.

The fact was that the editors and the production staff no longer needed an engineer to go mount a tape because it's just right there in front of them. I think they didn't believe that we would terminate them, and we did. So that was Atlanta. We did the same thing in Washington, DC, and New York. London was not big enough to really worry about; Hong Kong the same.

Stan Siegel: Did it take longer than you expected?

Garrison: Yes, because they were very resistant to change. Atlanta still had a bootstrap culture. Once again, Ted literally used to come down and get coffee in his pajamas, and these guys remember that. And you just have a different mindset of labor in DC and New York.

G. Donaldson: So how did you work through those issues?

Garrison: With help from corporate. This was not my decision. This was a decision that was made at the Time Warner corporate level—that we're going to change the way we do work because we can't afford to do it the old way anymore because we're leaving so much money on the table.

G. Donaldson: So executive sponsorship was important.

Garrison: It was huge. It was the hardest thing I've done. I'm still not as versed in television technology as I am in IT because I had not done it before. I managed it. By the time I got into television, I was managing it three layers up. But, still I surprise myself sometimes by how much I do know; how much I fully understand the audio process.

At the same time that was going on, we were building a very large building in New York called Time Warner Center where Time Warner Corporate, Turner, Warner Music when they were still there, and Warner Brothers would be located. There was a division from Turner and then there was CNN and production.

Time Warner actually was pretty crafty in how they used IT resources informally, in that they looked at the divisions and looked at where their best practices were and said, "We'll leverage."

For Turner, leveraging the infrastructure meant me. For application development, frankly, Time Inc. was a little further ahead, so they used Time Inc. for their app dev. But that meant that I had the Time Warner building as well. And that was a phenomenal project. It was a good three years where for three days a week, Tuesday through Thursday, I lived in New York. It was a great experience, building the building.

G. Donaldson: What made it great for you?

Garrison: One was the scale. I had done a lot of smaller buildings, and by that time I had done at least one or two in Atlanta as well, but not something that was of the scale of $1.6 billion. It was the most expensive building project in New York City since the Twin Towers. So it was very high profile. It had been around 10 years in the making. I had a big time construction site. And, it was a lot of fun also to be in New York for three years, three days a week.

So my career was changing a little bit. I was feeling like I'd done everything. I was a little bored. I saw at that point in my career that I wanted to be a C-something. I had done everything else it seemed.

One day I was coming back from San Francisco and a recruiter sat next to me, and we started talking about jobs and IT. She told me about a C level opening at ChoicePoint and asked if I would be interested. I said, "I've never heard of ChoicePoint." Turns out they were a north Atlanta firm, about a billion dollars in revenue. I'll be honest with you; I was wooed by a title. I wouldn't be now, but I was then. I took the job.

I went to ChoicePoint for 3½ years. It was tough. I didn't realize how tough it would be going from a big company to a small company. It was really hard for me to go to a company in the suburbs. I had always worked down-town—London, San Francisco, even downtown Atlanta or New York. I had misjudged it and the whole thing was really hard for me.

G. Donaldson: Well, the locations are different. Were there other parts of the job that were interesting?

Garrison: Yeah, it's an insurance-based company. They have about 85% of the market share in providing insurance companies with data on you and me when we go and get insurance. Insurance companies are a whole lot differ-ent than media companies. It was very stodgy. It was a mom-and-pop shop. There were just a lot of things that surprised me. I wasn't real happy there.

Siegel: How much homework had you done before you accepted the position?

Garrison: Not enough. I had been kind of wooed. You know, I made a mis-take, honestly.

S. Donaldson: So how did you make the transition to here?

Garrison: So, ChoicePoint was bought by Lexus Nexus. My position of be-ing the CTO of ChoicePoint was going away, and eventually went away. At that point Thomson Reuters contacted me.

I went and I interviewed. It was a big job; the biggest job I'd ever had. At Turner my largest staff was maybe around 600 people. At Thomson Reuters, it was about 1100. My operating budget was $360 million. My capital budget was at least that much. We were global, with a lot of offshoring and huge data centers. In Minnesota alone, I had 24,000 computers and servers and it was growing at 28% a year; so that's thousands of servers coming in a year. Honestly, that job almost killed me.

G. Donaldson: The scale of it?

Garrison: The scale. Seven by 24. It's multibillion dollars, about $13 billion; half of it comes out of those Minnesota data centers. About $6 billion with 38% margins, all online. If a server went down, the spigot stopped and soothe pressure was tremendous. I went into that job thinking that, "I've done this before. I was unhappy because ChoicePoint was too small, blah-blah-blah-blah."

[Mutual laughing.]

I had done my homework, but I was also very excited about that job. Enough to move to Minnesota and enough for my wife to leave Turner for Minnesota. It was a lot of money. But in my position, they had run through four people in the last five years. My ego gets involved, "Well, they just had the wrong people."

But the fact is the job was just too structured—literally, my health went—4 o'clock in the morning, three days a week, something happened. And I didn't have the lieutenants in place, so I had to be involved from top to bottom. If we had an outage, we had two, which if you look at their history was about average, and it went all the way to New York. The pressure was intense.

G. Donaldson: And the ability to recruit or develop these lieutenants was not there for you?

Garrison: Not at that time. They had reorganized that organization four times in the last four years, trying to find the right model. But all they were really doing was moving people around. So by the time I came in, they had just done a reorg. I wasn't even part of the reorg; I was just the guy they had brought in to run it once they had decided what they were going to do, so I didn't really have time. And, honestly, by nine months, I knew that this was bad for me. My wife was worried, my family was worried.

G. Donaldson: Unrelenting, it sounds.

Garrison: It was unrelenting, and it just drove me into the ground.

S. Donaldson: So they reorganized, but they didn't redo the business process.

Garrison: They didn't redo anything and they didn't change.

S. Donaldson: So what happened next to migrate you here?

Garrison: I took a year off. I went and said, "I've got to have a package. I'm not right for this." I actually had a wonderful boss and they said ok. My wife and I traveled around the world for a year. We went and did all of Southeast Asia and the Middle East. We just traveled while I tried to figure out what I wanted to do. Retirement was a possibility. Financially, I could probably do it.

My wife found this job at NPR on the Internet and sent off a resume to the recruiter. I came here and I just loved it from the minute that I walked in. For this stage of my career, it's perfect. I'm surrounded by really smart people doing really cool stuff with a mission. I couldn't ask for more in Washington, DC. I ride my bike to work. It's phenomenal. They're happy, I'm happy, it's challenging.

You wanted to discuss the infrastructure here. They underinvested for a number of years because the money that came in has gone to news and programming operations to the detriment of the infrastructure. They recognize that they underinvested. They made a commitment to change that, and they wanted someone who had done it before.

The other thing here is—it's a very cohesive place. You find a lot of people here who have been here 30 or 40 years. I was able to bring a perspective from the outside to a role that didn't exist before.

Right now what I oversee is distribution for the public radio system, not just NPR. NPR manages the distribution, the satellite radio system, for all public radio in the US. So I run that. I oversee audio engineering, which is exactly like my broadcasting engineering of years ago. I lead IT, both development and the infrastructure. I think the reason they hired me is that I have the background and I've done buildings all over the place. We're in the middle of the largest investment that NPR has ever made right now.

S. Donaldson: When you say the "development piece," what does that mean?

Garrison: We have your classic back-office development: finance, HR, legal, all your back office applications. But we also have internal homegrown news content and a workflow application. Actually, it's very elegant. It just cost about three times as much as what they thought it would. I got lucky on that one. I'm kind of taking all the glory for that and haven't done all that much because they got this together right before I came in. It works, and it's really cool, and I'm rolling it out right now. I'm in the last phase of that. The first phase was content management, so stories, writing stories, etc., rundowns. That's what was released when I first came in. What we're releasing now is actually the whole workflow, which is the multitrack editor, and that is where you're having production people and producers, actually doing their editing, and so it's downsizing my engineering shop by 13 people. And it's all done, and we're implementing it.

Siegel: Is cloud computing coming into your shop?

Garrison: Here? We're not big enough. However, NPR.org has around 15–17 million unique visitors. So it's a very large website. It's not hosted here. We outsource it. All the development is done here, all the content management, etc., but the actual servers are hosted on clouds by various vendors, actually.

Siegel: And that was in place before you got here, or you were part of it?

Garrison: No, it was in place before I got here. I have my own views on cloud. I mean, cloud is a lot of different things. It depends on what vendor you're talking to. At Thomson, we did not go external cloud. We were putting in 6000 servers a year because of security. We just built our own internal cloud because a cloud is nothing more than virtualized servers and storage. So I had my own cloud. It's just right over there in the data center. It's all virtualized servers and storage.

S. Donaldson: What virtualization technology are you using?

Garrison: VMware along with a variety of storage net apps. When I walked in there, they're using IBM XIV. I don't think we're going to stick with that.

S. Donaldson: Have you looked at VCE, the Vblocks?

Garrison: No, I haven't. We could spend a lot on technology here.

S. Donaldson: Who do you report to?

Garrison: I report to the senior vice president for strategic operations and finance, Debra Delman. Debra was brought in by Vivian Schiller, and they worked together. Debra was brought in specifically to professionalize the organization.

G. Donaldson: How is outside talent received?

Garrison: It depends on where you are. My organization loved the fact they had some outside talent that understood their business. It's very good.

G. Donaldson: It sounds like an academic environment where there's a great deal of highly intelligent folks.

Garrison: I think you're right. The amount of highly intellectually curious professionals along with Rhodes Scholars who are mission driven—I've never run into so many in my life in the corporate world.

G. Donaldson: What is a typical day for you? I know there probably isn't a typical day, but what do you do on a day-to-day basis?

Garrison: Well, it depends. Right now I'm doing a major project this weekend to fortify UPS systems and back up infrastructure.

So this weekend we actually have to shut this building down completely. That's very hard because we're radio; we're on the air. We have live shows all weekend. So we've shipped two full shows to LA. We're going to be doing Weekend Morning Edition, Weekend Edition, and ATC, "All Things Considered," off the air in LA. And there's a lot to consider especially in terms of disaster recovery.

I'm also overseeing an organizational audit to take a look at our technical infrastructure and what improvements we can make.

Siegel: I see that's up on your board there, right?

Garrison: It sure is. It's one of my main things that I'm doing. And this has actually been a great exercise because it's forced us to take it seriously. So when we leave LA after this weekend, I now have a warm site, which to get that kind of stuff done without an emergency is difficult. So now I'm replicating a content management system there.

Siegel: So how did you convince management to pay for this insurance policy?

Garrison: There was no other choice because this building has to go down. The choice was: (1) you can run for the next year like this because you're on street power, until we get into that new building and they knock this building down, or (2) you can move these shows out to LA because this weekend, this whole building's going to have to be down. And they said, "We've got to go," and rightly so. It wasn't even a hard discussion.

Siegel: So the business guys have very little to do with technology then. Is that correct?

Garrison: Nothing to do with technology. It had to do with their risk. I did the first half of it last weekend. We took the whole data center down for 6 hours, and we had 15 minutes of Internet outage and that was planned. And now we have to do the hard part, which is streaming the shows out of LA.

Siegel: So since you're going to be working on weekends, does that mean your current job is 24 by 7?

Garrison: It is 24 by 7, but one thing you should know is that we don't do any shows in the off hours. We do newscasts, which are on the top of the hour, right? You hear, "This is NPR News." You hear that on all radio stations. That's all we do after 6:15. The second thing to know is that I've inherited the IT group in place. The IT was thin in terms of seasoning. However, the audio engineering in the distribution regions that I inherited is well seasoned; they've been doing this a long time.

S. Donaldson: So you had the lieutenants in place?

Garrison: I had the lieutenants in place. And they had the lieutenants in place. So it's really great. It's 7 by 24, but manageable.

G. Donaldson: If it comes under your purview, I have a question about software development. Are you involved in agile development, and is it your preferred approach?

Garrison: Software development is under my purview, and agile development is our preferred method.

G. Donaldson: And why is it your preferred approach?

Garrison: Speed. It's faster, and so it gets the product in front of the customer faster.

S. Donaldson: How long are the sprints? Typically, 60 days or 90 days?

Garrison: More on the 60 days. Ninety days is too long.

S. Donaldson: So you've got bite-sizable chunks of things to get done.

Garrison: That's right.

G. Donaldson: So you've been able to transition your previous experience to help professionalize NPR. And you're involved in all aspects of infrastructure, from constructing the new building to how it's wired to the other technologies that supports the building. You also mentioned you connect with all public broadcasting. What kind of working relationships do you have with people outside of NPR? Are you in contact with people in other companies, other broadcasting stations, and so forth?

Garrison: Well, outside of NPR I have contact with our member stations.

So in the public radio space, we have three main distributors of programming and then a lot of little ones. You know, NPR, which is far and away the largest. You have American Public Media, which does "Prairie Home Companion." They do "Marketplace." They do a lot of classical music, and they own Minnesota Public Radio, which is one of the largest networks in the country. We also have a lot of interaction with our station colleagues at PRI, which is Public Radio International, a public radio producer and distributor. For instance, when we go down this weekend, my satellite system has to go down. Our hot site is Minnesota Public Radio in St. Paul. I actually pay them to utilize their network operations center. We will transfer the satellite distribution center to St. Paul Saturday at 2:15.

Siegel: So how much does your job involve doing that outreach to get the money and so forth?

Garrison: Really, in my job—very little, other than serving the board of trustees. The majority of the Board members come from member stations and the rest are public leaders. We also have a board of trustees whose primary role is fundraising. My involvement there is I built their internal website. I set up when they have conferences. I supply the technology and the support. It's behind-the-scenes support.

G. Donaldson: So you're a CTO and a CIO kind of combined? You report to the COO. Do you have other horizontal relationships with other C-level peers?

Garrison: I sit on the Executive Committee, which meets once a week for 2 hours.

G. Donaldson: Who else is on that committee?

Garrison: The general counsel; CFO, who's my peer and reports to the SVP of strategic operations and finance; SVP of development; SVP of news; chief people officer, which is the head of HR; VP of diversity; general counsel, VP of member audience partnerships, VP of policy and representation, general manager and SVP digital media, CEO of national public media, our sponsorship arm, and the senior vice president of marketing, communications and external relations.

G. Donaldson: So how do you see the value you add to NPR in your role? How do you define it?

Garrison: Experience, having done it before. They don't have anybody here who's ever done a new building at all, in terms of technology. It's not really something you want to learn on the fly.

G. Donaldson: How do you measure success?

Garrison: On time, on budget. I'm really proud of the buildings that I've been involved with. I love doing buildings. I love driving by. I love going into Time Warner Center and saying, "Wow, I was part of this. This is so cool." Or the Hong Kong Telecom Building or what have you. And this building is really neat because it's being designed as a building for audio and for radio. If you look at this building from the ground up, it is an old bank building that they've retrofitted. They've done so many things. At Turner, CNN Center was the same thing. It was like a hotel and an ice skating rink. And so everything was compromised. And this new NPR building is from the ground up.

S. Donaldson: What technologies are different about the building?

Garrison: This building is a 17-year-old plant that's all analog. The new building is all digital. The new building workflow is all based on a new digital infrastructure; hence, 13 positions are going away. The whole workflow changes in the new building. We're implementing that new workflow now with the new system that I talked about: news flex and multi-track editing. The only reason we're doing that now is that we don't want to change where they sit and how they work at the same time. We want to change how they work now. We call it "self-ops," by the way. It's a huge project. Self-ops: It means a producer does his own stuff. We're going from eight studios in this building to three. Because we don't need an engineer just sitting in a studio waiting for someone to come in; the guy can do it at his desk.

S. Donaldson: And you mentioned the workflow is a homegrown product.

Garrison: It's a combination. The content management is homegrown. It's integrated with a system called DAVID, which is a French company. DAVID has a multitrack editor so that when you go into the editing process, it's a canned project.

S. Donaldson: So what led you to that decision to use a French product?

Garrison: There are only two products in the world. There's DollaD, French and DAVID, French. The reason we choose DAVID is just that it's a better product for our own needs. DollaD has just refocused onto video instead of audio, so they're not putting their resources into it. So that was one reason. DAVID is a really small company, and whenever you have that you have to worry about them staying in business. This was exactly the same thing in the late '90s to 2000 that we encountered at CNN with small companies and startups: You had to worry about their viability. We bought them because we had the money to do it, because once we got in bed with them, we were so dependent on them. Well, we can't do that here. It's probably the best product. It's what WAMU uses; Discovery Channel uses. However, they're a small company.

Siegel: Going back to your success factors for a minute: on time, within budget. Are those your schedules and your budgets or somebody else's?

Garrison: Well, it depends. The budget's mine. I had to approve the budget though it was prepared earlier by others. They erred on the side of being conservative.

G. Donaldson: This is where your experience counts because you know how much it costs.

Garrison: Yes, I know how much it costs to put a network in the building, and we have enough money. The schedule was not mine. The schedule was already in place, and there are a lot of dependencies on that schedule where we can't be late.

Siegel: So you had no say in modifying the schedule because there were lines in the sand, as you just described that could not be moved. Is that correct?

Garrison: I can move them if I really want to, but I have to be aware that if I move them, it can be costly.

S. Donaldson: Where's the new building?

Garrison: It's 111 North Capitol Street in the NOMA [North of Massachusetts] neighborhood.

G. Donaldson: Are you involved in your role in any strategic planning?

Garrison: Very much so. I oversee all planning for PRSS [Public Radio Satellite System] or for the distribution side of the house.

G. Donaldson: What is your relationship with your research labs? And what do they do, and how do they connect with what you oversee?

Garrison: The labs report up to me. They are part of distribution. They used to be part of NPR. NPR went through kind of a reorganization. NPR moved the labs out about a year ago, actually, and into the distribution, but they are a self-funded and self-sustaining group.

G. Donaldson: What do they focus on?

Garrison: They are focused on research and development for all of public radio. For example, they are experimenting with new technologies in captioned radio that allow people who are hearing impaired to experience live radio. They rely on some competitive grants—meaning grants they seek out and apply for—around those activities.

G. Donaldson: Are you involved in helping set those priorities or areas of focus?

Garrison: Well, it reports to me and we do collaborate in some areas, however they have an incredibly resourceful team.

G. Donaldson: How do you keep future focus in terms of technologies that are emerging, that you need to be tracking, keep on top of, and that influence your industry?

Garrison: Well, I'm fairly plugged in with other technologists around the country and the world. I'm not much of a Gartner guy, you know. It's more about relationships. I do your classic Cisco every couple of years or EMC every couple of years.

G. Donaldson: What are you seeing as the technologies that are important toward the future?

Garrison: Well, virtualization, clearly. Unclear about storage virtualization right now. I'm not sure how big a bang that is or not.

S. Donaldson: Is that because of a financial payback reason or concern about the privacy of the content?

Garrison: It's a couple of things for me. We looked at it hard at Thomson. By the way, I kept up on technology at Thomson a whole lot more than I have to here because I spent a lot more money on it. For storage, it was hard to get the payback. It was hard to make a business case. And in addition, at Thomson why I shied away from it was [because] your major arrays, your major disk manufacturers have built in huge amounts of redundancies into their product. EMC's the top cheese. You could say IBM, but I consider them a second tier myself. At least a year and a half ago, when I was really looking at storage virtualization, you had these highly redundant storage systems on the back coming into a single point of failure of virtualization control. And so I thought, "Holy Toledo." I did not feel comfortable taking all this redundancy and putting it right through a single point of failure. So, it was the ease of management of storage, which in large environments takes thousands of servers. I think I told you we bought 5,000 servers a year at Thomson. I spent twice as much money on storage as I did on servers. Storage was my number one cost center for a number of years.

Siegel: So is that one of the reasons you're hesitant about diving into the cloud environment?

Garrison: The reason—well, at NPR I'm hesitant about diving into the cloud because I can't make a business case for it because we're not big enough to worry about it, honestly. I could save some money, but it's not that much money. I could outsource my e-mail right now to Microsoft and save some money. Here I'm not sure the savings are enough to worry about it.

At Thomson we were worried about security because we were selling data. We were selling data that included SPII. And if you look at what's going on with cloud right now, all the big vendors are bringing it in-house. Cisco's building it in-house. All the big vendors are doing it themselves.

We had a *big* shortage of data centers in '90, 2007–8. Now we're having a large data center constructed. In some areas you're oversupplied with data centers right now. In some areas you're not. But, Cisco, Google, the big guys are building their own data centers. They're not outsourcing it to Rackspace or what have you. The folks who are doing that are startups. I guess, mid-sized probably, but here, if I took you back to my machine room, you'd say, "No wonder you're not really worried about the cloud." It's about twice the size of this office.

G. Donaldson: So what are other forward–thinking technologies?

Garrison: Mobile.

G. Donaldson: Mobile? And could you give an example of what might be involved in the mobile technology space?

Garrison: Yeah, right now we're filing stories on iPhones. So what used to be a guy with a recorder and a microphone is happening with iPhones. We filed Osama bin Laden stories and a lot of the mideastern stories about Libya that you're hearing about are coming off iPhones over the internet direct from us.

G. Donaldson: So you think about the correspondents and what they need and what they would like to have. Is there a formal process you follow?

Garrison: There's an area that I oversee that I didn't talk about. I run what's called news operations," which are the people who gear up all the correspondents. They deal with studio bookings, kind of news operations. They're very close to the correspondents, the news correspondents. In fact, my head of news ops just came back from Baghdad. And if you look at what they need and what they want, they want more Panasonic Toughbooks. And then they just love this Tideline suite that turns an iPhone into a little mobile studio, and it's pretty cool.

S. Donaldson: Do you do any custom development in the apps shop to outfit the road warrior with anything?

Garrison: No, we try and do as little customization as possible.

S. Donaldson: Right.

Garrison: If they hadn't already been down the road so far on this in-house, I wouldn't have done it at all. It's crazy how much depreciation I'm carrying.

Siegel: So how does agile software development play into that model?

Garrison: I am in that business right now until I finish this product and then I hope, frankly, to turn that world into more of a support role; i.e., I don't plan on doing this again. You know, it's not really the business we should be in. I plan on buying canned products and configuring them and supporting them. That's the business we should be in at NPR. Now, a different side of the house is NPR.org. I don't run NPR.org, so that would be a different conversation. But we outsource the mobile application development here. We didn't do that ourselves.

G. Donaldson: Do you have an IT investment management process that you follow? For example, do you come up with a business concept and a proof of concept, and then you then take it to feasibility and then cost it out? Do you have criteria that you use in order to decide whether or not to select one technology over another or whether to go in a certain direction or not? Capital planning and investment control?

Garrison: We do. I'm not sure it's as formal as you're making it. We do an RFP [request for proposal] process. Right now, there are not a lot of choices that I really care to deal with. For example, I'm going to put in a Cisco network. I paid for the design to be done, but the technology choice was easy. Probably the biggest technology investment would be on the broadcasting engineering side, where we need to decide what audio controllers we are going to use. There's a fair amount of people in this business. We're doing the evaluation right now. In addition, we have products in-house. That's a multimillion-dollar spend, but the larger investment that we're making right now is the systems integrator for the audio engineering for the new building.

G. Donaldson: Do you have people that focus their time more exclusively on your IT investments? Building the business case and preparing it for presentation?

Garrison: No, we're not big enough.

G. Donaldson: And when you decide that you want to go in a certain direction, then you bring your investment option before an executive board or a committee? How does that work? What's the governance structure for IT investments and technology investments?

Garrison: It happens when deciding the budget. Those proposals are mine and we will go in front of an internal executive committee. We'll all discuss it. We'll throw stones at it, what have you. We'll make priorities based at that meeting. Now, having said that, there are investment thresholds that require us to go through the board of directors.

G. Donaldson: Yes.

Garrison: But the investments that I will be making of any size in the next 16 months are all building-related. My other investments are already approved.

G. Donaldson: One follow-up question about the future-focus technologies or the technologies that are emerging right now. Do you have any social networking–type technologies that are used or that you are planning on using?

Garrison: NPR.org, big time. If you go to the NPR Facebook page and look at the entry point into NPR.org, a large portion of that is now through social networks, particularly Facebook. I don't know about Twitter on my side of the house. However, Twitter is big on the content side of the house. Our head social media strategist is Andy Carvin who's probably one of the most famous tweeters out there right now doing ground-breaking work in using Twitter as a reporting tool.

We're producing a lot of news on the digital side of the house. The digital side of the house is a very interesting discussion. I'll just touch on it. Our distribution model is that we produce programming for the local radio stations, for example WAMU is a great example. Here's a good station. They are dependent on broadcasting "All Things Considered" at 4:00.

G. Donaldson: Could you speak a little bit about how social networking-type technologies are disruptive?

Garrison: Well, think about it. What if I didn't have to wait until 4:00? If you go to NPR.org right now, you can't stream "All Things Considered." And there's a reason for that because we can't cut out the local stations.

S. Donaldson: Right.

Garrison: What about Pandora? What about NPR on Pandora? What about connected cars? So when you are in Iowa, maybe you want to listen to WAMU, and not your local IOWA station. What does that mean to their economy and to their fundraising? If you do a little research on that; it is *the* disruptor in my view.

G. Donaldson: It's a game changer.

Garrison: It's a game changer. And so what it means, in order to stay relevant, the local stations, once again in my view, have to focus on local content so that they stay relevant.

S. Donaldson: Has mentoring played much of a role through your career?

Garrison: One of the things we didn't touch on and one of the reasons that I'm here, actually, is my greatest enjoyment and what I'm most proud of in my career is not building buildings. Building these buildings is fun and that's cool. My biggest achievement and what I'm most proud of is if you go back, for instance, to Turner Broadcasting right now, the SVP for development, the SVP of International and the SVP of Infrastructure were all hired by me. I hired all of them at or below the manager level and groomed them. And that is what I'm having a blast doing here because I'm taking people and mentoring them and coaching them. It's so much fun. So that's what I think about.

S. Donaldson: What keeps you up at night? What do you worry about? What's your biggest challenge or fear?

Garrison: It all depends on the business. I don't really worry about this building much. I really don't.

Siegel: So how do you see your role changing?

Garrison: Stan, I'm not sure I worry about it that much. You know, maybe I put myself out of a job in the next few years. Maybe I mentor these guys and I'm done. I don't know. We're quite a ways from that, I'll tell you that. We really are. I just now promoted a manager to director, and he's going to be a director for quite a long time because he has a lot to learn.

I have a very cookie-cutter approach to my job when I take over a new organization, when I'm the fixer. I look at people. I look at processes. And I look at technology. The technology is the simplest; it's easy; I don't worry about it. I don't really care if it's an EMC or a Hitachi frame. I really couldn't care less. I care if I have people who are skilled enough to manage it.

G. Donaldson: So your own advancement, your own career path, what are the next generation of issues that you will be tackling here? Have you had the chance to think about that? I know standing this building up and getting the infrastructure in place is all-consuming at the moment. Have you thought of the solution after next? Challenge after next?

Garrison: I'm not so sure it's a NPR challenge. I see myself probably as a consultant. It would be at the last part of my career as a consultant, working on a project and traveling. So consulting is really what I want to do.

G. Donaldson: So for someone who doesn't like to use consultants, you're ready to be one at a certain point?

[Laughter]

Garrison: That's right. I am, as a matter of fact.

Cherches, Loveland, Mosca and Natoli

Mind Over Machines

Dmitry Cherches Cherches is Chief Technology Officer at Mind Over Machines. His 15+ years in IT have been largely focused on the development of high-transaction databases and e-commerce applications, high-availability servers and storage solutions, and multi-lingual Web applications. For more than a decade, he has been responsible for setting the technology vision for Mind Over Machines. Under his direction, the company has increased its depth of expertise and certifications in web programming languages, tools and technology platforms.

A native of Belarus, Russia and one-time aspiring professional swimmer on the Junior Olympic team, Dmitry was disassembling mainframe computers and creating DOS-based games as a child. After immigrating to the US, he ultimately received Bachelor of Science degrees in Computer Science and Economics from the University of Maryland, Baltimore County. Dmitry previously served as Director of Technology at National Information Services Corporation (NISC)

Tom Loveland is Founder and CEO of Mind Over Machines. A largely self-taught software engineer, Tom founded the company in 1989 and continues to drive its mission to better business, government and society through the creative use of technology.

Tom's technology activism extends beyond Mind Over Machines. In response to the passage of Maryland's "tech tax" in 2007, he co-founded the Maryland Computer Services Association and, with other business groups, led a lobbying and grassroots effort that resulted in the unprecedented repeal of the tax before it took effect.

He was named by Baltimore's mayor to serve as "Google Czar," leading a drive to entice the search giant to choose the city for an ultra-high speed broadband access project. He continues to work with local and state leaders in efforts to create greater high-speed broadband accessibility and foster opportunity for the citizens of Maryland.

Tom has been recognized as an Influential Marylander, Innovator of the Year, and Baltimore's Extraordinary Technology Advocate. He attended the University of Washington, St. John's College and the University of Chicago.

Rick Mosca is Vice President of Consulting Services at Mind Over Machines. He brings to the role more than 25 years' experience in technology leadership, including product management, application development and business process analysis and re-engineering.

Rick held previous positions as Vice President of Products and Services for Gannon Technologies Group, where he led the transformation of technology research into the product stage for the defense and intelligence communities, and as Vice President of Strategic Projects and Applied Technology at T. Rowe Price, and Program Manager at Roadnet Technologies (a UPS company). Rick attended Towson University and the University of Maryland, Baltimore County.

Joe Natoli is Chief UX Architect at Mind Over Machines. With more than 20 years' experience, Joe is a recognized thought leader in interface design, information architecture and user experience. He marries technology user expertise with a background in brand and product strategy for B2B, B2C and government projects.

Joe speaks frequently on user experience, web engineering and design for the Graphic Artists Guild, the American Institute of Graphic Arts (AIGA) and other national forums. He has served as an adjunct professor at the Maryland Institute College of Art (MICA) in Baltimore and the University of Baltimore since 1992. In addition, he writes frequently about the roles of design and technology in business and organizational success.

Gary Donaldson: Tom, when we contacted you as CEO/Founder of Mind Over Machines to discuss interviewing your CTO, you suggested we consider an alternative to the standard one-on-one interview process that we have been following.

Tom Loveland: To understand the role of the CTO in our company, it helps to be familiar with our integrated approach. We address business strategy, technology, and user-experience together. I thought it made sense to include key people on our team who, with the CTO, reflect and even embody our approach, including my role as CEO. So joining us today, in addition to Dmitry Cherches, our CTO, are Rick Mosca, Vice President of Consulting Services who leads the business strategy work with our customers, and Joe Natoli, Chief User Experience Architect.

G. Donaldson: Let's begin with a brief overview of Mind Over Machines.

Loveland: Mind Over Machines is a consulting and technology services firm that delivers game-changing information systems to midsize and large firms and the federal government. Today we're about 70 people or so. I used to say we are an application development firm, because I just assumed that everybody thought about it the same as I did. It took me a while to learn that people were pigeonholing us as the guy that comes in after they've already figured out what they want and have laid it all out. "Now just call in Mind Over Machines to write this code." I realized that not telling the whole story was a big disservice. When we get involved with clients, we always ask them the big questions, "Why are you doing this? Who's going to die if you don't do it?" And we help them find new recurring revenue, enter new markets, get a leg up on the competition, or just do things more efficiently. One of our clients will tell you we've given them a third or more of the strategic business ideas over the years that have helped them grow.

G. Donaldson: It's a strategic, collaborative partnership with your customers.

Loveland: I like to think so.

G. Donaldson: What kinds of services do you provide?

Loveland: We offer services basically in three different areas. We provide high-level consulting services—strategy, analysis, innovation—as well as a strong specialty in user experience design and we match that with just solid application delivery: enterprise systems, standalone apps, legacy modernization, and data analytics.

G. Donaldson: Do you consider yourself a small or midsized firm?

Loveland: I consider us small. But I'm going to talk to a six-person firm tomorrow, and they're pretty impressed with what we've achieved, so it's all relative. There's always the next mountain.

G. Donaldson: Can you share more detail about your customer base?

Loveland: Historically, we've worked with folks like IKEA, Johns Hopkins University, the National Institutes of Health, and the US Army. We're quite active in financial services and the health sector. In all these cases we're building new systems, integrating systems or pulling things together. In some cases they're saying to us, "We want to have this thing done. Please do it for us," and in some cases they're asking, "We want to get to this place. We're not quite sure how to get there. What do you think?"

G. Donaldson: Tom, you moved through several career stages in the technology field to where you are now the founder and CEO of your company, and a business community leader as well. I'd appreciate if you could share your story and perspective on that journey so others may be able to learn from your experience.

Loveland: Sure. I'll step back a little bit and speed forward. In high school, I thought I was going to be a US Senator, something like that. And I spent a total of five years attending three universities, and I got zero degrees. I didn't know what I wanted to do for a career, so I just followed my interests. After five years I still hadn't found a path, but figured I was better educated than many graduates and finally had the guts to drop out. Bill Gates was smarter than that. He figured out after one year that he could drop out. But he also had a clear direction.

My first major was the Comparative History of Ideas. Then I went to St. John's College and studied the Great Books of Western civilization. Finally, I attended the University of Chicago to study a little bit of math. I think I took three computer classes the whole time, and one of them was to avoid getting a really bad grade in chemistry; you know, switch courses late in the term, grab a computer class and ace it.

Programming was just fun. But I thought even then that I would probably go to law school, because I didn't know what else to do. All I knew for sure, and I remember this clearly: I didn't want to go into computers as a career. I thought that making computers my job would ruin my love for them, would ruin my hobby. I tell you, I wasn't too smart about it! It took me a while to figure out, "Do what you love!"

Fortunately, one day my father sent me a magazine advertisement of a computer by Seequa called the Chameleon. "Here's yet another new computer I've never heard of. Nothing interesting about that, but check out the address." I was like, "Holy crap. I walk by this building every single day. It's an abandoned building."

It was a Saturday afternoon. I ran right over there, knocked on the door, and sure enough, they were actually building computers, a luggable. Much like the first Compaq, but one year ahead. So I talked myself into a job, "Can I please work for you?" And I convinced them to let me work two 40-hour shifts so I could make enough money to pay my rent at minimum wage. And that was the beginning.

Thomas Burke, who was 16 years old at the time, five years my junior, taught me how to program in dBASE II and how to test PCs. We largely ran the quality control department, where the machines came off the conveyor belt, and we tested them and sent them to shipping. We'd take support calls from all over the world; Italy, the Arctic Circle. A dealer would call so excited that he had received his five computers, maybe three of them weren't working, but he was just so happy they were finally there. So we're debugging over the telephone. And the manufacturing staff learned to call us back into the assembly area earlier and earlier in the process when they realized a machine wasn't working right.

Walking back there alone those first times, I panicked a little inside. "I don't know how these things work!" But I kept my mouth shut except to ask, "What seems to be the trouble? What have you tried?" And then the next obvious thing, you know, "Have you plugged it in?" And then at night, read the manual. Always reading. And, sure enough, you get a little bit ahead of the game and tomorrow you're a little bit smarter. Pretty soon you are the most knowledgeable guy in the room, you truly are the expert. And that's worked really well throughout my career. This is how I learned everything, and everything that has come since.

After I left college, Thomas pulled me into a four-person software development shop in Baltimore. I built software for Baltimore Gas & Electric Company and a local army base. More interesting, we were building the graphical user interface for a chemical weapon preparedness simulator used in NATO war games in Europe in the late '80s. The other guys on this project were a lot smarter than I was as far as coding, so I learned there that I wasn't the sharpest guy on the block.

Then a funny thing happened. I'd moved around a lot after leaving college, and hadn't kept the student loan people up-to-date regarding my whereabouts. When they found me, they convinced me that I had to pay it all back right now, or really bad things were going to happen. I fell for it and borrowed money from my friends to pay off those loans. Then I quit my job so that I could become an independent consultant to make more money more quickly to pay my friends back sooner. And that was the glorious beginning of Mind Over Machines.

I did anything for anybody related to computers back then, set up networks, whatever. But I quickly realized that my passion really is software, meeting challenges better through software, so I focused there. For example, I built the core system for a local registered agent services firm run by a guy named Jim Strott. I still have the invoice here. I charged $3,500 or something for the initial build. A few years later, Jim showed the system to Dennis Howarth, who had left Prentice Hall and was planning a national network of affiliated registered agent firms. He liked what he saw so Jim called me and I went running down there. I liked Dennis. We got along really well, so right on the spot I gave him my software with the understanding that he would engage me to enhance it. It's 16 years later now. NRAI quickly became third in the nation. Mind Over Machines has built nearly 100% of their systems. We have hundreds of employees and dozens of affiliate offices servicing hundreds of thousands of business units. We've built 45 or so integrated systems that handle corporate compliance, tax filings, entity search, and on and on for companies like Best Buy, eBay, Coca-Cola, over half of the top 50 US law firms, and all the rest of our client's customers. So that meeting with Dennis was really nice, serendipitous.

G. Donaldson: You not only gave birth to yourself, but you gave birth to another company.

Loveland: Yes, exactly. And Dennis and his partners just sold their firm to a multinational out of Europe. We helped them from startup to growth to exit. And we've done it for others.

Like OPNNA, the Office Products Network of North America. These guys were a spinoff of a local office products company. They had the idea of aggregating the buying power of the nation's largest companies, negotiating favorable rates with distributors, and creating a national order-processing clearinghouse to make it all work. Well, their prospective customers liked the idea. So it was like, "Oh man. Now we have to actually build the technology to do this!"

They hired a firm like ours, but gradually became uncomfortable. I was called in to do an assessment. "Are we getting what we're paying for?" I did the assessment and was stunned. Not that the code was particularly fancy, it was just so clean and better documented than any I'd ever seen. "I'm super confident it's going to do exactly what it says," I told them. "You've got nothing to worry about."

Later they called me in again. "We've got an enhancement that our current vendor is unwilling to do. We think it's going to take about 80 hours of work, and we'd like you to take a stab at it." So I sat down with the CIO, and we spent about 3 hours going over the system. And I figured out a solution on the spot, talking myself out of work a second time.

Well, then they just had to have me. So they fired the other company and gave me the project. I also got to hire Bob Mayo, the guy who'd written that super clean code in the first place. That's really where Mind Over Machines was born. OPNNA did well, too. They grew to $1.2 billion in annual sales before selling to Corporate Express.

S. Donaldson: So with these experiences, with the technical background, technical experiences, technical success, thinking like a CTO, how do those experiences help you now as you've migrated to the position of CEO? How did that technical knowledge help you set the vision for the corporation, the next step, the next plateau?

Loveland: Well, that's funny. I fell into this thing accidentally. I never really had the vision of building a company, and in earlier years I even fought being called an entrepreneur, the kind who can run any company he's given. I only do this because I love this stuff.

But the technical background has shaped our approach and what we're about in some important ways. First, we believe it can be better. "It" being everything. In fact, breakthroughs are waiting to happen. And we believe technology, specifically information systems, can make it so. We've seen it. We've done it.

We also know that this absolutely is not about us. Coding teaches you humility. Heck, the computer throws your mistakes in your face in a heartbeat. You quickly learn to take ego out of the equation, and you develop a certain integrity around truly solving the actual problem at hand. Wherever blame or praise may go. Heck, cast that aside. Simply, "Is this working?"

And we take that to the next level, because this also is not about technology. Technology is the last thing. Though it certainly has to be solid, that's a given. What this is about is the right business solution for our clients. In fact, honestly? It's about our clients' customers. In the end, are we really helping our clients help their customers? Because that's what makes the world go around. And that's where we go.

Finally, I think having strength in technology makes us very comfortable relegating it to a back seat. I mean, it's important, but it's just a tool. And we never forget that. Instead, we focus on the softer stuff: understanding our clients' strategy and goals, coming up with ways to make them competitive in their markets, and so on. And for ourselves, we just keep pursuing the next big challenge.

G. Donaldson: How did you become engaged as a business community leader? Can you share more about that experience?

Loveland: Sure. In the fall of 2007, Maryland's governor called a special session of the General Assembly to address the state's looming budget deficit. It was a short, rapid-paced session and one of the things that popped out of it at the last minute was a 6% sales tax on the computer services industry.

I thought this was really dumb. Business people are smart; they'll figure out how to move work where it won't be taxed. Which means Maryland's IT jobs would move out of state, and all the smart people and their salaries would follow. How dumb is that? And since IT drives innovation almost everywhere, Maryland basically had put a 6% drag on innovation across all its business sectors. Wow.

I started calling around to figure out what this new law meant and how it had happened. Turns out our industry had been picked because we weren't known in Annapolis—we weren't a lobbying force—and our estimated tax revenue solved their problem in one swoop. Plus most of the legislators didn't understand how integral technology is to nearly every industry. It was easy to go after us, the silent geeks. And they knew all the other possible targets would put up a big stink.

The more I learned the more I realized we had to jump into this. We couldn't just sit back and hope that the chambers of commerce and tech councils and other business groups would right this wrong. The stakes were too big. We in the IT community had to jump in with all our might and help get this brain dead law repealed.

So I co-founded Maryland's first statewide IT lobbying organization. And we started raising money, strategizing with other business groups and hiring some of the best lobbyists and political communications teams in the state.

The experts placed our odds extremely low. I heard over and over, "It's 1,000 to 1." "No chance in hell." "It'll never happen." But we had to try. We orchestrated some of the largest demonstrations Annapolis had seen in years. We used social media to bombard legislators with personal visits, phone calls and email. And we used data mining to educate legislators district by district that they had large IT constituencies and serious economic consequences to consider.

It was an intense 100 days. And we won! Afterward, a half dozen old-timers came up to me and said some version of: "In all my years in Annapolis, I've never seen anything like this. It always takes two or three legislative sessions to get any bill passed, and you did it in just one. On a budget issue, no less. And you took $200M OFF the table, during a DOWN economy. And you didn't piss anybody off! Yet you didn't even exist six months ago. Who are you guys?!?"

I gained a lot of visibility out of this very public success and was known by some as the guy who'd been able to get government and business to work together. So when Google announced its Google Fiber for Communities program in 2010, Baltimore's mayor named me "Google Czar." My task was to help Baltimore win Google's nod for a 1 Gb citywide fiber network. This was another intense community project, and Baltimore showed very well, but Kansas City took the prize.

I'm still active on the broadband front, seeking other ways to bring more fiber to Baltimore to help with education, health, economic development, and all the rest. And I've been evangelizing on the state level. In late 2010, Maryland won one of the largest Federal grants for broadband and will be the first state in the nation with all counties and major communities connected via high speed fiber. So I've been helping economic development folks appreciate what this means to their communities, helping them understand how to take advantage of it.

G. Donaldson: Now, let's talk to Dmitry about your journey. You're the CTO, and you've been here how long now?

Dmitry Cherches: Since 1999.

G. Donaldson: Well, that's a good long time.

Cherches: Well, in the IT industry, it's very long. My journey is a little bit different from Tom's regarding when I learned that I wanted to be a computer engineer. I was surrounded by computer scientists in my family. My dad was a director of a very large computer department in Belarus [Republic of Belarus], where I originally came from, for the polytechnic academy, running basically huge mainframes, calculating salaries for every state employee in Belarus. They bought IBM mainframes and then disassembled them and created Russian versions of those mainframes. This was a very popular approach to technology back in those days because America was decades ahead of Russia. The approach was very useful because it gave me an ability to see legacy systems in America, where these systems were already replaced by more advanced technologies. I learned mainframes when I saw how they used them. It was exciting when you were a kid to see punch cards, large tapes, etc. I was actually allowed to play on secondary backup mainframe, each taking two floors, each being, 20 to 30 ton humongous machines. On the secondary mainframes I was allowed to change tapes, I was allowed to punch punch-cards and use the long tapes. So that's how I got my hands-on experience. At the same time my mom was running a PC lab because PCs were coming to Russia. And, once again, they took a Swedish version of a PC and disassembled it and created the Russian version of the same machine. She ran the lab with all these PC computers for students from the polytechnic academy.

I had another friend who was the same age, very smart as well, and his mom worked at the same lab as a professor, too. We started building games together just for fun, simple little games using regular BASIC and Fortran under DOS [disk operating system]. So that's how I got into computers. I knew from a very early age that I needed to have a computer at home. I needed to disassemble it, re-assemble it, and install hard drives and other peripherals.

Education was very big in my family. I was pretty much forced to be very well educated in different areas, math, physics, chemistry, because for those who don't know, back in those days in Russia, if you don't have a good education, if you don't go into a college, you ended up in the army. You don't want to end up in the Russian army when you're 17 or 18. Basically, your career will be over. As a result, I had been taught to spend most of my time reading books on computers, and spent a lot of time doing math and physics. I got transferred to a special math school, when I was 14. That gave me a lot of good knowledge in computer science and math, and then we immigrated.

Prior to immigration, my family sent me to sports, but not regular sports, where it's just for fun. I was actually doing a professional sport. I was on a team that was trying to prepare us for the Junior Olympics. I qualified to be on the team and had the training sessions twice a day for about 8 years.

G. Donaldson: Which professional sport?

Cherches: Swimming. That taught me some very valuable lessons. I've learned how to handle stress. I've learned how to do multitasking, how to do time management, very, very important in swimming. I've learned how to be part of a team and at the same time being responsible for my own actions.

I think that my journey toward who I have become, was mostly due to sports and to my coach, who was very tough, as most coaches are, especially when you are trying to train as a professional athlete, where the government actually spends a lot of money on you, sending you to special camps and spending all this money on flying you to different competitions.

So when we immigrated to the United States, my whole family moved. We had relatives here. We had lots of different reasons why we decided to emigrate. I went to University of Maryland, Baltimore County, UMBC, but as an immigrant, you need to work. So, I worked throughout college as a computer programmer, which was a big deal for my college friends because they were just starting programming. I already knew it and it was easy for me and that was part of the reason why I went through college in 3½ years, earning two degrees while working 35–40 hours a week. I did Computer Science and Economics because I still wasn't sure, believe it or not, whether I would end up being a true techie or I might end up going back to maybe Russia or some other country. I did economics because my grandma was a very good economist and she influenced me in this field.

I still wasn't 100% sure whether I would use all of my computer skills or whether I would use them 50-50. While in college I had been a programmer doing hardcore C, C++. I was working for a company called National Information Systems Corporation, NISC. They were building an Amazon type of engine for searching books for the educational community. They created some systems that were pretty famous and used by many students. For example, Medline is this huge medical database, 20 or 30 gigs in storage. Back in those days, hard drives of this size were humungous. So we wrote custom indexes and algorithms for how to access big data. They were very hardcore, complex problems.

Then I finished college and stayed with NISC. I was trying to help them launch a new product for searching books for the Spanish community. The product was called LEER, which is "to read" in Spanish. And that product was very successful. Then I was instrumental in launching an offshore initiative with NISC. In 1997-98, they hired about 15 or 20 developers in India back to solve very hardcore database problems. They also developed techniques to access massive arrays of indexes and books in milliseconds and do that for thousands and thousands of students in libraries at the same time.

S. Donaldson: So did you head up a team there or did you help identify the right skill set? What was your role in that effort?

Cherches: My role was to transfer knowledge from NISC USA to NISC India. Everything that we had been doing was proprietary. So that's when custom solution development got introduced first at NISC. Half of my goal was to work with a project manager over there, who hired very smart people. And then we would just be on the phone. Skype I guess didn't exist yet, but there was a time difference obviously, and it was challenging, mostly for them. I would work from 9 to 9 right next to another individual who was from India. Most of the internet programming knowledge I've learned I actually learned from that guy. He was just amazing. I was surrounded by people who were a lot smarter in large scale databases than I was, and my goal was to absorb as much as I could.

S. Donaldson: Effective communication during product development is difficult and with outsourcing it can be even more difficult. Were you involved in the requirements specification and were there problems communicating effectively?

Cherches: Yeah, definitely. The problem is you say one thing and you hope that they got it and then, two weeks later they deliver and it's not the right thing. We learned to avoid that very quickly.

S. Donaldson: How did you avoid the miscommunications?

Cherches: Off shoring is different—it's a very interesting subject by itself. We learned very quickly to tell them what they needed to do and then said, "Tell me, please, what you understand?" Then I would tell them, "This is what I think I understood of what you just told me." And definitely the culture thing was important and we got along very well. I spent about a year working with this team. Again, I was transferring knowledge to them so they could support us and do maintenance upgrades to the existing system.

S. Donaldson: From that experience, what was your next experience? How did you come to know this corporation?

Cherches: One of the gentlemen who I worked with joined Tom's company. Tom was known and is still known as a leader who surrounds himself with a lot of smart people. I think that approach is part of the success of Mind Over Machines. We are surrounded by lots of smart people—whether it's in management or down on the floor software developers, architects, business analysts. Tom hired this smart guy who was working with me to do re-indexing. At the time, he was the director of the custom software development that we were doing.

Loveland: And this guy, by the way, has a Ph.D in English literature.

S. Donaldson: That's an interesting point. One of the best computer programmers who I ever met had a degree in English. And when you think about it, programming, in part, is syntax and grammar. He was very articulate—it was just a different language.

Cherches: So this gentleman said, "I just joined this company and you have to meet Tom. You have to—you can't miss this opportunity here. We're still building up the company." He wanted me to be part of the growth. I trusted the guy and I interviewed with Tom, accepted a position and started by heading a little group of fellow developers.

From the very beginning of my career, I've been in charge of building custom software for large companies. After being a developer, I was involved with databases. I've been a DBA [data base administrator] for some large systems and security administrator. Then I got involved with hardware. For a while, like Tom said, we used to have a hardware division, which we later sold, but I was heading that division for a few years. I got experience in managing hardware, servers, and all that stuff. I think that going through all these different departments helped me become CTO. I learned throughout being hands-on; being able to do many different things like routers, voice over IP, switches, firewalls. But, then at the same time, working with developers provides additional hands-on experience.

S. Donaldson: Learn by doing.

G. Donaldson: You both did. Tom was on a journey of discovery and self-teaching. You had a very focused career from the get go, yet you both share the passion of learning by doing, and succeeding by doing.

Given what you have described as your technical journey thus far, what is your role now as the CTO here in the company?

Cherches: I'm a CTO for a technology company, which is a little different from what most CTOs have to deal with. My clients—the ones I build systems for—are technology people. They are techies and they're tough, as you can imagine. They know what they want. They know the technology very well. Some of them want cutting-edge, some of them want very standard, established systems. So it's very tough to be a CTO for a technology consulting firm. My sensibility is to make sure that they get what they want, what they need.

Many of our customers also want us to host the systems that we build for them. We don't seek this business, but customers are so comfortable with what we do, they often want us to handle the systems that we build for them. And so we manage some hosting. I am responsible for these systems with 24/7 production support.

I'm also responsible for Mind Over Machines' infrastructure and vendor management, servers, workstations, routers, voice over IP, switches, firewalls, security and databases. In addition, I'm responsible for the company's vision in terms of technology, the tools that we need to use, and the tools that our developers need to be excellent at in order to support our customers.

S. Donaldson: How do you keep up with technology for your customers and for the company?

Cherches: We have a very healthy combination of government versus commercial business. Government technologies and commercial are very different. And as a result, we need to be good in both.

G. Donaldson: What is the difference that you notice?

Cherches: Government wants risk mitigation and very established enterprise systems. Initial cost is less of an issue, but they are focused on total cost of ownership. What will the system cost in maintenance? How well can we integrate this system with other vendors? The government is very focused. They will tell you exactly what they want.

With the commercial clients, they often say, "This is our vision. This is what we think we need, but how do we get there? What kind of technology do we need? Tell us what risks we will run into. What are the pros of open source versus proprietary systems from a particular vendor?" We need to walk them through these questions.

S. Donaldson: Do you see a trend of people using more out-of-the-box solutions, less custom software, or in the government, for example, maybe more custom than the commercial or is it the other way around?

Cherches: We constantly hear how one day it will all change and the customers will take commercial off-the-shelf products and start customizing them without any programming knowledge. And in some areas, it's true. Nobody now writes CRM (customer relationship management) packages, nobody now writes accounting, ERP (enterprise resource planning) systems, but believe it or not, most customers that we work with—and they are large, established businesses—still realize that it will cost them a lot more in the long-term to customize something that is not designed for them. They'll get 80% off-the-shelf, but the last 20% is going to cost them so much and they'll be forced to upgrade with whatever the vendor is dictating. There are some risks associated with going with the 80-20 rule.

S. Donaldson: Don't they have to live with the business rule that's encoded in the product, as opposed to live with their business rules which are more efficient?

Cherches: Exactly, so a lot of IT executives want to be able to control their destiny. When they hire us, they want to ensure that the software we write for them will work for 10, 15 years with some additional minor patches. But they don't want to be controlled by a commercial vendor who can go out of business, can be purchased, merged, acquired, situations like that.

Siegel: So given what you just said, how does the rush to cloud computing influence how you handle your customers?

Cherches: Cloud computing is a very big, emerging technology right now. In the old days, literally five years ago, I would say to someone, "It will take us two weeks, three weeks, or even a month to get the new server from the manufacturer, then configure the system, then patch it, then provision it on a network, then..." Customers (and our internal developers) won't take that answer anymore. They want something in days at most.

Virtualization and cloud computing are important technologies. Customers still want custom solutions, but that custom solution can now live in the cloud. If they are very successful, they can scale the solution quickly. It is a bit easier for us to develop something designed for a small system. With cloud computing, it doesn't matter if you design for small or large scale. You don't necessarily need to customize your system to be able to handle a large load. Scaling comes with the cloud platform. The moment you're successful, the solution can scale. And that's a huge cost saving to a potential customer. Being able to scale up, being able to provision new environments quickly, literally in minutes, being able to save money by not installing a particular software product on a particular platform—all very important capabilities. If somebody says, " I need this particular version," there's a good chance I can go to a cloud provider, and pick the instance that they already have configured for me, secured for me, and, as a result cloud will save me a lot of time. You just buy the instance, you ring it up, you pay for usage, for CPU, and for storage and you can very quickly provision new environments.

G. Donaldson: So you help your customers think that process through?

Cherches: Yes, and again, most of the large enterprises still want to stay away from the cloud, especially if it's government. It's a big subject for the government, whether they want to live in the cloud or not. I know fellow CTOs who are actually running data centers and they are, in fact, bringing up some private clouds for some government agencies. So it's happening. We're not going to be able to reverse it. Cloud is here to stay. For developers, it's exciting because they can provision development instances very quickly. When they develop, they can create multiple computer instances to simulate true application isolations, focusing on developing a system without ever worrying if it has any true hidden dependences or if the solution will be able to scale up.

G. Donaldson: So part of your role is to help them think that through and do you help them cost-out that investment yourself or how does that work?

Cherches: For a few clients, yes. They will ask questions like, "Should I consider cloud? Should I do it internally or with you?" We can definitely help our clients think through those cloud options. Again, for most well-established businesses it's still very early for them to worry about moving production to the cloud because of dependences on their existing legacy systems. Currently, many established businesses say to us that they need to develop this brand new system and host it internally, but enable enough hooks to transfer it to the cloud in the future. We help them with evaluating risks. Putting stuff in the cloud is not rocket science. It's not very complicated.

Loveland: There are times we've had clients come in and say, "We want to be in the cloud." That's when we said back then, "It doesn't make sense to do it."

Siegel: How much experience do you have going into a company and saying, "Well, we think you need to replace your desktop computers with virtual computers"?

Cherches: Well, I just helped my friend in the process of creating a startup and he runs it completely in the cloud. He wanted to have a zero dependency on a local office. He doesn't have an office yet. The idea is that he wanted to have a CRM in the cloud, mail in the cloud and desktops in the cloud. As a startup with minimal or no revenue, there is no serious reason for you to have a physical environment, worrying about switches, worrying about routers and firewalls. When you're an established business and you're fairly large, there's no way yet to be completely in the cloud 100%. For a startup, the cloud makes sense. I personally helped a few startup companies establish themselves completely in the cloud. When I say "completely," I mean virtual desktops, email, local storage and all the types of business apps.

S. Donaldson: Payroll?

Cherches: Yes.

Siegel: So getting back to Scott's question, how are you keeping up on the changes that are occurring now? What was the spark that got you into that domain?

Cherches: I'm a hands-on CTO and I take it seriously because in this industry you can get rusty quickly. Literally within two years or so, the technology changes so much that if you don't keep up, you'll be in trouble if you want to stay hands-on. I read a lot, a few hours every day. I have to keep up.

I visit the job posts sometimes for large companies—Facebook, Google—to see what kind of technology they're hiring. Here's a little secret for CTOs: if you want to know what your competition is doing, if you want to know what's emerging and what's well established, then go and look at who they are hiring, especially those companies that you trust.

I spend a lot of time doing web seminars. I also surround myself with people who can help me. In the old days, I would literally spend hours on a daily basis, trying to track down every new product that comes out, any new version that comes out because you need to be up to a certain latest and greatest patch. But lately, in a given day, there are probably at least 100 startups producing new products every day, hundreds and hundreds of new updates and new patches. So you need to come up with a good filter on how you're going to keep current. There are a number of IT sites that will show you the top 15-20 IT news stories. You don't need to learn about every new startup or about every new open source company that opens up. In the old days, believe it or not, I actually tried that.

Siegel: Does your relationship with Tom, does it include, "Tom, I think we need to look into this technology domain?" or does it go in reverse? He'll tell you, "I think you need to look into this technology domain?" How does that work?

Cherches: I think it's both. Tom, believe it or not, emails me saying, "I know you know it, but, hey, I like it," and that gives me incentive to go out and research it more. So when Tom runs into something that he sees as a cool thing to learn internally because we can sell it to our clients, he tells me. I get this weekly; sometimes more often than I want! [Laughter]

The next step after we identify something cool, we need to look at the ROI [return on investment]. We need to see if it's something that we need to learn internally so that we can become experts and then later on introduce it to our clients. If it's something that we're never going to use, I'm just going to hire a vendor. For example, I don't need to be an expert in voice over IP. I don't need to be an expert in external penetration testing and security.

Siegel: So, as part of your job, you have to give Tom the ROI?

Cherches: I actually report to a CFO and now COO, but I for a long time was reporting to the CFO. Part of any new initiatives that we do internally is to talk to the CFO about ROI, which includes not just the upfront cost but costs of ownership, long-term maintenance costs and how easily we can replace it in the future. There is a little secret in IT, everything changes at a fairly fast pace. When you need to learn something, you already need to worry about how you're going to retire it. We talk about all these factors and in the end the COO says, "Can we sell it to the client?" If it's not a technology's we're going to learn internally, or can't necessarily sell, there's a big chance the COO is going to outsource it and hire the vendor to do it for us.

G. Donaldson: This is a good time to discuss about how Dmitry works collaboratively with Rick, Joe and Tom as a team.

Loveland: To start the discussion I'd like to talk to the world about what we do. I think of what we do as three "Olympic" rings or circles. These are the three areas of focus that we referred to earlier on. The top one is basically strategy. What's the strategy of the organization? Where are they going, what are they trying to achieve? And our story is that if you don't know where you're going and you're launching some venture, well, you're probably going to fail. You might get somewhere, but you've really got to figure out your strategy, so we ask those questions. Then let's say you get the strategy figured out; you make a pretty good guess at where you need to go and you start heading down that path and build an integrated system of some kind. If it ends up being a system that nobody really wants to use or it's hard to use, you're probably going to fail. You really need to pay attention to user-experience design, the second circle. The third circle is technology. If you know where you're going and you got that right, and the people like using the system, and holy cow, you're successful, but you built it with toothpicks and the thing falls over or collapses on itself, or you can't enhance it or whatever—you fail. So you've got to have solid technology as well. You need all three circles.

Joe Natoli: If you give any one of those three areas short shrift, you fail on some level. And what happens is, whatever it is that you're building—or providing or guiding somebody through—fails to provide value for the client's organization and its customers.

Loveland: Rick, Joe and Dmitry are like physical embodiments of those circles, and when they go in front of clients, the clients see these guys embodying the philosophy I just talked about and they see the chemistry and the light in this organization going on, and it's like, "Holy cow. This is great." So Rick represents the top circle of strategy and analysis, and Joe represents the user experience, the human side of things. And Dmitry represents the technology, making sure it's there, it's solid.

G. Donaldson: Tom, that's very well-put; it frames it very well. So let's go over some examples of how this actually plays out via Dmitry's hands-on CTO role.

Cherches: We have a variety of different clients and often what happens is a client wants to open a new line of business or build a new product. This situation is very complex. In building a new product, you need to know what you're doing. We've been in business for 20 years and we've had to learn how to build a good product so that the customers later on call you to upgrade or support or to call you again for another new product. Joe mentioned that the reason for success is that when we approach the problem, it's going to be about strategy: What will it take to deliver it? What are the risks? —being a good consultant. And that's where Rick comes in. Rick's background expertise is building large systems for financial companies, for insurance companies, for a variety of industries. And being able to work with developers and know the whole development life cycle, what it takes to develop a new product. Then Joe comes in from a usability point of view. It is a science. You didn't learn about usability in US colleges. They were not teaching you user experience and what it takes to develop a new good product. After using Apple for a while I kind of knew about innovative interfaces and what it takes to build an intuitive product, but then Joe proved to me that it's essential. You can't build a good product, especially if it's consumed by hundreds of thousands of people without a human interface. It's a science.

G. Donaldson: Well, can we walk through step-by-step? Does it begin with Rick meeting with the customer?

Rick Mosca: I think so. It's all about corporate strategy and position in the industry, right? You need to be able to understand where that client is positioned on a bunch of different levels: where they are currently in the marketplace, where they want to go in the marketplace, how they want to present themselves or project themselves in the marketplace, not just from a business perspective but certainly from a technical perspective. Quite often the technology's actually the easy part. You need to be able to figure out the social and political aspects internally with the people that you're talking to. How are they trying to further the business, their organization, their product, and their standing in their particular industry? But it's also important to recognize and understand the individual that you're interacting with and how that individual is going to benefit by the success of any particular engagement that's going on.

G. Donaldson: When do your respective roles enter the picture to work with the customer?

Mosca: When it is a technical sale, it's a technical relationship, so we tend to get involved very early in the cycle.

G. Donaldson: Do you go as a team and meet with the customer?

Mosca: Eventually, we will come in as a team. I will typically go in first, but in some situations, it depends on the intel that I've been given about the particular engagement or about the particular client. It may be two of us. Quite often it's all three of us.

G. Donaldson: Well, can we walk through a real case? Do you have a company in which you all work together?

Mosca: A top fulfillment house in the area that services many of the top financial services firms is an example. They are the back-end physical distributor of all the financial performance materials that show up at your house. They were faced with a crossroads in their development as an organization to be able to take the paper-based, US Mail delivery and make it electronic. It's one of those obvious things; why hasn't someone done it before? But the transformational idea that we've helped them envision and then ultimately build for them is to transform that whole experience of a 401K, a fund prospectus, any kind of portfolio evaluation performance updates, and all of that material that we all get in the mail.

The simple use-case that we talked about often is that when someone first joins an organization and you're there for a short period of time, now you have the opportunity to join the 401K program and you have to fill out the 401K enrollment booklet. Ultimately, you have information about the funds, the mutual funds that you're able to select, sign up, for an enrollment beneficiary, rollover, those kinds of things. Well, the idea was to make whole experience electronic. We first got introduced by way of Joe and the user-experience expertise that he brings to the table and the connection that he had inside the company. Why don't you take over, and I'll jump back in?

Natoli: Here's essentially what happened. I ran my own firm for 10 years and a very good friend of mine who also was my partner for five of those years, called me on Friday and said, "We're trying to take a leap forward and develop this new product. We've got market demand. Our customers are saying to us, 'You guys need to be more innovative. We've got a company we're ready to contract, but I asked everyone here to wait until we talked to you.'" This is a $2.4 billion organization. They talked to other consultants but didn't have any confidence they could do the job, so our company was approached. He told us that we needed to get their staff in the room and, and talk. They knew they had to have the user-experience part on the innovation side. "Innovation" is a term that gets bandied about a lot, but what it really means is solving problems the company doesn't know it has through strategic design. We've got to identify those areas and deliver on them. They couldn't afford to get this wrong. The company also knew that this was a huge technological undertaking. They needed some folks who really have some muscle in the area of technical discipline, enterprise-level knowledge and user-experience expertise. The company wanted to decide which contractor to hire in less than a week.

We called a team meeting on a Friday to put together a presentation for Monday. We essentially sat around this table just like we are now, talking about the sort of three ways to approach this, and nicely, you know, it goes back to the three circles, right? There's a hardcore strategic part to this. There's a hardcore user-experience part to this. There's a hardcore technological part to this.

On Monday we presented our understanding of their situation and discussed how we could address what they needed. Rick went first, Dmitry went next, and I went last. And we each approached what we knew about their problem.

The customer was telling us they needed to maintain their position as the market leader, and this particular problem would pose an existential crisis for the organization if not resolved.

They're at a real pivotal point, so it'd be easy to go in and scare them with 'what if' scenarios. But instead, we approach it like a working session, not a pitch. We go in there and talk facts, "Well, from this side, you need to do X. From this aspect, it's probably Y. From another aspect, it's probably Z."

G. Donaldson: Those aspects are based on the three circles: strategy, technology and user-experience?

Natoli: Yeah, and essentially the reason we got the work is because they felt like we had a lot of cross-disciplinary expertise in all those areas, that all these areas worked together collaboratively and that we had an equal degree of strength in all those areas. And those are their words, not ours.

Siegel: And you got the work on Tuesday?

Natoli: Yes, with one conversation.

Mosca: In the room on their side, they had the primary business owner, but also the primary technology owner as well and so you had to sort of get both of those people comfortable. They both had different aspects of what was going on. There was some experience between the two that were in some ways positive but in some ways not so positive, and for them to take that leap in bringing a firm in, it's one of those steady hand and confidence-building exercises that you have to go through pretty quickly. But then the combination of being able to bring to bear enterprise architecture, software architecture, as well as user experience and application development; that combination is not completely unique, but it's relatively unique in our space, and we'd better be able to project that with a high degree of confidence.

S. Donaldson: Yes, solving problems is more than technology.

Natoli: Yeah, you have multiple players doing things together that each couldn't do alone. I think what's important there is that this gentleman sitting on my left, Rick, is no stranger to innovative product development. There's a lot of confidence I think generated as well that this path, again, in all three areas, is one we've been down before. This is not new because it's where we all live, so to speak.

S. Donaldson: So I understand the strategy kind of going first, getting the owners, but then why was technology second?

Mosca: Why was technology second in the presentation? Because I guess as we went in there, we felt as though—it was a huge business play that they were undertaking and they were putting chips in the middle of the table. There's certainly a big technology element to it, but, I think the real overriding factor was the combination of the two. I don't think it was really so much who went second and who went third. It was sort of the combination of the complete package that we rolled before them.

Natoli: I think it wasn't necessarily ordered, more that the flow came from the way that we talked about their situation. But by having the user experience part last, it sort of takes those other two things and ties them together because what they were talking about is a consumer-facing application, a consumer-facing system. At the end of the day, what a user sees and manipulates onscreen is the delivery vehicle for all of those strategic and technological decisions. So I think to us, it just sort of made sense that way.

S. Donaldson: And it goes back to what Tom said, it's that you've got to know where you're going strategically. You've got to be able to have the technology to get you there, but you've got to have the experience to make it easy to use all this stuff, to get there.

Cherches: Technology is always second. That's one of the primary reasons why Rick went first and discussed the ability to build a new product and build it around various risks. We had to describe how our developers will work with their team. What will be the process? What will be the software methodology? And then technology comes second, always. Whether it's internal or external with the clients, we first discuss the business goal, what we need to achieve, and then technology is secondary.

G. Donaldson: Part of that meeting was for you to help them think these three things through, and they gave you the go ahead to move forward. You established yourself as a trusted advisor and resource to help them improve their strategic position.

Natoli: We go in and we have conversations and discuss what really is happening, and Tom alluded to this earlier, it takes the three circles to uncover the true nature, depth and breadth of the problem. It's my favorite thing. You're essentially asking one question—why? —in all three layers. Why are you doing this? What do you want out of it? Instead of us coming in with a dog and pony show and saying, "Well, okay, we could do this, we could do this, we could do this. It could look like this and act like this and this," it doesn't matter. What are you trying to accomplish?

Cherches: They described what they wanted out of the system in terms of innovation, user experience, and IT technology. Then, we have to prove that we can do it. So how do you prove it? We had to describe and show what we've done in the past for other customers. The biggest thing is being able to project confidence and demonstrate that you can do it and you've done it in the past. It's all about trust.

Loveland: A measure of success I want to point out is that often when a CTO or somebody like us walks into an organization that already has an IT group; we could be seen as a threat or an annoyance or whatever. Well, the IT division of this company has since, a couple of times, brought our team into other projects. They brought us into one project to help them land a marquee client because they knew we could add value, so I see that as a success. Rick and the team have done a fabulous job at negotiating the politics and so forth.

S. Donaldson: You're an extension of their company. You represent them.

Loveland: Yes. The champion of this project absolutely trusts and respects us and the IT department also respects us and trusts us.

G. Donaldson: So you get the work and now you follow up with actually doing the work. And what did you do as CTO in actually doing the work?

Cherches: We had to work with their IT and it's a big organization. They wanted us to build a prototype and work with their offshore team. So we had to figure out what our developers needed to be successful with this project, what our technology platform needed to look like, what kind of tools we needed. Then, we had to figure out how we are going to be interacting with their enterprise systems and their developers.

G. Donaldson: How did you do that?

Cherches: We had to bring stakeholders together and discuss how we were going to do it. Very often we develop using their standards. It's a financial organization. It has to be all FINRA-compliant.

Loveland: You spent time over there. Dmitry, in particular, spent a lot of time over there looking at their current infrastructure and processes. How does all this stuff work? What's it built on and what's the process?

S. Donaldson: So you're dealing with the IT shops. Did they have a life cycle or did you have to come up with a blended life cycle to help march through the development process? How did that work? Plus you've got the overseas aspect.

Mosca: They had some sort of a life cycle, but they really weren't in the business of building a bunch of new products. When they got a new client, they actually would instantiate a whole new environment that was a duplicate of a current environment. The whole idea of starting with requirements and going through a development life cycle was not something that they were really all that familiar with. They really looked to us to guide them through that process. We started out with a functional prototype. It was far more than just wireframes. It certainly told a good story about how it was going to be. In fact, the end system changed a good deal after the prototype because it got the feedback and the reaction.

S. Donaldson: You know what you want once you've seen it.

Mosca: Yeah, and they were able to put it right in front of sample user groups to get feedback.

G. Donaldson: So was agile development involved in this?

Cherches: Yes. The solution evolved through iterative prototyping and incremental requirements with the initial external vendors not being identified for the final build. I was involved in helping them pick a few vendors for the particular feature that they wanted. It was a page-flipping technology.

Natoli: There was some fancy page-flipping catalog technology, which we didn't build.

Cherches: The architecture was designed so that if they decide to change any kind of a layer, they can. If they decide to switch to a different presentation layer, they will be able to because it's all XML-based. Presentation is just a simple part of it.

G. Donaldson: So as part of your hands-on involvement, you helped them think through technology-related considerations.

Cherches: Yes, I also helped them mitigate risks, comprehend a particular technology and understand the licensing.

Loveland: Dmitry, talk a little bit about the back-end component and the integration because that's a really key part.

Cherches: Sure. A new product, in a large organization, especially if it's a multibillion-dollar organization, needs to integrate in the least painful way.

G. Donaldson: And that integration is part of what you did?

Cherches: Yes. They had a very complex ordering system. Once you get enrolled, a lot of business triggers happened at the back end. We had to figure out how to minimize integration points and how to minimize changes they had to do to the existing system. As I discussed before, changing existing systems is costly and not desired. So, we tried to architect the new ordering workflows relying on the dynamic attributes which their existing system could handle without any major adjustments.

G. Donaldson: So would you develop those ideas separately and then present to them for reaction or did you, as part of the development process, collaborate with them to come up with this approach?

Cherches: We collaborated with them in this room and on this whiteboard. We got a bunch of smart people in the room at the same time to work the technology problems—it's not just Dmitry. It's a whole bunch of architects, business analysts, developers and project managers sitting together and trying to draw the architecture.

G. Donaldson: From your company and from your customer?

Cherches: Initially, it's just internal people. We make sure we're on the same page. We talk about risks and how we're going to present the solution to the customer. And then, of course, the customer got in the room to collaborate. One of the work products is a huge diagram that is in my office and it will show you the complexity of the system.

Natoli: I think we had paper stuck on every available surface. It was all over the full wall and the whiteboard here.

G. Donaldson: Well, there's a lot of depth and angles to go over when you are working with your customer. We won't be able to cover all of that today. I want to go back to that word "innovation" because that is a word that you feature in your company. Joe defined it a certain way, which was to get things—it does what it was supposed to do.

Natoli: Well, innovating to me is delivering something that exceeds expectations, because as I said before you're solving problems people may not realize they have. Innovating to me is really about what happens on the receiving end. We can say that our technology is innovative. That's one thing to say, "This is a scientific breakthrough or a mathematical breakthrough," or something like that. I'm certainly not giving any of that short shrift. But what innovation is to me—and these guys can certainly weigh in—from an industry perspective, is when you put something out there—the reaction you get or the value derived from it is off the chart—that's what innovation is. It's doing something which jives with what our mission is. It's doing something that's smarter and better and more efficient than anyone on either side ever thought possible.

G. Donaldson: I've frequently heard the words "user adoption" associated with the word "innovation" as well. It's one thing to have a good idea or a clever solution, but if it isn't adopted, then it hasn't innovated and changed the way business is done.

Natoli: Well, that's my motto all the time. If you deliver this thing that everybody in this room thinks is amazing, but no one uses it, who cares? If you're first to market but no one wants or needs what you have, what's the point?

G. Donaldson: Dmitry, how do you define innovation as the chief technology officer?

Cherches: Well, the CTO has to be very innovative. An innovative CTO needs to figure out how to use technology in order to do two things: either bring more revenue or cut costs. Typically, these are the two most important things that technology can solve for business. At the end, IT can cut costs by automating things, by making people more productive from using better products and tools. In addition, technology needs to contribute to additional revenue. The CTO needs to work with marketing departments, work with other business executives who are trying to launch a new business line or launch a new initiative.

G. Donaldson: And so as the CTO, you're helping them keep focus on that, not just the technology, but the return on that investment in order to increase revenue and decrease costs or some combination of that?

Cherches: Yeah.

G. Donaldson: What about the degrees of change in innovation? What would be the difference between fine-tuning something—is that innovation? Or does innovation represent a more transformative way of conducting business for the company that technology helps enable?

Cherches: I would define innovation as something that most people wouldn't think about; you come up with a product or you come up with a feature, a tool that just wows the client. You know, it's a wow factor. They would never have considered it. It could become a game-changer. That's being innovative. We have lots of examples. We developed products for our clients where their competitors couldn't figure out for years how we were doing it.

G. Donaldson: Did you design the platform or tailor an existing platform?

Cherches: For example, we built an application which scraped public data from the web and then massaged that data in such a way as to bring more business. We had to mash together multiple unrelated databases into one relational coherent data structure. Our client's competitors were trying to figure out where our client is getting that information? What kind of database were we using to target specific clients? But, again, the idea came from us. We implemented it, the ROI was amazing and the application was extremely innovative.

S. Donaldson: Let's switch topics just a little bit. With everybody being mobile today and needing to have access wherever they are, do you see mobile computing and social networking showing up in your client mix yet?

Natoli: I think to the degree that it makes sense, yes. I'll be honest with you. You want to say, "Everything's mobile"—and almost everything we build has a mobile component to it because it's becoming part of the cost of admission, so you do have to present it as an option. I think for us, though, it's about making sure that mobile decision is a smart one for the client. If they're going to spend X amount of money with us and they expect to get a return on that investment, we want to make sure there's actually a chance of that happening. So sometimes a heavy investment in mobile can pay off tremendously. But other times it doesn't. It really depends on the user base, what they want and will use on a mobile phone. Social networking to me is the same thing. It's great, it's amazing, and it's capable of wonderful things. But you have to be very careful about how many eggs you put in that basket and what you expect in return.

S. Donaldson: Well, I guess some of this is tied to the workforce change that we're seeing with the younger generation.

Natoli: Absolutely.

S. Donaldson: With the way they approach programming, they go get 20 apps that already exist and knit them together to come up with an innovative way to present information—and they are a sophomore in high school. [Laughter.]

Cherches: Most CTOs will tell you they hate these changes where they now have to worry about social networks and media compliance, about data flowing out of corporations, about partitions being installed, and things that happen that accidentally tell competitors what you're working on. It's a big subject in the enterprise now, in the business world, but most clients still— when we develop products, they want web-enabled, mobile-enabled solutions. They don't necessarily need to build it yet, but they just tell you they need it in the future. For example, they tell you, "Oh, and while you build the full system that we actually need and will use now, can you make sure that in the future we can run a lighter version of this application on a mobile device? Not now, because our clients are not ready. Make sure that your architecture can support it." And once you hear that, you will design the architecture where the user presentation is abstract enough and can be driven by multiple presentation layers, including mobile.

Natoli: That's absolutely right. We had a conversation with a large client last week about an intranet and about a client-facing extranet, and then there's a public website. There are pieces of all these things that certainly have a place on a mobile device that would be useful because people are using these products, but certainly not every part of each product. And there are some things you're simply not going to do on a small screen with tiny buttons.

Mosca: So sometimes they just want it to put a check in the box to tell the customers that they have it. If they want to be able to go out to clients and say, "Yes, we can run on mobile devices, we have that," in some cases, it does not make any sense. However, some clients want to say that's a capability that they have, so we have to include that as part of the software architecture that we roll out for them.

G. Donaldson: As part of your strategy involvement, do you help them think that through, how they're positioning themselves?

Mosca: Absolutely. That is one of the most important areas where we can add value. To be able to wade through all of the technology hype and shiny objects and get to where they will receive a maximum return on the investment.

G. Donaldson: So from your three perspectives, is that where you work together as a team to think that through to present a unified solution?

Mosca: Yes. There is a lot in all three fronts.

Cherches: We tell the story and the client makes the decision, obviously, on what we tell them.

Mosca: But is it technical capability? Yes. Can it be built in a manner that can be displayed and useful on a small form factor? Yes, if, in fact, the strategy is to be smart about what you're going to present at that point.

G. Donaldson: As CTO, what do you see are transformative and emerging technologies that need to be tracked?

Cherches: Definitely cloud, definitely virtualization. It's now part of the enterprise, and if you don't have it, you'd better do it now because it cuts costs and makes IT very flexible. Another one is the ability to handle large data. A lot of companies are going to be facing issues regarding enormous amounts of data, how to present it, and how to create business intelligence solutions out of it. There are not a lot of standards yet how to handle these petabytes of data, how to access it in an optimal, cost effective way. There are some open source applications to manage big data, and some very well-known large companies are starting to support those standards.

S. Donaldson: How about cyber security?

Cherches: Cyber security—well, that's a big subject. I always talk about one day walking into the office and everything is wiped out. A new, unknown threat, often called zero-day attack, may come out and computers will be wiped out. So, you need to have a good data recovery strategy in cyber security. Hire a good expert. Hire a company that can do penetration testing for you and can just come from outside and the inside and then report you their concerns.

S. Donaldson: How do you handle technology investments for your own company?

Cherches: What we try to do is to find at least three different vendors to try to present their solution. I try to make them do the research for me. You can Google and you can try and learn, but my advice is always to call them and they'll go above and beyond to help you with your research. Saves time and human capital.

S. Donaldson: Do you have a procurement shop that helps do that for you and then you guys take a look at that?

Cherches: We do it internally and then there are three or four people who get involved in vendor selection. I interview at least three vendors. Like I said before, if we are buying a product internally, which will also become part of our future solution to a customer; we learn how to support it internally. But if it's not, we are just going to buy and outsource the support to the vendor. That's part of the ROI that I'm looking for. Also, I consider the long-term costs, what will it take to maintain it, what are the true license costs, compliance costs? How easy will it be to retire in the future?

G. Donaldson: How do you help identify the ROI metrics that your customers use?

Cherches: If it's a new product that we built for them and it brings new business, that's an easy one. You run a report, you know the cost that they spent on us, you help them project cost of supporting the product, maintenance cost, and you calculate ROI. It translates into dollars. There are a lot of people who joke I see the world in green, not just technology. [Laughter]

If you're trying to cut costs and be efficient, that gets a little more complex. Typically, we don't necessarily get involved in that. Clients tell us, "Please automate this part of the process," and then we'll calculate ROI.

G. Donaldson: Do you have a formal process that you follow for calculating whether or not to go in with a certain investment or not? Do you have an IT investment management process?

Cherches: I do it on paper because I have an economics background and I know what we need for the investment to be acceptable. And, of course, our CFO helps me figure out the total cost of human capital and what we will save.

Mosca: And in our place, there's always sort of two answers because we're a little different from a consulting perspective than the other folks you're talking about. From our perspective, when we're faced with a new technology or we feel like a client is pulling for a particular technology, we have to make the decision internally whether that's a good technology that we're going to invest in as an organization, that's going to have legs going forward.

G. Donaldson: That's a very good point.

Mosca: Because it could be good for that individual company, for reasons that make sense to them, but it might not make sense to us because of the human capital that we would have to invest in training and making sure that we have critical mass to support, not just for that client, but is there a market beyond that one client that makes sense to invest in?

G. Donaldson: So as the CTO, you're involved in taking a look at what markets to be in, what customer niches you're going for, and that sort of thing?

Cherches: Absolutely.

G. Donaldson: Are you working on any big projects right now?

Cherches: The short answer is yes, absolutely. We have a few initiatives where we are trying to launch new product lines for our customers.

Mosca: I think that healthcare quality is an interesting story. Think of an organization that is a combination of the Good Housekeeping Seal of Approval and Consumer Reports Top 10. It's really their place in the industry to be evaluating health care and providers of healthcare services across the country. Their business, so to speak, is a bunch of statisticians, healthcare industry experts, actuaries, those kinds of people who cull through and come up with interesting calculations that they can perform for healthcare provider data that they're bringing in from all over the country. They currently do it all in SAS (Statistical Analysis System). It's a complete mess. There is no master data management strategy. There's really even no great data warehouse. There certainly aren't any data definitions and there's a language and a vernacular that's well used and well understood across the organization within different companies.

So imagine the amount of data that's coming into said organization from all the healthcare providers across the country in sort of a uniform format, not necessarily, but that's not the interesting part. Really, what we call the data factory: to be able to bring in all this data, go through ETL (extraction, translation, load) processes, ultimately load the data into a data warehouse and queue with master data management, where there are aliases for definitions of the data, what that data is. There's a very strict governance process on the calculations that get applied to different data sets and ultimately produce the user reports.

Siegel: So, just to follow up on that. Are you guys in the role of establishing a data dictionary for all that or is that something you hand off to someone else?

Mosca: We are involved with the data dictionary, master data management, all of the attributes as well. Yeah, it's ultimately going to be a large business intelligence initiative.

Siegel: Okay. So you're hired in this case to get down to the blade-of-grass level.

Mosca: Absolutely.

G. Donaldson: Dmitry, what do you see as some of the important issues confronting your industry today from a technology perspective?

Cherches: Security and hacking are going to become more of a daily normal event. Unfortunately, many still believe that it's a lot easier to steal versus innovate. So, the CTO is responsible for making sure data is protected and mobile devices are not creating a threat. Being able to manage data and doing a lot of business intelligence from the data. That area is starting to become fairly standard. The technology is fairly affordable and if you don't have good KPI's (Key Performance Indicators), if you don't have good alerts that you can deliver to business stakeholders, you need to look into it ASAP. There's a big chance that a business executive wants to know when on this particular day some indicator is not right. These tools are now emerging and affordable for companies of any size. Before it was extremely complex and it required a lot of custom solutions.

G. Donaldson: How do you see the role of chief technology officer changing over time?

Cherches: It will probably become more complex. You have to be hands-on more and more and be able to deal with all kinds of technologies. Ten years ago there were maybe 20 vendors that I had to track. Now it's hundreds and hundreds. And for each vendor that comes up with an impressive product, you need to read, you need to know their strengths and weaknesses, you need to know their license model, and you need to know their pricing. That's the only way you could intelligently go about proposing to your prospects and also to your internal organization. It's going to get very, very complex, so the CTO needs to manage huge volumes of information

G. Donaldson: How are you handling those challenges?

Cherches: I'm a big believer in learning technology from YouTube. You'd be absolutely surprised what's available there. Almost every technology and its description are available on YouTube. It's also a good indicator that if you find some cool technology and there are only, say, five videos on YouTube—run away. You might have a chance to implement it now, but vendor support and a development community are not going to be available. If you see developers talking about a product, hosting videos on how to use it, that's a good indicator of a product we'll be looking at.

G. Donaldson: You know, there's a question that we like to wrap up with, and Scott you usually ask it.

S. Donaldson: So what keeps you up at night? What do you worry about day to day?

Cherches: Keeping up with all the new technologies and innovations, making sure our clients maintain their competitive advantage. Working with fresh technology on cool projects also means that we will be able to attract the best and the brightest, another big concern in the current IT market.

S. Donaldson: It's the lifeblood of the company.

Cherches: It's the lifeblood of the company.

G. Donaldson: We really appreciate you all taking the time today to share your thoughts.

Loveland: Thank you, we enjoyed it.

Darko Hrelic

Gartner, Inc.

Darko Hrelic is currently the Senior Vice President and Chief Information Officer (CIO) at Gartner, Inc., the premier IT research and advisory services company. He leads the Strategic Technology Group, ensuring that Gartner fully leverages the capabilities of technology to deliver exceptional value to clients, and further develops its technical infrastructure to support long-term corporate growth objectives.

Darko joined Gartner in January 2007 from ADP, where he led all aspects of ADP's client facing technical strategy, architecture and technology as VP and CTO of Employer Services. He played an instrumental role in driving the SOA (service-oriented architecture) vision and strategy, making legacy systems on-demand SOA capable, defining a successful implementation of an Enterprise Service Bus (ESB).

Prior to joining ADP, Darko spent over 21 years at IBM, most of which were at the TJ Watson Research Center, working in areas such as videotext, high speed communications, electronic commerce, among others. He also helped form the IBM Internet Division in the mid-1990s, where he spearheaded the technical strategy for ecommerce, also known as "eBusiness." In 2000, Darko was also a key technical driver in helping found e2open.com, a high-tech industry electronic marketplace consortium startup.

Darko holds a Master of Science degree in Computer Science from Stevens Institute of Technology, Hoboken, NJ.

Scott Donaldson: Let's begin with your journey to your position. Can you provide us with an overview of your professional background and how you landed where you are today?

Darko Hrelic: I have spent a lot of time in my career being very deep into technical issues and technology and across the board in the technology stack, from micro-code to operating systems to middleware and to applications. I've been fortunate in my 20-plus years at IBM to have had a chance to work in all of them in a very significant and deep way. That experience allowed me to really understand computing end-to-end. I always felt that whatever software stack layer you're working in, unless you understand what's happening at least one layer below you, you're at a disadvantage. So if you're in applications but you don't understand how middleware works, you're not going to build very good applications. And the same thing for the middleware layer and so on, so IBM was an outstanding place to give me that background and learning experience. For various reasons, I took my time over the years moving up. In the first 15 years of my career, I wasn't very ambitious. I just wasn't looking to move up. I can't claim that that was by design. It was just that I was interested in many other things, sports and things. I just enjoyed what I was doing. I mostly had fun. IBM Research, with its sandbox environment, was kind of hard to give up. But it turned out to be a tremendous asset and it really built a foundation for me as I progressed in my career. I spent five years as a CTO with ADP (Automatic Data Processing, Inc.) in their Employer Services division, the biggest part of their business. Then for the last five years here at Gartner.

Donaldson: During this journey, did you have mentors who became important in your life to help you navigate your journey to where you are?

Hrelic: Absolutely. I think it's critical to use other people as models, in good and bad ways. You see people do things and you think, "Nah, I don't think I want to do it that way," and you see people do things and you say, "How can I do that?" I've had many, many people along the way that I think are responsible for many of the things that I do today. So I think it's critically important to develop skills that way, and it's one of the things I wish we could do more of in my organization today.

Donaldson: If you had a lesson learned to pass on to those coming in the next generation, in the next wave, what might you tell them about taking their professional journey?

Hrelic: A big part of it, I truly believe, is to take your time. Don't be overly ambitious and try to get there before you're truly ready. Make sure that you do things that will get you ready. Too many people make the mistake of focusing on area A, whether it's a technology or business area, whatever it is, and then see this great job in area B and want to go for it. Hopefully, they don't get it, because they shouldn't get it. They've been in A. They should have been working and preparing themselves for B and they haven't. So think about what is it that's important to you and prepare yourself for the next position. That way, when you get there, you're likely to stay there—not just stay there, but stay there and advance from there.

Donaldson: Right. I understand in your position here at Gartner you have CTO responsibilities, CIO responsibilities, there's a blend. Could you tell us a little bit about your main responsibility and who reports to you and who do you report to?

Hrelic: Sure. I am responsible, essentially, for all technology at Gartner. That includes client-facing systems, both products and service- and support applications. That includes our back office function that is product-related, like authoring and publishing. A big part of our business is publishing research.

Donaldson: Okay.

Hrelic: It also includes all of our corporate business systems, CRM, HR, finance, and all of that. And it includes the data center. So those are the primary areas that report to me. I manage them as functional components, but given the business that we're in, they're all highly related. On one hand, they have very focused and well-defined areas that they need to work on. On the other hand, they reliably depend on each other. So everything runs in the data center, whether it's a product or whether it's an internal system. The test organization tests across all of the areas. Internal systems are key even to products from the perspective of the rights granted and what a user has acquired; what products do they have that they should be given access to on the front end? So all of these things are interconnected technically. It's critical that they work well together.

Donaldson: As much as you can have a typical day, what might a typical day look like for you? A lot of meetings? Meetings with vendors, customers? What's it look like?

Hrelic: Quite honestly, I keep my meetings with vendors to a minimum.

Donaldson: Right.

Hrelic: I meet with vendors, obviously, I have to. I meet with the biggest vendors that are critical to success either because things are working well and you want to keep them going well, or more often than not, things are not going well and we need to see what we can do to address them. But most of my time, I would say at least half, probably closer to 70%, is dealing with product-related issues, customer-related issues. Those are things that move the needle on the business side. It's the stuff that my boss, who's the CEO, cares about most. It's the stuff that my peers care most about. And I would be out of sync if I didn't also focus in those areas. So it's a lot of time just working and understanding both business and technical issues, but primarily technical as related to the business objectives.

Donaldson: It sounds like you spend a fair amount of your time customer facing and then maintaining internally as well.

Hrelic: That's right.

Donaldson: How do you see your role evolving over the next five years or so?

Hrelic: It's going to become mostly business-focused. In general, IT has tended to step back and let the business people handle issues and then wait for the order to come, so to speak, to IT or technology people. I think CIOs as CTOs are going to have to be as much business managers as they are technology managers. Clearly, in my opinion, job one is about managing technology and making sure that it's leveraged and its use is maximized to the advantage of the corporation. But it has to be in the context of the business. And because technology has been moving so fast and is becoming more and more complex, it's becoming harder and harder for business people to understand just how to best leverage it. What are the possibilities? So it's up to technology people to step up and proactively provide some of that leadership to the business people to show them what's possible, to show them that there are technology-enabled business opportunities. I think that's been going on for a few years. It's really nothing new, but I think it's accelerating.

Donaldson: Thanks. So with your other C-level peers in the corporation, how do you interact with them to help shape the strategy for the corporation to move to the next level?

Hrelic: I try to have a very close working relationship with my peers. There are about 14 of us, and in addition to regularly scheduled management meetings, we meet on an ad hoc, as-needed basis. Any one of them can walk into my office any time they feel like it, and the other way around. We all view ourselves as the number one team. So, for example, if you were to ask, "Well, who is your number one team?" too many managers make the mistake of saying, "Well, my organization is my number one team," or "The people who report to me are my number one team." No, they're actually my number two team. My number one team is the team of my peers. And that causes me to look and say, "Okay, what do I do to make that team successful?" Or, in effect, "What do I do to make my peers successful?" which means, literally, I'm saying, "What do I need to do to make the business successful?" It's difficult, but I talk to my organization the same way. I tell my direct reports, "I love you guys, but you're not my number one team. And you know something? Your number one team is not the people who report to you either. You, my team of direct reports, are the number one team for each of you." And so on and so on, right? I realize that it may almost look like it's a game, but it's just a completely different perspective. What's really, really important might be nuanced, but it's actually profound.

Donaldson: So on a day-to-day basis, weekly, monthly, what external organizations do you interact with? You know, professional associations, university affiliations, partnerships, and meetings that are important for you to help shape strategy?

Hrelic: That's probably an area right now that I feel the worst about. I do talk with universities. Do I give it the time that I'd like to? No, I just don't have it. Do I speak with those people anecdotally or at our conferences? Absolutely, but I would love to do a whole lot more in that area, and time is the only enemy to it.

Donaldson: Are you involved in any of the research parts of the Gartner business?

Hrelic: Yes and no. We obviously enable all the technology for the authoring process, and all that is quite extensive. From an actual content perspective, we do work with analysts, in both directions. One, when we look for technology we use our analysts, probably more than a typical client would. But the other way around is also true. The analysts often call us and say, "Have you guys deployed technology X and what's your experience?" So we give them our honest feedback. Do we write anything? No. We do try to separate the two areas of the business. And they stay very, very objective in what they do and how they do it—the process basically forces them to stay very objective. So obviously we honor that process and make sure that the objectivity is not compromised in any way.

Donaldson: Are you using new technology or technology in new ways, creative ways, to help the analyst do what they need to do?

Hrelic: We try. The difficulty with trying to use new technologies is that there's always another new technology and you haven't even really gotten juice out of the previous one. So, we look at things like mobile, and we look at things like social technologies to see how we can improve productivity and processes. It's a challenge. People change slowly, and so it's one of the biggest challenges in the corporate world. By the time you get going with something new, something else is almost around the corner.

Donaldson: Yeah, I guess one of the trends with the technology is with the new generation coming into the workforce; they're much more mobile.

Hrelic: True.

Donaldson: They all have their own iPads and their own iPhones. That situation creates its own unique set of challenges. What's your experience in dealing with that aspect of the technology?

Hrelic: We have embraced mobile in a big way since I came on the job about five years ago. Our workforce is unbelievably mobile. Analysts are from all over the world. Most travel at least 60% of the time. Obviously, between analysts, sales, and executive partners, they essentially work at the hotel room, the airplane or their home. So we do not buy desktops at all. Everything's laptop based. Mobile smartphone devices, we're very liberal on. All we care about is that a password is on a device and we can wipe it clean if it's lost or stolen, which means that essentially if we can connect to the device with ActiveSync or BlackBerry we will support it. We don't force people to use any one specific mobile device. I would say it's worked really well for us. We have VOIP [Voice over Internet Protocol] as a phone system, which essentially allows people to answer their office number via their PC, literally anywhere they are on the planet. So that aspect has worked well. From a business continuity perspective, knock wood, we are actually very, very flexible. We're not too concerned if something happens to an office somewhere—unless people are harmed, obviously. People can be very productive regardless of where they are.

Donaldson: Right. With respect to supporting the Gartner symposiums worldwide, mobile has an extended meaning for you in this case. So how do you support this global reach that you have?

Hrelic: It's a challenge, but it's a fun challenge and the team loves doing it. We have over 60 events, and it's growing. And you're right; our mobile challenge is to essentially mobilize part of our data center. As an example, here in Orlando, we overlay our wireless network across all the facilities. Actually, this is the first year we've done that here. And finally, customers are saying, "Okay, you've figured it out, Gartner." We weren't doing it before. It's amazing how hotels are just not keeping up with the technology in their venues. But it is not a simple thing to go across these four major hotels and provide seamless wireless connectivity and performance and all that. We have applications that are local on-site replaying certain sessions—we record every single session. There are over 500 sessions. So this morning, people are viewing keynotes they might have missed or some sessions they might have missed yesterday. Obviously, we have registration and all of that, so it's running in dual mode. We have copies of those applications back at a data center, but we also have copies here locally. In some cases, the backup is local, the master is back at the data center; in other cases, it's the other way around. For instance, with video, just so that it performs better, the master is local and the backup is back at the ranch. It's a data center that we actually built in about three days here, run for five days, and then tear it down.

Donaldson: That's amazing. Gartner runs many webinars. Does that pretty much run on its own now? It seems to function very well.

Hrelic: You wish everything ran on its own. We've outsourced much of that, although we were integral in defining what it needed to do, picking the technology, and architecting the capability in the first place. We just felt that this was an area that made sense for us to partner with somebody else to provide that reach and the capability needed there. So we work with our business people and the external provider to make sure everything is running smoothly, but the actual day-to-day operations are outsourced.

Donaldson: What are some key lessons learned that you'd pass onto other CTO/CIO peers in the industry?

Hrelic: The biggest one is relationship management, which is critical to success across the board. You know, it's a big part of what I talked about earlier—who's your number one team? That just means, are you managing relationships appropriately, at the right level, looking at things in the right way? Managing a relationship with my boss, with my peers, with the CFO, is paramount. Business leaders have to be part of the team. We have to be part of their team; they have to be part of our team.

Donaldson: Right.

Hrelic: And the only way that happens is if there's a good, strong relationship there. So it starts with that. All the other things, be it technology, be it functionality and usability—I mean, all of the things that are critical to success can be figured out if the greater team's working together.

Donaldson: Thanks. So let's talk a little bit about Gartner here and spend a few moments on that. Who do you see as your main competition and what do you think makes Gartner different in your space?

Hrelic: We actually have a boatload of competitors; Forrester and IDC (International Data Corporation) are some of them. The biggest one is probably Google, in a sense, the Internet, at least in people's minds and perceptions. The advantage and the reason why we exist is that we have a very credible process for gathering information on a scale that really nobody else can touch. We have almost 800 analysts that meet with vendors in real detailed discussions. I think it's over 10,000 meetings a year. They meet with end users of technology in over 250,000 to 260,000 meetings a year in typically one-on-one half-hour discussions; it could be bigger. The knowledge that you get through those discussions, the visibility that you get and the depth that you get is unparalleled. So our research and our findings and our advice is based on all of that. All of that is pulled together and the patterns are recognized.

Donaldson: That's an interesting point—there's an enormous amount of data and information that you're collecting. The process by which you synthesize that into something and distill it into something is bite-sizable. Are there special technologies that you're supporting to do that or is it more of a business process procedure supported with run-of-the-mill-type technology to do that?

Hrelic: It's a combination of both. If the business processes are not right or are broken, no technology is going to make it work. So we try to look for technologies that make it easier, but it's a constant battle, and it's very difficult, especially since we're talking about traditional publishing, which is writing and a combination of voice and video. I mean, these are all data or information that we have. Graphics is also a huge goldmine of knowledge that we have. We have toolkits, we have surveys, we have benchmarks. It's absolutely amazing, and quite honestly, I have no doubt that we still have a huge opportunity to leverage the raw content and the raw knowledge in a better way than we do today. So I think that's going to be an ongoing and continuing challenge and technology is going to play a key role. Technologies such as searching by voice directly, not by text or transcribed voice into text, or searching video directly or searching graphics directly—those technologies are starting to make their way into the forefront— and will make a difference for us.

Donaldson: So to make all this work, you need good people. Where do you look to recruit people?

Hrelic: Anywhere I can. [Laughter] It is by far the most difficult part of the job. You're absolutely right: without good people, it doesn't happen. Rather than try to find those diamonds out there, which we will continue to do, but it is very, very difficult, especially if you're selective. We're going to universities early on and getting people sometimes in their freshman year and we bring them in for internships. We actually pay them.

Donaldson: Sounds good.

Hrelic: And college kids, at least with a little beer money, are happy. But it gives us an opportunity to see them, understand their chemistry and whether they're a fit or not. They hopefully see it the same way, see if it's going to be a challenge for them that they will enjoy and hopefully a relationship builds. So we bring people up that way. We started a couple of years ago. Slowly it's gaining momentum, but it's a challenge everywhere.

Donaldson: What do you look for in the people you're hiring? What characteristics are you looking for?

Hrelic: Personally, I like somebody that has the horsepower between the ears and a good work ethic and I'll probably be happy right there. Because with those traits, you learn everything else. The thing that you really try to look for, but it's not easy to find, is: "Do people know how to learn? Do they know how to figure something out?" So, it's not so much what you know, it's do you know how to figure it out? Do you know how to find it? So you look for that quality—they don't wear it on their forehead, but it's obviously important to us.

Donaldson: Okay. What do you see that might be issues confronting your customers both internally and externally for the corporation?

Hrelic: I think the traditional job of just sinking yourself into the technology and closing the door and just having fun—I think those days are for the most part over. Businesses are looking for more value-add than that. In fact, just managing technology very little of a value-add nowadays. With things like cloud, the infrastructure play for the IT organization is really over. So I think the change is how does IT or how do technology leaders become business leaders? I think that's a huge change. They fundamentally have to think that way. They have to brush up their interpersonal skills, and develop much more relationship management capabilities. But that's not simple. On the other side of the road, business people are not just opening up their arms and saying, "Come on in. Take my job over." Or "Yeah, things that I used to be doing, you guys can do it better." There's finesse in how that's done. It absolutely has to be done and nobody needs to lose their jobs or anything like that.

Donaldson: So let's shift gears just a little and talk a little about technologies. Given that many people consider Gartner, I'm quoting here, "… the best first source for addressing virtually any IT issue…" and given your job, how do you leverage your Gartner in-house expertise to help you do what you do?

Hrelic: We leverage our analysts in a huge way. But the truth is, we just pick up the phone and call the analyst directly and probably talk for significantly longer and more than a typical client would. The good thing is that with so many analysts, you will get somebody that probably lives and breathes whatever is on your mind, regardless of what it is.

Donaldson: Right.

Hrelic: And addresses one of the things that often concerns you. It's really difficult for a chief architect or CTO or whatever, to be up to date on literally everything that happens. I'll say it's impossible, right? You try to focus on what's important to you and be up to date on those things, and you probably are as good as anyone on the planet, but you're likely not paying attention to many other things. The good thing here is that I can pick up the phone and call an expert in pretty much any area.

Donaldson: Excellent. What do you see as transformative technologies?

Hrelic: There are many of them. I personally believe context-aware is transformative. I believe cloud is transformative in a big way. Social technologies along with the kids coming into the workplace—that's sort of hand-in-hand.

Donaldson: Okay.

Hrelic: All of these I think are fundamentally changing or are going to be changing business and business processes. So, for example, social technologies—the whole concept of workflow is probably going to have to be rethought. I think with social technologies, things can be a whole lot more collaborative, a whole lot more real-time, and decisions can be made in quick, short interactions rather than long, sequential, step-by-step processes. So cycle times as well as quality will improve tremendously.

Most IT people don't really have time to burn and aren't just sitting around with nothing to do and saying, "Let me read some research." They have something they need to accomplish and they need help now. To the extent that we can provide a toolkit or we can provide expert advice or we can provide a research paper, just in time, that include our services, our research, our capabilities in the context of the needs of that customer, then we provide a real value.

I think that generally, businesses are going to be thinking that way more and more, not just in the context of people, but in the context of business processes.

Donaldson: Given that content generation is key to everything the organization does, cyber security must be a concern about intrusion or malicious things happening to your content. What's your strategy for dealing with such a thing?

Hrelic: It's a delicate balance that never has you feeling good. We try to give people as much freedom as we can. So there are sort of two aspects to it. There's the client side devices and obviously, there's the business side.

So talking on the client side device first, we don't want to restrict people; we don't lock the laptops down. We manage them with technology. We automatically refresh software and all of that, but if people want to install their own versions of iTunes, whatever, cool. Nothing is stopping them from doing that. And they need to do that for often very legitimate business reasons, where our users have a need to run certain software and so on. So we're looking to allow more flexibility on employees using their own devices. We're not entirely quite there yet, but we're experimenting in that area.

We want to give end users flexibility with the assumption being that they'll be more productive, but obviously, not risk the corporation from a security perspective. So we use technology as best as we can to mitigate those risks.

Donaldson: Do you encrypt the hard disk?

Hrelic: Yes. So that's an example of what we do. We encrypt the hard disk. We automatically ship patches, fixes, and install them. We check to make sure that firewalls are not shut off by accident, use antivirus software, and all of that.

Donaldson: What do you do with thumb drives, which you're probably seeing, and other externals that you don't know about?

Hrelic: It's an exposure, it's an exposure. The software will check it and make sure that any file that's on the drive is clean and so on. In terms of data leakage, it's an exposure. We offer, free of charge, thumb drives with . . .

Donaldson: Encryption.

Hrelic: Yeah [laughing]. And with built-in biometric fingerprint readers. So we try to do the best we can there, but it is almost impossible to be totally water-tight on a lot of these things.

Donaldson: Do you have your favorite few technologies or technologies that you keep track of maybe for yourself?

Hrelic: I love playing with everything. I enjoy looking at new things and how they work. I personally love tablet computing. I don't know why. And so I play with the Android devices, with the iPad, obviously.

Donaldson: Alright.

Hrelic: I'm looking to see what Windows is going to end up doing in this area. I personally feel that in many professions, the tablets are just such a superior solution primarily because the traditional laptop is just not as personal. I think the tablet is much more natural. It's down on the table in front of you and it's not threatening. And, you can already do pretty much anything on it.

Donaldson: That's interesting. I'd like to spend a couple of minutes here talking about technology investments and how Gartner invests in technology and what your role is in the investment process.

Hrelic: At Gartner, we start everything with business priorities, the key initiatives that the business decides upon, are led by the CEO and the operating committee, which I'm a part of. Business priorities are essentially established there. The CFO manages the investment dollars that we can we afford in a given year.

Basically, we start the planning process by saying, "This is how much money we can afford to invest and here are the general areas that we want to invest in." The money is allocated that way from the top. The CFO and I chair, essentially, an investment committee that meets on a scheduled basis every six weeks—it can meet the next day if necessary—to review projects. So the CFO and I look at every proposal for projects to determine if it is in sync with the overall business priorities, if there is a fighting chance for that investment to be successful from a technology perspective—which is primarily in my court. Or does the business case look like it holds water? We don't really go into an enormous amount of detail with business cases. We just like to understand at the back-of-the-envelope level, have you thought about what the business benefits are at the highest level? Does it make sense? Does it feel good that this investment is the right thing to do? Because we build small and incrementally, we don't put a lot of money at risk with big expensive projects. We believe that we're better off trying and doing little things than thinking or planning big things for a long time.

Donaldson: Who can bring forth proposals to be considered?

Hrelic: Any business unit. And it typically is a business unit. The way that we work is that I have people in my organization who work with the businesses to put together four or five pages that basically say, "This is the proposed project." Any business unit can propose a project.

Donaldson: Excellent. Do you get involved in mergers and acquisitions? Do you do due diligence or get involved in other M&A aspects?

Hrelic: We are an integral player in evaluating or helping evaluate potential mergers and acquisitions, to understand it from a technology perspective. What will we be getting? What are the potential challenges? Is there actual value to the technology that we will eventually acquire? Or is it something that we would just scrap and not use? Is there value to it? You know, does it increase the value of what we are acquiring? So typically, it's not a surprise for us after the acquisition happens to say, "Okay, what do we have to do in terms of the integration?"

Donaldson: Okay, so let's shift gears again here and spend a few minutes on your vision of the future and what you see happening. Are you helping to lay out specific strategies to take Gartner into adjacent market spaces and/or new markets? How do you play in that analysis?

Hrelic: To the extent that I can lead with technology, strategy has become a high priority item for me in my organization, and I encourage my entire organization to identify good ideas, technical ideas that we can propose to business. "Is there business potential with something like this?" Given that Gartner's business is IT, it's us—my organization should understand IT, right? So there are often very, very good ideas that we come up with that we propose to the business, which is probably a little different from most other IT organizations. I think we play an even bigger role or should play an even bigger role in helping business with new business ideas. Do we go much into adjacent areas and all of that? We get involved, but we're not as deeply involved in those things.

Donaldson: Do you get involved in evaluating your competition as part of the strategic road-mapping?

Hrelic: In a minimal way, yes. We obviously pay attention to what our competitors are doing. We're not obsessed by it. We really feel that our future success is in our hands, not in our competitors' hands. And if we're looking at what our competitors are doing, then we're following. So it's more important for us to understand the needs of our customers. What are our customers trying to do? Not even necessarily what they're doing, but what should they be doing. How do we help them be successful? If we can solve that problem really, really well, it's really irrelevant what our competitors are doing. It doesn't really matter.

Donaldson: That's right. Okay. What do you see next in your career?

Hrelic: It's kind of strange and you may find it odd, or people may find it odd, I've never had a long-term plan for myself. I enjoy what I'm doing! At some point, I suppose, if I'm no longer challenged and if I'm no longer contributing, or making a difference, then I'll probably step back and say, "Where do I go from here?" I know it goes a little bit against what I said earlier about "Plan your future out."

I'd like to think that almost everything I do is well-rounded. I don't pigeonhole myself into any area. And it's something that I struggle with my own people within the organization and tell them, "Yes, it's really, really important for you to be the best possible Java expert or .NET expert, or whatever technology expert, but you really need to understand the adjacent fields." By being involved and trying to understand adjacent fields as much as you possibly can, you'll get that experience and knowledge. And when you're no longer challenged in the area that you are in, you'll actually be prepared to move somewhere else.

Donaldson: Does Gartner have a process for helping people cross-train, if you will, or cross-experience?

Hrelic: We do, but would I say it's working really well? No, I think we can do a better job than we do. We have individual development planning, and career planning, and managers working with people who work for them. We force people to do a lot of that themselves. Managers are there to coach, mentor and help them. Managers are not there to do people's individual development planning for them.

Donaldson: Right.

Hrelic: And the basic theory is kind of obvious: if you don't have the incentive to go and figure it out for yourself, I'm not sure that you're ready for that position or that next level job.

Donaldson: Which gets back to your earlier point, which is that you look for people who know how to learn.

Hrelic: That's right.

Donaldson: And that kind of completes it.

Hrelic: That's right.

Donaldson: So I've got one final question for you. What keeps you up at night?

Hrelic: It could be a list of many, many things. But the biggest one is, do I have the flexibility and the agility in the organization to keep up with the changing business environment and the changing business needs? Looking back at the legacy, which we all have, it's not flexible. It's not easy to make quick changes and move on, and all of that. Architecting, designing for flexibility and agility is a guiding principle that we really work hard at.

It's because if you don't have that flexibility and agility, it is not clear that when my boss comes to me and says, "Can you guys do this in the next three months?" whether I'm going to be able to say yes. And not saying yes or not being able to say yes is what keeps me up at night.

Donaldson: I want to thank you for your participation and time today. It is much appreciated.

Hrelic: Thank you. It's my pleasure to participate in the project.

Jan-Erik de Boer

Springer Science+Business Media

Jan-Erik de Boer is executive vice president of IT at Springer Science+Business Media where he is responsible for leading Springer's technology development and innovations in addition to standardizing the infrastructure across Springer's many business units. In 2000, he became Manager of IT Operations at Kluwer Academic Publishers and two years later was in charge of all IT. When Kluwer merged with Springer in 2004, his role was to merge the infrastructures. In 2007, he was promoted to his current role.

Prior to joining Kluwer, Jan-Erik was IT manager at Housing Corporation "Binnen de Ringvaart" and at Relan ICT. He is married with two children and lives in Roosendaal, Netherlands.

Gary Donaldson: Jan-Erik, thank you very much for agreeing to participate in this interview.

Let's begin with an understanding of your organization and your role in that organization. Then we'll drill down on some specific issues related to, and challenges to and trends, etc., focusing on publishing, where you're involved. So can you give a little background about Springer?

Jan-Erik de Boer: Springer is a publisher that is divided essentially into two main parts. The biggest part is the STM part. "STM" stands for "science, technology, and medical," so it's academic publishing. The other part is professional publishing or B2B publishing as you would call it, primarily located in Germany and in the Netherlands. Without a doubt, STM is the most important part of the organization. It contributes most to our revenue on an annual basis, so that's where we focus most of our time. IT is different because basically we provide services for the entire organization. At Springer, in total, there are roughly 5,500 people working, of which the vast majority are in India. In India we have a typesetter called SPS where most of our content is sent and then typeset, so that we get back XML to put on websites and send to printers.

G. Donaldson: And this is for hardcopy documents?

de Boer: Well both, the typesetter creates PDFs to be sent to the printer for hard copy, but they also send XML for us to display on the web.

G. Donaldson: And that would be for e-books then?

de Boer: Well, e-books and journals.

So if you look at the product lines basically, we're talking books and journals. Journals is probably an even smaller part of the knowledge pyramid, so we publish journals for, let's say, the top 200 or 300 researchers in the world, whereas the books depend a little bit on the field but are slightly more accessible for professionals. Since, I think, 1997 all our journals are being published online, and we've done the same thing with e-books.

G. Donaldson: Okay.

de Boer: And we have had those online since 2003, and we've started major projects to digitize all content. So for journals, we have issue 1, volume 1 online, and everything moving forward, and currently we're in the process of doing the same thing for books.

G. Donaldson: What would you say are your overall revenues?

de Boer: I would say, roughly 900 million Euros.

G. Donaldson: Okay.

de Boer: And then our profit, I think the latest report is 286 million Euros.

I think you can verify that on the annual report that you can find on our website.

G. Donaldson: What is your role in Springer? I see on the organizational chart here that it mentions IT. Is that all-inclusive of the chief technology role and technology investment management and CIO responsibilities?

de Boer: Yes, it is. I report to the COO, Martin Mos.

G. Donaldson: Okay.

de Boer: If you would look at the org chart, it shows some sort of a round-table thing, which I think had to do with King Arthur. I don't know whether it's been democratic.

[both laughing]

de Boer: But, basically, I started out roughly 10 years ago with a predecessor of Springer, which at that time was part of Wolters Kluwer. It was called Kluwer Academic Publishers and I think seven years ago we were bought by two investors, Candover and Cinven. They quickly acquired Springer-Verlag, which was a German-based STM publisher, and we merged the two companies. So Candover and Cinven bought these two companies; they hired Derk Haank, who was the CEO of Elsevier Science, and Martin Mos, who was the CFO of Elsevier Science, to head up this integration. In the meantime, Candover and Cinven sold us to a Swedish equity firm called EQT.

G. Donaldson: So when these purchases and mergers happened, there had been a previous chief technology officer on board and then you came in?

de Boer: Well, essentially what happened is the two companies merged, so I was IT director within Kluwer Academic Publishers.

G. Donaldson: Okay.

de Boer: Springer-Verlag was a lot bigger. They had an IT director too, Werner Fischer. Basically we started the merger and I started out as the, what I call the "cable guy." So I was responsible for networking, help desk, desktop support, and standardization of all these entities. At that point in time, I said, "Well, probably that will take me three years." And, well, that's essentially what it took.

G. Donaldson: Okay.

de Boer: Three to four years, and then Martin Mos called me and, well, we had a conversation about the future and I took over the role.

G. Donaldson: What is your official title? What are you now?

de Boer: I'm Executive Vice President of IT.

G. Donaldson: And in that role, you are responsible as the chief technology officer and for the typical CIO-type roles, which is making sure the ship runs?

de Boer: Yes. So it's a bit of a combination of things. I'm not only doing strategy, I'm involved in the day-to-day business-making decisions—well, at least managing the people that actually do the work, of course. But I'm also involved in making sure that we do the right things and then do them in the right order. The focus has very much been on efficiency the last couple of years. Of course, when you merge two companies, you try to find as many synergies as you possibly can, and so we standardized heavily. At that point in time, it was mostly an internal IT task.

G. Donaldson: Okay.

de Boer: And now we're principally thinking about how to expand the architecture that we have, which we are convinced is very good, and to make sure that we benefit from this and the back-end systems also on our website and in delivering content in an electronic way.

G. Donaldson: You had mentioned previously both an internal and external focus. What you're referring to now is the internal focus?

de Boer: Yes.

G. Donaldson: Primarily?

de Boer: Well, it used to be very much … we integrate all of these locations because we're pretty much distributed. Off the top of my head, I think our company is located in 48 locations, or something like that, maybe even more.

G. Donaldson: Okay.

de Boer: So it took a lot of time to make sure that they all are on the same standards, they have active directory, mailing environments, back-end systems, and so on and so forth. Now that's more or less done, so we can use all the information that we centrally store and make sure that we push it out in the most effective and efficient way.

G. Donaldson: When you put your CTO hat on, is your focus involved in more strategic thinking about where you're going or technologies that you are evolving and how you might be able to leverage that?

de Boer: Yes. Our most important product is our website because it is by far the biggest contribution to our profit. I think in 70% of what we sell as a product, there is an online component at least associated with it. So without the website, we're basically doomed.

In December of last year, at the board meeting, we decided that we needed to be in control of development on this online platform. So far—well, up until today, actually—we used a service provider to deliver our content on the web. We were getting, well, slightly dissatisfied with the throughput that they produced, so we decided that we needed to be in control of development. There were a couple of more reasons. Seven years ago, in STM publishing, the general thinking was that it was very important to own the search engine on the scientist's PC, so that's when a lot of publishers invested heavily in search engines. Of course, in the meantime, we know that Google won easily. So that's a done deal. At that point in time, seven years ago, we decided that fulfillment of the electronic content was not really important. It was more or less a commodity. We used to sell huge packages of content, but now with the iStore and Amazon, we see the granularity of the content change, and we want to be able to serve the individuals and the corporate market more than we used to. Our current site is not really geared toward servicing these groups of users, so that's why we decided we had to be in control. So then we started talking to the service provider, and well, we are evaluating whether we will build just the GUIs for these target groups or we will start completely doing it ourselves.

G. Donaldson: So part of your role is taking a look at your investment strategy and where to go.

de Boer: Yes.

G. Donaldson: In terms of the strategic portion of your role, how does that play out? How do you conduct that part?

de Boer: In large part, it has to do with talking to other parties within Springer. Well, having some RSS feeds, reading pertinent blogs, and following websites. I don't go regularly to conferences. We do have, of course, a number of strategic partners, from a technology point of view, where I very much try to keep updated, but that's an easier thing because I can just ask them to come to my office and they can tell me what their roadmap is for the next couple of years.

G. Donaldson: Are you involved in selecting the strategic partners then?

de Boer: Yes. Well, sometimes I am, sometimes I'm not. Sometimes it's just an inherited thing. For instance, Marklogic is, let's say, an XML database, roughly, which is used throughout the STM world. We happen to use that for a number of our sites, and now we're thinking about extending that to the main site as well.

G. Donaldson: I've got a question about your day-to-day responsibilities. Can you give me a sense of what your typical day might be like for you? Like what do you have planned for today, other than talking with us?

de Boer: Well, right now we're working with Thoughtworks in setting up this corporate site. They're finishing an iteration today. We're expecting the first batch of code coming in. I travel to London today. Then I have three telephone conferences and an interview, and then two meetings with the team that's sitting in London. That's more or less my day for today.

G. Donaldson: When you mentioned "team," what team were you referring to? Who's on that team?

de Boer: Oh, the developers, business analysts—so more the development side than the maintenance part.

G. Donaldson: Okay.

de Boer: We're building up a team in London for development, because that's where we think there is a large pool of highly qualified people.

And the time difference is okay. I mean, New York would also be feasible from a resourcing perspective, but the time difference is a little bit too much, so we decided to go with London instead. We already had a couple of developers over there, so it's more for pragmatic reasons than anything else. Most of the maintenance team is in mainland Europe, basically divided over Germany and the Netherlands. The IT department as a whole, consists of roughly 90 people.

G. Donaldson: Okay.

de Boer: It's also distributed all over the place, so we have a true matrix organization without any local responsibilities. People just report in to a team, and they have their area of responsibility.

G. Donaldson: Does that include your external partnerships?

de Boer: For external partnerships, it depends. For instance, we've outsourced help desk and desktop support. We started out with outsourcing desktop support because we are not capable of delivering services in every small office. Otherwise, it becomes too expensive, and that's why we were looking for a partner that was global on the one hand but on the other hand, not too big. We are just a midsized business for the IBMs of this world, or the EDSs. They pick up the phone and they pretend to be very interested, but when it comes down to the details they say, "No, thank you very much." So in some cases it's difficult to find an external partnership that's in the sweet spot for us and for them.

G. Donaldson: And how do you do that? As a CTO, how do you determine what the sweet spot is?

de Boer: Well, it's very different. With IBM it becomes extremely clear, because in those cases I just contact any sales rep that I know. First, they start to be very interested, and then they hand it over, to Germany in this case, and then the German person doesn't return my calls, and then I know enough.

G. Donaldson: [laughter] Okay. Determine the profile of the kind of strategic partners you need, both for your internal IT focus as well as your strategic focus. How do you go about formulating that?

de Boer: It depends on what type of field it is. So for internal focus, it's very important that it's cost-effective and that there is a fit between the companies. I would say that for anything that has to do with the website, cost is, well, not entirely irrelevant, but there we want to excel. So then the costs are less important. Let me put it that way. And there we just look for the best people, whereas internally, we can say if somebody is unable to work for two or three days, we won't go bankrupt over it.

G. Donaldson: For strategic planning for your company, do you participate in that as with the other C-level folks?

de Boer: Internally—yes, I do.

G. Donaldson: And how does that work? Do you have an ongoing, annual process, that sort of thing?

de Boer: We have an annual process, but we also have what we call a "platform group," which consists of essentially all stakeholders that have to do with IT, development especially. So I would assume internal communication consumes probably 20% of my time, if not more. If you add the traveling time, it would definitely be more.

G. Donaldson: But you have ongoing meetings with the executive staff?

de Boer: Yes. With the nonexecutive board, the executive board, you name it. And basically the nonexecutive board is every two months. The executive board is every month. Then we have platform groups, and, of course, now that we're determining what the website should do, we're in almost continuous talks with internal stakeholders, and external, by the way.

G. Donaldson: So you're finding, your company is finding itself in a very rapidly changing environment, I suppose, with more and more shift toward paperless-type publications and so forth, more e-based.

de Boer: Yes, I would say so, cautiously.

As far as I can see, what we publish still very much resembles an electronic version of what used to be a paper book.

G. Donaldson: Okay.

de Boer: Whereas if you look at companies like Inkling, for instance, they more or less reinvent the book in a different way. So they can completely make it an electronic learning tool. And in the case of Inkling, it's specifically for iPads and touch devices. The drawback is the investment per title is tremendous.

G. Donaldson: Okay.

de Boer: Typically, we don't sell huge numbers of paper copies of our books. If we sell 300 paper copies of an STM book, we would be perfectly happy.

G. Donaldson: Are you implying that it is more important to be focused otherwise? What do you mean?

de Boer: Well, the entire field of publishing is changing, but not as rapidly as you would think as an outsider.

G. Donaldson: Can you talk about that a little bit more?

de Boer: If you're looking at companies like Inkling that require a huge investment for a title to be really electronic, that is not applicable to us because we cannot afford that investment on a title-by-title basis.

G. Donaldson: Okay.

de Boer: I would say the focus is very much on speed, which is primarily true in the journal area. So imagine you're a researcher, you just spent two years of your life doing research, and then you submit an article at Springer for a certain journal, and then it takes three months to publish the article. Between submission and us publishing the article, somebody else publishes more or less the same results. Then you just threw away two years of your life. So for the authors, and for Springer, it is important to be quick.

G. Donaldson: And how are you doing that, from a technology point of view?

de Boer: Well, basically, we reduced the publishing time in the last three to four years. Every article has to be peer-reviewed. After it has been peer-reviewed, it used to take 80-something days. Now we're aiming for fewer than 20.

G. Donaldson: And how does technology play a role in that?

de Boer: Well, technology plays a role in everything that we do. We did a couple of things that made this possible. First of all, when we started out with merging these two companies, we decided on using a DTD for all our STM publications, and the DTD is called A++, which was a huge simplification from what we were using. We created a system around this technology to push the content through our organization, to the typesetter, and then back again. So we monitor the process of what is happening to the content on a day-to-day basis.

G. Donaldson: And so the technology and the project management focus is helping with the workflow process to accelerate that along?

de Boer: Yes. We used to have a system which was specific for the publishing industry, called Klopotek, and we switched over to a document-based system, which is workflow, or workflow-capable, let me put it that way, and we are using the workflows extensively.

G. Donaldson: In terms of other technology-related things, such as the type of ink you use and the type of paper you use and so forth, are you involved in those kinds of decisions?

de Boer: No, not at all. We don't have any printer in-house.

G. Donaldson: You outsource everything along those lines?

de Boer: Yep, yep. Well, I mean, it's even better, to be very honest. I mean, we have ... if an order for a book comes in, we say, "If you order a book, you will get it electronically. If you want it on paper, you can have it on paper." So, if somebody buys a paper book, the order goes to a printer, and then it's printed on demand.

G. Donaldson: And you have a worldwide operation, are you using any particular technologies to help with the translation into the various languages?

de Boer: No, 95, 96 percent of what we publish is English. We used to have a program in Japan, specific Japanese language. Well, we try to focus more and more on English—let me put it that way. The only exception to that rule is the German-language program, which I think is pretty successful. Apparently, the market is big enough, the usage is tremendous. So, we'll keep on doing that, but the focus is on English.

S. Donaldson: I've just got a follow-up question. Why the focus on English? Is that because it's becoming the international language?

de Boer: No, it's always been. It's a worldwide business, and English is the worldwide scientific language. So everything we publish is English, or almost everything.

G. Donaldson: As an aside, Scott and Stan both have been published in Chinese, so they found a way to transfer their books into that language.

de Boer: Yeah, well, the exception that I'm aware of is the website, where you used to be able—let me put it that way—used to be able to choose a language, which changed the interface only, but the publications would still be in English. So for Springer books where the market is hundreds of people who certainly understand English, we're not providing translations for our scientific works.

G. Donaldson: I want to focus on a couple of other areas if that's okay with you.

de Boer: Yeah, sure.

G. Donaldson: How do you lead the development of the strategic technology vision, priorities, and implementation planning? How do you lead development of the strategic technology vision for Springer, its priorities and implementation planning?

de Boer: Well, that's very much, as far as I'm concerned, very much on an annual basis prior to the budget rounds, where we talk to all stakeholders as to what they want to accomplish. Then, typically, it's like, in using a German word, wunschkonzert, so it's like a big wish list, which exceeds the budget probably four times.

G. Donaldson: [laughter]

de Boer: [laughter] And then we have some serious talks. In all honesty, especially if you look at the capex (capital expenditure), the discussions that we have on an annual basis, we see that there's a demand—I mean, our capex budget is roughly, let's say, 30 million a year. Then you see that there is demand for 50 million, which always sounds very nice, but in the end we don't have the people to spend that kind of money. Basically, every strategic initiative, if there is a sizable financial impact, would be capitalized.

G. Donaldson: So the stakeholders you're interviewing—do they include your target customer markets?

de Boer: Well, marketing basically is talking to the customer markets and sales, so we take their input as being the customers' wishes.

G. Donaldson: Okay. So they provide you the direction that looks like you need to go in, and then you take a look at it from the technology implications?

de Boer: Yes. For instance, last year, we did another usability study among our customers, which was driven by marketing. We also have library board meetings with librarians and users all over the world with our customers and prospects to make sure that we supply them with the information that they want in the way that they want it.

G. Donaldson: Now, you're briefed on what your marketing people are finding. You're not directly involved in those conversations?

de Boer: Nope.

G. Donaldson: Can you give an example of how you've worked with your marketing folks to translate a customer expectation and need into a technology-enabling approach?

de Boer: Well, a very good example is a specific detail on the corporate side. So, for instance, if a corporation has a contract with us, they have a couple of e-book packages and, let's say, 500 journals in their package, whenever they are searching for something, they are searching the entire content base. So if they find something that is interesting to them, they might end up with a pay-per-view page because they are not subscribed to the content that they actually want to see. So especially in the corporate market, there has been a very explicit wish also to be able to only search within the content that they have access to.

G. Donaldson: Okay.

de Boer: Which sounds like a very reasonable request. On the other hand, we want to be able to upsell as much as possible, of course. So it's not primarily in our interest, and that's why we've come up with a new business model, on one hand, and on the other hand, we'll also enable this board of corporate users to search only within their content.

G. Donaldson: And by this "new business model," you're referring to what?

de Boer: What we used to do is bundle content in certain packages, or you would have the atomic book or chapter level availability. What we are now doing is we have the deposit level, where we say if a corporation pays us, let's say, $100,000, they will get a reduced pay-per-view price, which is a lot lower than the normal $34.95, and then they can use this reduced pay-per-view price to view the content that they are not subscribed to.

G. Donaldson: So the technology side of that is that you help make sure your company has the kinds of technology it needs to make that happen?

de Boer: Yes, so in the project that we're currently executing, we took that one step further. And we said, "Why shouldn't we have the customer define his own package?"

G. Donaldson: Okay.

de Boer: Because, for instance, if you look at, and as I said earlier in the beginning of the interview, the content is now organized in a way that is specific for the academic market. Which is not necessarily of interest to the corporate market. So we have to be able to slice and dice our content in a different way and in a more advanced way.

G. Donaldson: And how have you done that from a technology point of view?

de Boer: Well, by using Marklogic. Marklogic plays an important role there. It's an XML database.

G. Donaldson: Okay.

de Boer: And, essentially, what it allows you to do is that by creating queries, you can define whatever package you want. You can create a query that is updated as we add content. So we can basically create a unique query per each contract, where the customer defines his own set of content. As we add new content, this is automatically added to the results of the query.

G. Donaldson: Okay. It's much more tailored.

de Boer: Very much more tailored.

G. Donaldson: Do you, in terms of your communications internally, do you find that you spend time trying to help bridge between technology and business speak and so forth, so that folks understand what can be done and what cannot be done?

de Boer: Very much so, yes.

G. Donaldson: Can you give an example?

de Boer: It's always a difficult balance, because I have counterparts who write their own programs, and I have counterparts who don't know what a computer looks like. So that's always a difficult thing. With the one person, you have to be a little more patient, whereas the other one will tell you exactly what they want, which may not be the right thing, as far as I'm concerned.

G. Donaldson: Right, right.

de Boer: I mean, the counterpart, the people outside IT, should ask for, or should have requirements, rather than come up with solutions.

G. Donaldson: Okay.

de Boer: Whereas from the IT side, we should try to point out what the possibilities are and what possibly the drivers could be for the future.

G. Donaldson: Okay.

S. Donaldson: The question here would be that as you look to the future, as you lay out the technology roadmaps that you have, as you interview people, platform groups, etc., do you see the process maturing as you move forward with new technologies?

de Boer: Well, yes, the process is improving internally. I would not say that it has to do with the technology on its own. No, I don't think so. I do think that what changed in the relationship with external parties is that they, in general, have become more knowledgeable about IT. For instance, I remember that the platform that I was talking about—it used to be considered rocket science, and now, people have found out that it isn't actually rocket science because they've worked with other companies where they had their own platform and were able to deliver their content. So I think such experiences change the maturity of the process itself.

S. Donaldson: Right, because they've gotten more, a better understanding of what can be done. It opens their eyes, they're asking even for more, and I guess that's why your 30 million budget is expressed as 50 million.

de Boer: Yeah.

G. Donaldson: Are you involved with mergers and acquisitions and so forth? What kind of a role do you play in that as a technology leader?

de Boer: Well, I've gone through data rooms to determine risks, but I also assess the opportunity. Right now, for instance, I'm sitting in the office of what used to be Biomed Central. They're an open-access publisher, part of the Springer family that we acquired three years ago. Then, of course, you talk to all the stakeholders. You go through the data room and try to figure out what all the synergies are and what the risks are. To be very honest, the last two years, we didn't acquire a lot. The financial markets were not in the position where we could easily get a couple of million just to buy a company.

G. Donaldson: Well, when you form strategic alliances or partnerships with other companies, are you involved in analyzing the technology fit and what needs to be in place in order for that to work and do they have the horsepower that's needed to do what you want?

de Boer: Yes, yes. Well, we have, of course, our CFO, who regularly gets updates on companies that are for sale and if they're IT-related, I certainly get the summaries to figure out whether it's a company suitable to be bought by us. At the same time, if we're buying a publishing house, I am part of the process to figure out whether they actually have the technology to make it work.

G. Donaldson: How do you do that?

de Boer: We go through whatever documentation that is there and take a very close look at their finances to figure out whether they're underspending, overspending, compared to what we are doing and compared to whatever, for instance, Gartner is saying about what should be spent.

G. Donaldson: So you're taking a look from the financial point of view and the efficiencies on their end and providing good costs for you. Do you take a look at all at the types of technology that they use?

de Boer: Yes. In all honesty, most of the time, the data rooms are just a lot of data without any coherence. So most of the time it's pretty difficult to figure out what the actual state of, let's say, a platform is. Being from Europe, I feel a little bit more comfortable with Java-oriented stuff than .NET-oriented stuff. But then again, it wouldn't stop me from giving positive advice, just as an example.

G. Donaldson: Okay.

de Boer: So I tend to take a financial but also a personnel perspective and a little bit about what they are doing or are trying to accomplish in the next couple of years. This approach gives me most of the information, most of the time.

G. Donaldson: Do you focus at all on the technology roadmap and so forth? Do you focus on potential transformational technology that the company might want to take a look at?

de Boer: As I said, if we get a report from, let's say, our accountants or some other people who talk to our CFO, I will be involved. For instance, I remember seeing a couple of opportunities for social media–related companies in the academic world that were for sale. Then we decided that at that point in time that it was not interesting for us. Not from a technology point of view. But maybe I would think differently now. Let me put it that way.

G. Donaldson: And why would that be?

de Boer: Because I see an increase in demand for collaboration, for, let's say, messaging. I can imagine if you have a very strong foothold in the academic market that collaboration could be interesting.

G. Donaldson: A question about your organization, your company, your enterprise, its culture. How does that influence the technology focus that you pay attention to? What's important?

de Boer: What probably is more important is that we try—if it's not necessary, we will not build it. I think that's an important point of view that we've taken. So that also means that you cannot be too picky on your technology level either. It's not like we're only Java or we're only something else. We probably have most operating systems that you can find in the world working within our company somewhere. And if we find that the best product to, I don't know, create ads in our German-based newspapers only runs on an AS400; we will get an AS400 in. Does that answer your question?

G. Donaldson: I believe so. Having worked for a company that's very pragmatic, I know how that keeps you focused.

de Boer: Yeah.

Stan Siegel: Jan, as part of your role in strategic planning, are you involved with decisions like, "Are we going to do away with printed books?"

de Boer: No.

Siegel: You're not involved with that at all?

de Boer: I'm not involved.

Siegel: Or are you ever asked that question?

de Boer: I'm listening to the discussion, let me put it that way. But I'm not the person that makes decisions on business models or our content.

G. Donaldson: So you do not advise on business models.

de Boer: Oh, I advise on it, but I'm not the one to decide on it.

G. Donaldson: Okay. How is your position, how is your success measured?

de Boer: Well, right now IT is starting to shift. So it used to be very much the internal operations. Now I see a big shift toward our platform, which is probably 30% of our profit.

G. Donaldson: And so—how would success in that area be measured?

de Boer: Well, it would be a lot of things. The number of downloads is probably the most important success factor because that's also what the librarians use to find out whether they think they've paid too much or too little, which is really the only measurable usage for a librarian. It would be the referrals, the referrals from search engines. And without a doubt, for the future, it will be very much focused on revenues in the individuals' area; "individuals" meaning persons we do not have a contract with, and the corporate market, because we do intend to grow there.

G. Donaldson: What would be an example of a metric that would be used, because that seems to involve forces other than you to capture that kind of market share, to get the librarians to use it? What technology metrics are used?

de Boer: Oh, for instance, that we see the number of downloads going up is a very easy metric, so we have to report to our customers what their usage is. That has to grow. It used to grow typically by 10% per year.

G. Donaldson: Well, how is that differentiated from the content that they're downloading because it's great content or they're downloading because of ease of use and access, flexibility, that sort of thing? Did you use measurements like that?

de Boer: Well, we know they're an influence, because if we take away all the restrictive rights, then the usage will go up. The problem is it won't land in a usage metric for a certain customer.

G. Donaldson: So usage is tied to your success measures?

de Boer: Yes. It has a lot to do with ease of access, it has to do with making sure that the site is available, that it's up and running. Our negotiations right now with the vendor or the service provider we're talking to are running okay and moving forward for the corporate site. That would mean that we are able to get a better product for the corporate market up and running.

G. Donaldson: Well, the better product would be the content plus the access and …

de Boer: Well, it would be a different organization of the content, for instance, to make the usage go up.

G. Donaldson: Okay, good.

de Boer: Because what the corporate market is saying is—we have, I don't know, 5, well, I do know, 5.2 million content items.

G. Donaldson: Okay.

de Boer: On our website. And, typically, the corporate market says, "They are definitely not all interesting to us, so we don't want to pay you for the entire bucket." So what we have to do is prove to them that we can create a bucket for them that is specifically of interest to them, and then they are willing to pay.

G. Donaldson: And the technology is the enabler for that? And the proof is in the pudding and if they use it.

S. Donaldson: One question I have would be is there any one area or areas, a number of areas that keep you up at night?

de Boer: Well, when I used to be in charge of the internal stuff, we had a storage area network crash two years ago. We had to rebuild everything from tape in one weekend. That was not a moment I would like to relive again.

[mutual laughter]

de Boer: At the same time, if I see what is worrying me right now, it is our capability of influencing the referrals we get from Google. We have been on the top 20 companies most heavily penalized by the new algorithm by Google and we're somewhat in a Catch-22 on how to mitigate those effects.

S. Donaldson: Oh, did Google give you a heads-up on what the new algorithm was going to be?

de Boer: Nope. And they will never. We also tried to talk to them. We said, "Hey, we give you our books to sell on Google's Editions," or Google eBooks, I think it's called now, now that they're live in the US I think roughly 25% of all their books are from us, but they said that the algorithm is nonnegotiable. They are not talking about how that works. We know why that is affecting us so much. The problem is because of the setup with our vendor; there's very little we can do.

S. Donaldson: Right. So you reverse-engineer what you can, in effect, to organize appropriately so you'll get better hits.

de Boer: Right. But that's really agonizing, to be very honest. I mean, what it comes down to, the basic problem is that we have a user site and we have a robot site. The robot site is being indexed only by Google, by the way, which is already not good enough, but the link is then to the robot site. So, if the user clicks a link, it goes to the robot site, and the robot site determines, "Hey, this is not a robot, so I will refer you to the user site." This means that if anyone links in to the user site, considered an external link, it will not be accounted for because Google doesn't see it. Furthermore, there is no internal linking, so it's all a big mess. Typically, some of this you cannot easily change and effectively have a robot site. It has to do with the fact that the main, the user site is not able to handle the load if we switched on the robots. So there's your perfect Catch-22.

G. Donaldson: You know, listening to what you're talking about, it also suggests you may have a big focus on cyber security. Is that accurate?

de Boer: No.

G. Donaldson: No?

de Boer: No, not at all. Well, "not at all" is not entirely true. But no. We distribute our content without DRM. And our customers love us for it. At least that's my point of view. We can use DRM, and then probably we'll penalize all the right users so that they're not able to do something with the content that they should be able to do. And there is always a person who will break the code and put it on a Russian server so that everyone else can download it, and you only need one of those.

G. Donaldson: Now, what about security for your IT systems as a whole?

de Boer: The internal stuff, it's slightly different, of course. But, basically from the content point of view, yes, we are concerned, but we're not frightened to death.

G. Donaldson: Okay.

de Boer: I mean, in the book, in the paper area, people could borrow a book in the library and copy it. Essentially, they can do the same thing; they're just not allowed. What we do is we monitor, or we have a company that monitors, well, some blog sites and make sure that bogus links are placed to the same content, then if you place enough bogus links, people get slightly frustrated, so they abandon the project and buy the content. The internal systems—well, we're not a bank, so we're not completely strange on security. At the same time, we have, let's say, our financial systems in separate VLANs so that only the right persons can access it and so on; the normal stuff.

G. Donaldson: I have a couple final questions. One of the questions has to do with any lessons learned being the CTO of your company that you feel would be good to pass on to others or even to, you know, advise yourself and your career development.

de Boer: Well, I mean, in general, I would say—I don't know who mentioned the word "pragmatic."

G. Donaldson: You can ask Scott, Stan, or me, and we can tell you that one.

de Boer: I like the pragmatic approach, and I think it makes a lot of sense to just use common sense, which is basically applicable to every position whatsoever. On the other hand, what I try to do is make sure that my people have the right tools and environments. I mean, I'm not doing anything, actually. I'm just thinking about things, I'm listening to stories, and then I'm forming opinions. Then, eventually, if we're not coming to a conclusion, I will make a decision if it's up to me. But making sure that your people have the right tools and the right environment to be able to excel is probably the most important thing I can do.

G. Donaldson: And then the selection of your people as well, I would imagine.

de Boer: Yes. And, well, what I would like to add to the selection of people is that I find a very dangerous thing: you've all done job interviews, and if you do so, within three minutes you know whether you like someone, yes or no, and then the danger is you try to hire the people that you like, but it's very good to have a diverse team as well. So you need some people like me who are very pragmatic and goal-oriented; but you also need some, well, highly academic people who will play the role of … the advocate of the devil—is that English?

G. Donaldson: Yes.

de Boer: Okay.

G. Donaldson: It's the diversity of views, and some don't always agree with what you're doing but help give counterpoints. One last question, and if you don't mind just going on a minute on this one, is your journey to become a CTO. You had mentioned how the companies had come together. You had worked for another company and the companies were bought and merged and so forth, but how did your path toward becoming a CTO happen prior to all of that?

de Boer: Well, in all honesty, I would say luck, being at the right position at the right time, and then having the ambition, and apparently the ability to execute.

G. Donaldson: What part of your role do you really find the most interesting?

de Boer: Basically, I like it all. Sometimes, of course, when I'm in too many meetings with stakeholders, I get sick and tired of that. Sometimes I get sick and tired of certain people explaining to me why a certain RAID level on a storage area network is the best thing to do. So it is the combination of being technical, economical, and the integration with the business that's making the business interesting.

G. Donaldson: Okay. Well, thank you very much for taking the time to speak with us today.

Paul Bloore

TinEye/Idée

Paul Bloore is CTO and co-founder of TinEye/Idée Inc. He is the visionary behind TinEye and Idée's image search technologies. Paul has over 15 years of experience designing and implementing innovative commercial software. As CTO, he is responsible for product direction as well as research and development of visual search and image identification technologies.

Prior to co-founding Idée, Paul was co-founder of TrueRisk Inc. which developed large-scale market risk analysis software. TrueRisk grew to become one of the leading developers of quantitative financial software for trading and risk management. In 1999 SunGard Data Systems Inc. (NYSE: SDS) acquired TrueRisk.

Gary Donaldson: What we'd like to explore first is your journey to becoming the current CTO and co-founder of your company. Could you give us a little background about your journey from early on to where you are now?

Paul Bloore: Sure. As a kid, I was pretty nerdy. I was your classic kid who would disassemble things to understand how they work, and reassemble them if I possibly could. I certainly had an interest in really understanding how things work and exploring ideas on how to either make things better or come up with entirely my own ideas on what would be something worth building. I still think of myself a bit of an inventor in that respect.

G. Donaldson: Was this through childhood?

Bloore: That was me as a kid. As I grew up, I did have a fascination with computers. They're the most complex thing around to look at, so I had a fascination there. When I was in high school—it was so far back of course that the first computer they had at our school had a card reader attached to it. In grade 9, I wasn't allowed to actually use the computer, but it had a special glow for me. I'd watch it in the back of the room, and if anyone was ever using it, I would be over there in a second to learn as much as I possibly could about it even before I got my hands on it.

G. Donaldson: What was the fascination about?

Bloore: What you could possibly do with it, what the potential was. How does it all work? We had a card punch machine in our school, and when the teacher wasn't watching, I would open it up and learn how various parts of it work just for the fun of it. I ended up knowing that machine probably better than the teacher did himself, just for the pure pleasure of knowing how it worked.

G. Donaldson: Did you have any initial speculations about how it might be applied?

Bloore: I must say I didn't really grasp it. I couldn't see to how far we would come today. Computers have taken over in such a tremendous way. They are so much more powerful than when I was a 14-year-old kid. I couldn't have envisioned just how commonplace they have become in everything we do. That was a little bit beyond my grasp, but I could tell that they were very important and essentially the wave of the future. But at the time, I would not have thought that I'd be carrying around in my pocket a phone that is capable of doing all the things that it does. It was harder at that time to understand the importance of networking and the internet because, really, there wasn't an internet that was accessible to a high school kid at that time. I wasn't able to envision all of what we have today back in the early '80s.

G. Donaldson: So how did this passion move forward for you? What did you go through?

Bloore: I spent as much time as possible around computers in high school and then went on to university and studied computer science. I wasn't really academically inclined though. I dropped out of university, disillusioned with that a little bit. I still ended up, almost by chance, working at a very small software company that made financial software, which was curious because it was a field that I had no interest in. Finance seemed to me to be dull spreadsheet-type work and accounting, and I really had no interest in that. But the company that I worked at, which was called Algorithmics, was a five-person company at the time and the energy and enthusiasm of everyone who was working there was tremendous. That really was a terrific experience for me. I ended up co-founding a company in financial software and working in the financial software field for a full 10 years, in fact, and working in a bank as well. I had a great time, but it wasn't ultimately what I really wanted to do. So when we sold my first company, which was called TrueRisk, that allowed me the freedom to do what I really wanted to do and that's what led me to co-found Idée and start working in the image search field.

G. Donaldson: You were working for a company and learning your software development by actually doing it for this small company. What was behind you deciding to go out on your own and form your own company? Where did that come from?

Bloore: Even in high school I wanted to do something on my own. There I would come up with ideas that didn't necessarily have to do with software development. The first idea I had came from reading an article in *Scientific American* about some scientists who developed a magnetic fluid called "ferrofluid." It had some very interesting properties when you would introduce a magnet near this magnetic fluid. I was so taken by it that I actually ended up writing the scientists who developed the fluid and describing a product idea I had for a fascinating display of the capabilities of this fluid, and corresponding with them. Unfortunately, the idea wasn't viable due to the instability of the fluid, but it gave me confidence that I could come up with an idea and it would be a viable product that would be marketable. I so enjoyed doing that that I knew from that moment on that I really wanted to start a company, but I didn't know what it would do. I didn't know if I'd have the opportunity to start one, as much as I wanted to.

G. Donaldson: Were the scientists encouraging to you?

Bloore: Oh yes, absolutely. They were very straightforward. They thought it was a very good idea, and that was terrific, but they told me that if the ferrofluid, was mixed with another fluid, it would break down over the course of weeks or months. So it couldn't be a long-lasting product, and that's what ultimately ended that idea.

G. Donaldson: So you went from physical sciences to computer science with your programming?

Bloore: The physical science was really more just fascination with compounds that I was looking at. For me, it was more about the idea of what you could do with something and not about whether it's software or something physical you're working with. I like to take ideas and play with them over in my head about where this can go. I would say I do that in the software we develop today as much as I did back then when I was reading an article in *Scientific American.*

G. Donaldson: So you went on to work for the banking and finance community, and you developed a software product?

Bloore: Yes, one of the main products we ended up developing at my former company was risk management software that was able to measure the risk exposure of a bank's entire trading portfolio. This is a large-scale problem so one of the things we did was to use distributed computing to solve it, essentially, small clusters of computers. At the time, in '92 or '93, this was not a common thing to do. Most people were essentially just trying to build bigger and faster computers to tackle problems. But we said, "Well, wait. You know, that's not really going to work in this case. So we have to break the problem down, get a bunch of computers to work on the problem, and then aggregate the results." I worked on the system that did all of that, and that gave me a tremendous passion for using compute clusters to solve large problems. So that played right into what we do here at Idée with a number of our services, that we immediately started using clusters and distributed computing for.

Scott Donaldson: As you went through this transformation through your different jobs here, did you have particular mentors to help shape your direction?

Bloore: Certainly, the people around me had a tremendous influence in shaping where I am today. From the scientists that I corresponded with, their encouragement was a pivotal point. From watching my older brother become a computer programmer. That was a major point I would say as well; playing with his early HP calculators, learning how to program them was certainly an influencing point. My partner in my first company, who handled most of the finance, while I worried about the computer science side of things, was a large influence in learning how to put a company together and how to run it.

Other influences? I would say reading Richard Feynman's autobiographies was something that I think influenced a lot of technical people, including myself. These were terrific books telling the story of a brilliant physicist and his random path through life. There were many random events that influenced his life, and reading his stories would always show so much humor and so much pleasure in what he was doing that I wanted to get a lot of pleasure out of what I work on and work on things that I have control over.

Stan Siegel: Paul, I take it then from what you mentioned earlier regarding dropping out of the university, that you taught yourself math and physics and software engineering. Is that correct?

Bloore: Well, mostly it was software engineering after dropping out of the university. I was studying physics, chemistry, computer science and mathematics at the university, but most of what you learn in software development comes after. Especially at that time, I would say it was the early days of teaching computer science to young minds, and probably they weren't very good at it, I would say. Now they're much better at it, but back then, they weren't great. The vast majority of software development I learned afterward by reading other people's code and by essentially staying up most hours into the evening to work like a maniac on whatever problem I was trying to tackle at the time. It was largely hands-on learning when it comes to software development.

Siegel: Did you study physics from some of Feynman's work?

Bloore: Loosely, but I'm certainly not current in physics. It's something that still fascinates me, but I've never really used physics in an applied approach in my work.

G. Donaldson: So you moved away from the financial services world and established the company that you currently run. Can you tell us a little about that transition and what your company does?

Bloore: Sure. So what our company does is make images searchable by looking at the patterns within the pixels themselves. We are entirely focused on using computer vision and pattern recognition algorithms to make large image sets searchable. It's very different from using keywords to search images.

G. Donaldson: That's a big shift from developing risk management software to pixel imagery and software. Where did that shift come from? What was your interest in going in that direction?

Bloore: I would say that it's entirely personal. I have a very visual memory, and that's what ultimately drives what direction the company took. The specifics of how we started is that after I sold my last company, I happened to hear about using digital watermarking of images to make them identifiable. Digital watermarking is a procedure where you put an unperceivable pattern of changes in the pixels of an image to embed an ID into it. That fascinated me immediately because it was based on images and it just sounded like an interesting technology. So I started researching that a little bit, and I realized that it's the wrong way to try to identify an image. Really, I felt very, very strongly that what you should do to identify an image is not add a pattern to an image. You should identify an image the same way a human does, which is look at the pattern that naturally occurs within the image already. And that was really the start of Idée, when I said, "I think that we can do things in a very different way here that will be a much more valuable, much more powerful technique." And then I set about developing a company that could do exactly that.

G. Donaldson: How did that insight emerge? Was it creative inspiration?

Bloore: It was mostly research, my own online research into what you could do with watermarking of images—and my immediate suspicion that it wouldn't be very effective. Just because that technique doesn't work doesn't necessarily give you a new technique that will work, however. The technique that I thought would work is what we're using today, and that came from sitting down and really just thinking about it a lot, saying, "How would you, how could you identify an image just based on the patterns within the image itself?"

G. Donaldson: And that interest and just focusing on that particular area, where did that come from? Watermarks?

Bloore: Somewhere from the depths of my mind.

G. Donaldson: [Laughter] Was it a small extension of your focus on security and risk management?

Bloore: The two aren't related. It's interesting, I fell into the field of financial risk management and stayed in that field for 10 years, but it was never really a passion of mine. This area that we're in now certainly is a very strong passion of mine. I guess the question isn't so much how did I transition into image searching from financial software; it's how did I accidentally end up in financial software for a full 10 years when that wasn't something that I wanted to do, necessarily?

S. Donaldson: Who are your major competitors in this space, and what's different about how you go about what you do?

Bloore: There are certainly a handful of smaller firms, and the largest firm right now would be Google, who has entered into our space a little bit. They have their own image search very similar to what we do with TinEye. But I'll tell you one of the best bits of business advice I've ever received from a friend of mine, Charles Marston, who runs a financial software company called Calypso Technology. I was speaking with him over dinner about various trials that you have as a small software company, and in particular I was asking him about competition and how we should position ourselves and what we should worry about. He said to me, "Really, you shouldn't worry about your competition so much because it takes so much to get a company together, to develop actual working software, to deliver it, to sign on clients, to get every piece together to make a company viable. All of your financial competitors are struggling with the same issues as well. Let them struggle on that and focus more on where you want to go with your company rather than what everybody else is doing. Because if you're constantly looking over your shoulder, it will get you into a paranoid state and you won't focus on the things that you need to do." And of all the business advice I've received over the years, that one's always stuck with me as a very sensible thing, so I do that as much as possible, worry less about my competition and more about what we need to do.

S. Donaldson: Could you talk about TinEye a little bit and maybe provide a story or two about how it's used, how it's applied?

Bloore: TinEye is our reverse image search engine. It works very differently from most image search engines. Image search engines prior to TinEye worked by somebody typing in keywords and then finding images that had those keywords associated with them. You search for "dog," it shows you pictures of dogs. TinEye is very different and it doesn't use any keywords at all. You give TinEye an image. You upload an image to it or you point it to an image using a URL, and then we download it. We look at the patterns within that image, and then we're able to identify identical and modified copies of that image, purely based on the patterns within the image. This is what we refer to as "reverse-image search," and we do it on a very large scale, I think on a scale that really stunned people that this is even possible when we introduced it. We now have over two billion images in our index, and a search takes about a second or so. So that in a nutshell is what TinEye is. It was something that I wanted us to do for quite some time. We released it in March of 2008, but I'd wanted to make a web-wide search for a couple of years prior to that, but we didn't actually have the computing capacity to do it. In late 2007, Amazon was developing their AWS, their Amazon Web Services, and cloud computing platform. I was immediately taken by it because I thought, "Aha. Now we can manage to get ahold of the computing capacity we need to launch the search engine." So we started work on it immediately, and I think it was about four or five months later when we first put TinEye on the web. And, of course, that was about three years ago now.

S. Donaldson: Right. So what's an application?

Bloore: There are a handful of different applications people use TinEye for. One is that they've got an image, they don't know anything about it, and they want to find more information about it. We had a great example where there was a small group of people who were researching and documenting old World War II photographs. They wanted to know who the people in the photographs were, and so they would essentially hunt down people by doing web searches, by trying to identify different people and label them. After we released TinEye, we got an email from one of these people saying what a fantastic job we'd done for him because he had a photo that he sent us which was of a woman colonel sitting talking with some troops, and her identity was unknown. He entered the image into TinEye, and two seconds later he had a series of links to other people who did know who she was, and he had the answer to add to his collection. So that was, for us, pretty exciting, pretty nice to see that we were actually helping people out who had questions they wanted to answer, "Tell me more about this image."

S. Donaldson: Excellent.

G. Donaldson: It's applied in commercial settings as well. Is that correct?

Bloore: Yes, absolutely. To touch on some of the other applications—photographers will, of course, use it to track who's using their images because they always want to know where their images are appearing. There are other commercial uses too. One of the biggest commercial uses is that if you are accepting images to, say, print on products, there are a number of companies that will do this. They'll accept images from designers. They'll print them on products, and then they will sell the products and give a cut of the money to the designer who put the design together. The images will go onto, say, t-shirts or mugs or promotional products, what have you. One of the difficulties they have is that it turns out the designer who submits a design isn't always the original author of the design, so they have to be concerned about this. With TinEye, they can very often find out, in fact, that a designer didn't create that image at all, that somebody else did, or that it was done many, many years prior to when they said they created the design. So that's an idea of a commercial use for it.

S. Donaldson: What's your interaction with Adobe?

Bloore: Adobe was an earlier licenser of our technology. They embed our visual similarity software inside their Photoshop Elements product. So Photoshop Elements allows users to organize their photos. It's similar to iPhoto in the sense that it lets you keep all your digital photos in a digital shoebox and organize them. They wanted software to allow their users to be able to sort their images and find images based on visual similarity. So if you've got one picture of a beach, you might want to find the other pictures of a beach. So they use our technology to do that, and they embed our technology into their product for that purpose.

G. Donaldson: While you're rolling out your products and in the initial uses, have you discovered unexpected uses of it that have helped expand your market?

Bloore: Certainly. One of my favorite stories of an unexpected use is when we were trying to license our visual similarity software to Getty Images. They're the world's largest stock photography company. We wanted them to use the technology on our customer-facing website, so that if somebody searches for an image, they can find all the images that have a similar appearance to that image very, very easily. We'd had several meetings with them but we were still having a hard time convincing them that this was a good idea. At the end of one of the meetings we had, one of the senior executives said to us, "Boy, you know what I'd really love if you could do, I'd love it if you could identify every use of our images in, say, this magazine here," and held up a magazine. It was an off-the-cuff remark that she didn't expect anything to come out of, but I explored the problem much more with her and why they needed to do this. It wasn't for copyright reasons. It was to automate their own business practices, so they could bill a publisher for the images used in a magazine automatically because, at the time, they'd been using a manual approach to flip through the magazine and look at photo credits. She described this problem to me, and I said to her, "Yes, we can, I think we can do that." And she didn't take me seriously at all. She thought I was crazy because we'd have to look at every page of a magazine and tell if any of, say, 10 million images appeared anywhere on any page in a magazine. And that's a big problem, but we took that very loose problem description and we've actually built the world's only print-monitoring solution for photographs—our product is called PixID, and it does exactly what I described. It will tell our clients where their images appear in printed publications. And we've grown that to a sizable business, and it came really just out of an off-the-cuff remark by an executive at the close of a business meeting where we were trying to accomplish something entirely different.

G. Donaldson: I would assume that you've had other ideas presented to you that you've had to help the customer sort out the feasibility of it.

Bloore: A lot of what I end up doing is trying to sort out the feasibility of product ideas. The unfortunate truth is that many times clients will come to us with problems we can't solve. We have to tell them, "No, it's not solvable. We can't solve it, and we don't think anyone else can." The classic example that I get incessantly would be somebody wants to be able to walk up to a person, take a picture of, say, the dress they're wearing with their cell phone, and then immediately be told where to buy that dress and how much it's going to cost and any details like that, whether it's a dress, shoes, pants, what have you. But that's something that so many people have come to us over the years wanting to do, exactly that product, and I end up telling them that it isn't a problem we can solve, telling them why that is such a difficult problem, and that I'm afraid that they're trying to develop a business where the technology can't solve their problem for them. The reason we get this is that people will take a look at what TinEye can do and they will tend to extrapolate in their minds what the next step is and how they can apply it. And they extrapolate in ways that aren't really viable. The problem is that humans are very, very good at processing visual information, at understanding visual information, so we tend to assume that computers are equally good at doing things that we find naturally simple. But the truth is that computers are good at very different things than what humans are good at when it comes to visual information.

S. Donaldson: Are there military applications for this technology?

Bloore: There are none that we've explored. As a company, we really aren't interested in going into the military area. We've gotten some inquiries, though, from DARPA companies.

G. Donaldson: Did those discussions you had with your customers suggest to you other potential ideas for product development?

Bloore: I hate to say it, but no, nothing immediately from that area.

G. Donaldson: Do you see the capability eventually being developed at some point in time?

Bloore: I think it's a very different world when we have that level of capability in our algorithms.

It's a huge leap to go into that direction. Today we don't even have anything that's coming close to solving that problem. It's something that we'd love to be able to do, but there are so many other problems that are addressable today that I tend to focus on the addressable problems, and not necessarily ones that are just research and get you 5% of the way there. There are other things you can tackle that you can solve 80% of the way there.

G. Donaldson: And besides the things you've spoken about previously, what are some of those other areas?

Bloore: Searching video, for example. We do quite a bit of work in the video search space. Video is a much larger problem than searching—searching is still limited just because of the volume that you're dealing with. But, then again, Moore's law works in our favor, and we're able to tackle larger and larger problems as far as being able to search through video to identify specific frames or to identify things within a video. Another area that interests me a great deal is to be able to make, maybe not dresses and pants and shoes searchable, but you can make many objects in the real world identifiable, whether it be, fire hydrants and parking meters to the books that you're reading to packaged consumer products, or products out of packages. And our ability to get a digital impression of the world around us is just continuing to take off at a tremendous pace. Soon we'll be able to cheaply record all the video of everything that we're seeing, 24/7. If we wanted to capture that data and put it onto a storage medium it would cost us only a few hundred dollars in a handful of years. So being able to make some sense of that volume of data, visual data, it can be very valuable to be able to search anything that you can identify within, say, a continuous video stream.

G. Donaldson: Do you anticipate the convergence of technology such as the ability to identify objects with voice software that would be able to inform, say, a person with visual impairment what's ahead?

Bloore: Certainly. That is an area that has particular interest for me because I think a great deal about aids for the visually impaired. I've seen quite a bit of research in the area of trying to identify things and inform somebody who's blind about what's going on in the world about them. I think there's still a lot of work that I would personally like to tackle in that field. So, yes, I think that we're going to see tools that make a blind person's life much better by allowing them to see to some degree what we see, as a person with vision.

G. Donaldson: Do you see that your technology is converging with any other technologies?

Bloore: Well, I see that its convergence with the ability to capture visual information is exploding. In the last five years alone, it's just really taken off. And the ability to capture visual information and then the ability to search through the visual information certainly have resonance. It is worthless to capture all the visual information around you if you can't make any sense of it, so that's something that I see will be an area for us to focus on, making sense of the visual world around us.

S. Donaldson: With respect to the technical people you need to create these products and explore new areas, where do you look to recruit people and what do you look for in employees when you hire them?

Bloore: When it comes to algorithms, computer vision algorithm work, of course we're looking at people who have advanced degrees in that field. Despite my own lack of a degree in that field, people who are able to write robust algorithms are usually coming out of an academic background. And we are very often recruiting through our network of other technology people, who are telling us about very talented people that they know. Word of mouth ends up still being a very important consideration, and the recommendation of somebody who we trust is always a crucial factor in deciding who we would consider.

Siegel: How big is your company?

Bloore: Our company is just 12 people, so we are tiny for the level of the services that we offer. I would say people are often shocked to find out how small we are. As the developers of TinEye, they're picturing a company with dozens or hundreds of people within it. On top of that, we offer many other services, so I would say we are a very small firm for what we do.

Siegel: What are the important issues confronting your customers today and in the future?

Bloore: All of our customers have large image collections and the issue facing them is that their problems are getting larger and not smaller in dealing with these large image collections. So it's a matter of scaling; it is a crucial problem for all of them. That's where we will spend a lot of our focus, on the ability for dealing with collections of images that are in the hundreds of thousands to hundreds of millions in size. This ends up being our primary focus—how to deal with them efficiently and how to deliver our technology to our clients in such a way that it becomes a tool that they can easily make use of. So we're, we usually are developing, delivering our technology as an API (Application Programming Interface) or a web API.

Siegel: So given that your business may explode in the future, what are your plans for growing from a 12-person company to a much larger company?

Bloore: To be honest, Stan, it ends up being rather organic how we end up growing the company. We see where we need help and we do our best to hire in those fields. For example, right now we are looking to hire a product manager for one of our services that will free up my time and free up the time of my co-founder and allow us to focus on the new business areas.

G. Donaldson: Speaking of focusing on areas, let's talk about your actual role as the CTO.

Bloore: Sure.

G. Donaldson: What's it comprised of and how do you do it?

Bloore: Okay. Well, because I'm also the co-founder, I'm really setting the technology direction, and it's up to me to make sure that we're headed in the right direction when we're building the software products and solving our clients' challenges. So I am also very involved with our clients. One of the greatest pleasures I have is going to a smart client, listening very carefully to the problems that they are having, and understanding how we could use our technology to solve their problems, then actually going back with my team and working on how we are going to tackle this problem and produce the software that does it.

G. Donaldson: Do you target those customers or do they come to you, or some combination of the above?

Bloore: It's a combination. In the early days, we were going to them much more than we do now. Now they are generally finding us because we are quite a well-known name with the TinEye product. So very often they are coming to us and bring us problems that we've never encountered before. One of our clients is, for example, doing automatic monitoring of products on eBay and essentially buying products that are of interest to his company based on the actual pictures of the images that appear on eBay listings.

G. Donaldson: So you're involved in setting the technical direction. You're also in strategy, and you're also involved in engagement with the clients in helping to define their needs and how you may meet their needs. Are you involved in any internal research and development?

Bloore: Yes, certainly. I'm constantly pushing our algorithm engineers—I know what our weaknesses are—to come up with new ideas on how we can improve things. Often my ideas are shot down by the team, but often they work out quite well. So for a small company, we do an unusual amount of research and development into trying to solve problems that we would just like to be able to solve. It doesn't mean we have a client in mind for the problem, but it's something that we know it would be worthwhile if we could tackle it.

G. Donaldson: How do you do that?

Bloore: So, usually, it starts with me driving in my car.

G. Donaldson: [laughter] Okay.

Bloore: If I'm taking a long road trip somewhere, I will spend many hours thinking about what I'm seeing through my eyes, how our algorithms view pictures that we give them, and what the differences are between how I'm seeing things and how our algorithms see things, and why it's so different and how we can make our algorithms behave a little bit more like a human does.

G. Donaldson: Can you give an example?

Bloore: Most algorithms, when they look at a picture, tend to ignore white space or areas where there is no information available. If you give an algorithm, say, a pure white photograph, all it can do is, say, find other white photographs. It's not going to be able to tell very much about that photo because there's not very much information contained within that. I see that as a detriment because if there's just a large white patch within an image and there can be other parts of the image that have a lot of detail and texture in them, our algorithms will tend to focus on the detailed and textured areas and ignore the large empty areas. In certain applications, that's a big mistake because those empty areas—just the fact that there's a big empty area, can be important information. So one of the areas that we're focusing on right now is trying to get our algorithms to look at areas that they traditionally haven't looked at and try to make that a valuable attribute of a picture as opposed to something that our algorithms ignore.

G. Donaldson: Do you lead the technical team then in exploring how to flesh that out?

Bloore: Yes, I do, but certainly, they're bringing forth many of their own ideas and keeping me in check when I come up with ideas that are patently absurd, I would say. It happens from time to time.

G. Donaldson: Well, sometimes your customers expand your horizon, and sometimes I guess your staff expands horizons.

Bloore: Absolutely.

G. Donaldson: Well, what are other aspects of your job, as a CTO? What are they? A typical day, for example?

Bloore: A typical day? Ooh. Because I'm a co-founder, my days are never typical. They involve working on everything from working on client proposals to dealing with, say, a particular weakness in our cluster architecture that's causing us problems, to recruiting new software engineers.

G. Donaldson: Do you guide your team? What kind of interface do you have with them? Is it directive, advisory?

Bloore: It's much more advisory. Certainly, I'm setting the direction of what they're working on, but it's much more advisory. Because we're a small team, we're generally working on one floor of the building we occupy and everybody's within a few steps of each other. That's an environment that I really enjoy, not having an office and being very accessible and meeting with everybody at least once a day to find out what their challenges are and try to help them work through it.

G. Donaldson: What are some of your challenges as a CTO?

Bloore: I would say one of my challenges is to get my head up from my desk and look at the world around me and keep connected with people. I would say I look up—I'm still ultimately a bit of an introvert, and if I'm not forced to get away from my computer, I would spend way too much time in front of it. I try to stay in touch by organizing some meetings with my peers to essentially get together and geek out and talk about different aspects of technology that are on the horizon. Once every month or two, we will get together with some friends and one of us will present on a new technology that they're exploring using within their own companies.

G. Donaldson: And is this a formal association or kind of an informal network?

Bloore: It's a pretty informal network. There is no title to it. It was started by a friend of mine, and we've just been continuing on for about the last year.

S. Donaldson: Are there key CTO lessons learned that you could pass on to other CTOs?

Bloore: Thinking of phrases that I'm really drawn to, one of the strongest ones that comes to mind is "implementation trumps innovation." I have no idea who that quote is attributed to, but I think it really is important to realize that it doesn't matter what great idea you have, if you haven't implemented it well, it doesn't mean anything. Ideas are a dime a dozen, but getting it done, making something workable is where the focus needs to be.

Another is, in the field we're in, in image searching, there are more dead ends than there are viable paths. To give you an example of what I mean by this, in the early days of image searching, many people seemed to think that you would be able to replace keyword search by image search. So instead of going to a search engine and saying, you know, "Show me pictures of a dog," you would give it a picture of a dog and then it would find all the other pictures of a dog automatically. This has never come to be, and won't anytime soon because it is a very, very difficult problem to understand that this is a picture of a dog. And that's an area where I can say there is kind of a dead end. There were a number of companies that attempted to do this, and they ultimately failed. We learned from that, and we don't attempt to do that. We think that there are many other good uses of image search technology that don't try to do exactly what a human does but still ends up being a very valuable thing to have.

G. Donaldson: In terms of keeping current and where the future is going, are you aligned at all with any universities or research labs?

Bloore: Yes, we certainly are. We keep in touch with academics at both the University of Toronto and the University of Waterloo. We've done joint projects with the University of Toronto in the past, and we're likely to in the future as well, especially in the computer vision department.

G. Donaldson: Do you see your role evolving over the next several years?

Bloore: Well, as the team grows, at a certain point there will be less direct contact day-to-day with all the development staff. I'll see that as an unfortunate day, but it's probably a necessary step.

G. Donaldson: You have a lead engineer for your technology staff? Is that how the chain of command works?

Bloore: Right now I probably play the role of the lead engineer, and then I have engineers who have specific domain knowledge. For example, the actual coding of the pattern recognition algorithms resides with a lead engineer.

G. Donaldson: Well, let's shift and talk a little bit about your technologies. You've being doing a very good job of outlining what you've encountered. If you had to summarize, what are the most important technologies to your company?

Bloore: Certainly, the technology behind TinEye is the most important one we have, and that's the ability to find an exact or modified copy of an image. We license that technology out to our clients, and they find their own uses for the technology. It can be as simple as, say, a client has two very large image collections, and they know they have overlap between these two image collections for one reason or another, and they need to find out where the identical images exist so they can create a union of the two sets without any overlap. So they will apply our technology to a problem like that. Another example would be one of our clients has an iPhone application that lets anybody take a picture of a bottle of wine and immediately recognize the wine based on the label. And they use our technology for doing that.

G. Donaldson: Speaking of that, how is your technology fitting in with the mobile computing and social networking environments?

Bloore: On the mobile side, the example I just gave of the wine recognition, and there are other people who are looking into recognizing logos or printed pages or advertising using a mobile device. And on the social networking front, one of the more interesting applications other people have told us about is helping them spot fake profile pictures. Fake profiles are very common, as it turns out, and you can do a TinEye search for a profile photo, and you may find out—from the links returned from TinEye—that a person may not be who they say they are. Many people have sent us email thanking us because they were about to be taken in by a scam artist, and they were able to find that that person they were chatting with was not who they were pretending to be.

G. Donaldson: And that could be the same for online dating and things along those lines?

Bloore: Absolutely, yeah. Identifying if somebody is who they say they are.

S. Donaldson: Have you been approached to do applications for the police, for example, missing people?

Bloore: Yes, and we're still interested in doing things there, too, to help them identify abusive and illegal images and try to help them deal with that problem as a whole. It's still a direction we're trying to get them to move in.

G. Donaldson: Are there other technologies that you track as well because there may be some convergence at some point or if a change happens in these other technologies, it may influence opportunities for you, applications of what you can do?

Bloore: It ultimately comes down to Moore's law. We can tackle bigger and bigger problems as the equipment becomes available for us to tackle these much larger problems. Video is a good example of that because in video, you're usually dealing with data sets that are, say, a thousand times the magnitude of what you're dealing with in still images. So the hardware that we're dealing with there is a crucial component. We're constantly looking at new equipment that's coming out. We make great use of things like solid-state hard drives because they allow us to do things much, much faster than we would by trying to access things on a regular hard drive. So we're looking at a lot of the technologies that are available. Some of the newer emerging things that I'm personally excited about is the Microsoft Kinect product—it came out of the video game area—that allows you to get a depth field for the scene in front of the sensor, to get a reading of the people and their actions in front of the Kinect sensor.

The Microsoft Kinect is a video game controller where the end user is watched by the Kinect controller, and they can jump around and, say, do dance moves or pretend that they're skiing. The Kinect controller can identify what they're actually doing, the motions that the person is making, and they play the game very interactively in that sense. But the actual sensor that allows them to do this is being released as a development package for other firms to start building their own products on top of. So that's a very exciting area for me personally when I think about giving vision to the blind.

G. Donaldson: You deal a lot with more static images and you want to delve into 3D motion picture technology. Will that technology change the type of service you could offer someone?

Bloore: It's a little early to say, to be honest. That area for me is probably more of a personal interest in helping the blind, and it doesn't necessarily align directly with the products and services that Idée is offering today. But who knows? It certainly could.

G. Donaldson: What is your interest in working with persons with visual impairments?

Bloore: Currently, somebody who is completely blind is aided by—for walking purposes, they're aided tremendously by a white cane—essentially a stick. It's such a very basic tool that somebody who cannot see has to work with, that I feel strongly that we can do something better with technology. I've seen that there have been many attempts through the years at doing everything from glasses that have sonar embedded in them to trying to tell you when you're approaching an object to very sophisticated systems to try to replace the retina in your eye with a patchwork of sensor arrays that actually excite the optic nerve. My feeling is that we will be able to, within our lifetimes, have very useful, very affordable tools to help out somebody with vision impairment that makes their lives better. And that's just something that I've always wanted to do. It doesn't stem directly from, say, bad vision on my part, although I don't have particularly good vision. It stems from an interest in knowing that this is a problem that we can tackle and I think that I can make a contribution by thinking about this and trying to develop the technology that can help.

G. Donaldson: In terms of the development, do you follow an agile development process?

Bloore: Loosely, I would say. We try to in the sense that it does make sense to pair up developers and get people working in small teams on things. But I wouldn't say that we specifically ascribe to any one particular development methodology.

S. Donaldson: What's the native language that they are programming in?

Bloore: All of the core work is done in C++. All the algorithm work is done in C++, and that's really necessary because we optimize the code very, very heavily, and you need a compiled language for that. We use a tremendous variety of other languages surrounding that, from relational databases to scripting languages. In particular, Python is the main one we're using as a glue language for many other purposes in the services that we deliver. It's a fantastic language, but we could not optimize it to run at the speed we need to for the core image comparison algorithms we run.

S. Donaldson: Do you use a lot of open-source software?

Bloore: Certainly. We're all tremendous fans of open-source software. I have a UNIX development background, which tends to automatically point me in the open-source direction, so certainly, in the databases that we use and many of the coding libraries. Python, for example, is open source, and that—for me, the entire open-source movement has just been fantastic to see it come about. When I started working in the commercial software field, there was no open-source movement at all, and I saw it develop. I'm so encouraged to see everything from Linux being available to many very powerful packages and languages that are all fully open source.

G. Donaldson: Are you in partnership with other companies for co-development of product or do you outsource?

Bloore: No, we do not outsource really anything. And co-development, no. There's a short answer for you. Usually, we are taking input from many potential clients, and we're distilling them into a general idea that considers all of the potential clients' needs by making it more general and packaging it in a way that we're never trying to solve just one person's needs. We're trying to solve a class of problems.

G. Donaldson: Can you give an example?

Bloore: Sure. When I talked about the fact that some of our clients would have a need to compare two very large image collections to find out where there's overlap in these collections, that's one problem. There is another problem that would be to find all the wine labels, or to be able to take the mobile phone and take a picture of a wine label and find that particular wine label in a collection of, say, hundreds of thousands of wine labels. We actually package those as the same technology and we acted in such a way that there's an API available that you can solve either one of those problems using the same package from us.

G. Donaldson: How do you collect your images for your database? How do you go about doing that?

Bloore: Well, for TinEye, we actually crawl the web ourselves. There we do have help, there's a group in California called CommonCrawl. They're crawling the web in an open-source fashion and giving that crawl of the web to anyone who wants it. They've been tremendously valuable in helping us with our ability to crawl the web. Otherwise, we'd crawl it directly on our own. Most of our clients, however, have their own image collection, so they come to us and say, "Here's my collection of 10 million images," and they want us to do something with that collection.

G. Donaldson: I wanted to ask another question about the coding part. When we spoke the other day, you mentioned that, in a way, software coding is like poetry. Can you explain what you meant by that?

Bloore: Sure. It was actually a friend of mine who was writing an article on the concept of source code as poetry and she had asked my opinion on whether code could be considered a form of poetry. And what I described to her was that I feel a very well-written code has a beauty to it. You can see it in an elegant solution to a complex problem. But to really appreciate the beauty of a piece of software, you usually have to get very, very close to a very specific problem or try to tackle the problem yourself and fail at it and not do a great job. Then, when you look at somebody else's solution, if that person has been really talented, you can immediately see some of the elegance of how they very simply solve the problem in fewer lines of code than you would ever possibly have imagined. And most developers, I would say, have developed an eye for seeing elegant solutions and want to strive to develop equally elegant solutions themselves. I think most software doesn't fall into the elegant category, but when you see it, you usually know it.

G. Donaldson: Let's spend a few minutes talking about technology investments. How does your company invest in technology?

Bloore: Well, most of our investments are in development time, in software, and to some degree they'll be in hardware purchases. Often we're very client-driven, so it will be what our clients are asking us for. But equally, I would say that when I come to the example of TinEye, this was me pushing forth the idea that we should develop this engine, that it is a valuable thing, not just for us as a company, but for the world at large to be able to search large collections of the web, of images on the web, by using an image as the search term. In reality, it was just saying, "We need to do this," and it wasn't really justified in any sense of a cash-flow projection or hardware. Certainly, we did hardware estimates for what we'd need to do this because it had to be feasible to do it without requiring hundreds of thousands of machines. That is an example of how we decide to budget for and do the biggest things that we'd ever tackled before.

G. Donaldson: Do you follow a formal process such as developing a business case and costing out alternatives and then selecting an option?

Bloore: Very, very loosely. Most things end up being maybe a quick spreadsheet, maybe a back-of-the-envelope calculation. Usually, it's very much, "Are your estimates correct within an order of magnitude?" And things can be that loose. Sometimes you make a mistake and it ends up costing you much more than you expected it to and you can't go down a particular road, but for the most part, if you're getting it coarsely correct, that's going to be fine. I don't usually see that there's tremendous value in going through such a painful formal process of, say, trying to estimate the size of a market. It's very difficult if it's a brand-new market to estimate how many people you'll sell something to.

G. Donaldson: How do you address return on investment? Do you have a formal review process for that?

Bloore: One of our products, which is our print-monitoring service, where we will suggest to our clients how they should go about doing their own re-turn-on-investment estimates and they will often go through this. Whenever you try to do a return on investment for a client, they will tend to be very suspicious of that. Rightfully so, because a vendor's estimate can be overly optimistic. So usually, they're not done for us internally so much as we're advising clients on how to do return on investment calculations. How this is going to benefit them and how they should measure the benefits for themselves.

G. Donaldson: The next topic we want to talk about is your vision of the future, where things are going. What assumptions do you have about the future of your technology and other related technologies, and how's that informing you now to make strategic decisions?

Bloore: I've touched on a few of them already, which is that being able to tackle larger problems, especially more cheaply as the cost of computing goes down, is a very valuable thing. So we see that our technology can start to be applied to much larger problems than we have to date, video being one of the main areas, and getting things into the hands of consumers and users. People who have cell phones on them, can take a picture and make that picture something that you can automatically look inside of and it can tell you something about what you're taking a picture of, and that is a valuable thing. So there's that, along with the idea that storage and the ability to gather visual information is just going to continue to grow at a tremendous pace. That's a lot of what's also driving the direction that we're looking to go to in when we are creating new products. You have to look out five years from now. What's the world starting to look like, and how should we position our services so we take advantage of what the world's going to be in five years' time?

One future vision I have is currently counter culture. One of the things that I'm kind of known for is that I do worry about costs. I'm kind of referred to as a cheap guy when it comes to spending money on equipment. So we started TinEye completely using cloud-based services on Amazon's Web Services. Pretty soon, though, we realized that we could do it much more cost-effectively on our own equipment. So this means that we moved away from cloud computing and we do everything ourselves in-house. And that's just interesting because it seems to be swimming against the stream as far as what I see when I speak with other technology people. Many start-ups I see are afraid of buying their own equipment. They don't really know how to manage hardware effectively at all, and they're afraid of what would happen if a hard drive crashes. So they tend to do everything in the cloud. I think it's really short-sighted. I think that if you're going to grow anything large and sizable, you need to do it on your own equipment, and it's far, far more cost-effective to do it on your own equipment. I have the data to prove it from our own experience, I would say. So that's just something that—I'll put that out there as a future direction—although the cloud is a very valuable thing, it can be a very expensive thing to run your business on the cloud. And I think that over the next five years, many other firms will realize that. The cloud is still potentially a very, very useful thing to many companies, but I don't think it's as cost-effective as many people are thinking it is.

S. Donaldson: Paul, what keeps you up at night?

Bloore: What keeps me up at night? Well, beyond the usual things of what happens if we have a tremendous crash or we have a fire in our data center facility—because those would end up being tremendously painful to cope with. Usually what keeps me up are ideas on where else to apply our technology. What's the next direction we should be going in? I try not to be fear-based in what keeps me up at night, and I try to be focused on what's exciting me to keep me thinking in the middle of the night, what's new?

William Ballard

Gerson Lehrman Group, Inc.

William Ballard, a software engineer by profession, is currently CTO of the Gerson Lehrman Group. Founded in 1998 and based in New York City, the Gerson Lehrman Group provides access to primary research for a wide range of companies: financial and investment institutions, life science companies, the Fortune 1000, and entrepreneurs around the globe. It connects clients with essential and timely expertise that can lead to understanding the industries, markets, and issues integral to shaping your business's success. Its extensive and rigorous compliance framework improves its clients' best practices while connecting them to the most relevant insights.

On his way to his current position, he has gone through a progression of VP of engineering and CTO jobs. He began at a startup and then participated in a number of startups, increasing in size and scale.

At Gerson Lehrman, he runs engineering and products units. Previously, he was at Demand Media, which is an online media, search engine optimization, and domain registration company. Prior to Demand Media, he was at Pluck, which was a social media tools startup. He was the founding CTO. He built products and public ratings reviews, answers, all the social media functionality that went on the major media sites.

In the early '00s, he worked as a VP of engineering at NetSpend, which was a very early prepaid debit card provider. Before NetSpend, he was an engineering manager at Works.com in Austin, Texas. He worked at Trilogy Consulting for a while and worked at Quarterdeck in Southern California, as a development manager. His journey to CTO has been about ever-increasing scale and his ability to manage more engineers and more systems.

His degrees are in mathematics and computer science from Claremont McKenna College and Harvey Mudd College.

S. Donaldson: Let's begin with your professional journey to where you are now. Can you provide us with an overview of your professional background?

Ballard: Sure. Currently, I'm CTO at Gerson Lehrman Group in New York, and I've gone through a progression of VP of engineering and CTO jobs. I began at a startup and then participated in a number of startups, which were increasing in size and scale. Probably the easiest way to think about my professional journey is through reverse chronology. Currently at Gerson Lehrman I run engineering and products units. Previously, I was at Demand Media which is an online media, search engine optimization, and domain registration company, and which went public earlier this year. Prior to Demand Media, I was at Pluck, which was social media tools startup. I worked there for three years and was the founding CTO. We built products and public ratings reviews, answers, you know, all the social media functionality that went on the major media sites. We had all the Gannett papers, and actually they still do. So it was basically MySpace in a box back when everyone was concerned about competing with MySpace. And then ironically Pluck got acquired by Richard Rosenblatt, CEO of Demand Media Group, the chairman of MySpace.

Quarterdeck was my first management job out of college. So I've sort of always been either a senior engineer or a manager. My journey to CTO has really been about ever-increasing scale and my ability to manage more engineers and more systems.

Stan Siegel: What are your college degrees?

Ballard: My degrees are in math and computer science. I went to Claremont McKenna College and Harvey Mudd College.

S. Donaldson: As you worked your way through your career, did you have different mentors along the way who helped shape your journey and provided guidance?

Ballard: I actually had really limited mentorship along the way, and that's one thing that I really struggled with. Up until about the last three years, one of the partners at Oak Venture Capital, David Black, has been a really great mentor to me. He's a guy who's literally been programming since the late '60s and has a lot of historical perspective. His perspective has enabled me to improve the way I manage and improve the way I do technology much faster than I was able to by rumbling along on my own and reading consulting books.

S. Donaldson: What did you enjoy most throughout your career?

Ballard: To me, it's the variety of the people, the variety of the technology, the diversity of ideas, the diversity of folks, and the changing problems are the things I enjoy most. I can imagine having a job that's sort of repetitive, you know, like manufacturing or accounting, but the imagination that goes along with such jobs is bad. The technology is much more open-ended and you can build your own future with it.

S. Donaldson: Let's switch gears and focus on your current job. Could you tell us about your current company?

Ballard: Sure. Gerson Lehrman is the market leader in the global marketplace for expertise. What that means is we match up business executives, investors, fund managers, and investment bankers with experts, who are doctors, lawyers, executives, technologists, academics, and consultants, so that they can get multifaceted advice on their business planning and investment decisions. You can think of it by analogy to consulting, but instead of having to hire consultants for long engagements, you get to choose from a huge network. We have hundreds of thousands of experts, some with very niche, specialized expertise. And we have a staff of researchers to help you pick the right expert in order to answer your business question. So technology-wise, it's a search engine. We are a search engine that matches up people who have business questions that really haven't been asked yet with experts in order to get them advice.

S. Donaldson: How do you screen the experts who you connect people to? Is there a process?

Ballard: As I mentioned, decision makers need to do research to make well informed decisions. Mutual funds and other investment firms have a duty to do research before investing customers' money. Corporations and non-profits as well also need specialized consultants to inform their decisions.

We provide access to insight within a rigorous and hard-to-replicate compliance framework. All GLG experts are subject to training, to contracts, appropriate incentives, transparency and audit trails. And we've invested significantly in this compliance system of processes and procedures to ensure it remains the very best in industry.

For example, every GLG Council Member, upon joining, signs a contract and completes on-line training on the company's key compliance policies. Each year, experts are required to complete follow-up compliance tutorials and sign updated contracts.

It should go without saying that Council Members may not disclose anything confidential.

We've also built a database of more than 13,000 publicly traded and private corporations whose policies prohibit employees from participating in external consulting projects such as ours. Applicants employed by those organizations are automatically prohibited from joining the GLG network.

Speaking a little more about the technology involved, on a per-project basis, we use a system of profiling questions, which is a database, almost like a template system. We design the questions in conjunction with the customer and then present the questions to experts. The experts answer those questions and then the customer reviews the answers to make the final selection of which experts to hire. In the end, it's sort of a structured interview process, but not as heavy as a full interview because you're not actually hiring a person full-time. You're going to consult with the experts for half an hour to an hour, so you're trying to establish an a priori notion of their expertise. All the data is logged and tracked in our database so that we can evaluate experts for our customers over time.

S. Donaldson: Are there categories of experts like "junior expert" to "platinum expert"?

Ballard: There are, and there's leveling based on prestige and seniority. We also have what we call Councils, which are groupings of the experts based on their seniority and prestige and influence. We also have practice areas, which you can think of as major business segments. For example, we have technology, media, telecom, or consumer goods and services councils. The councils are broad collections of industry expertise so we can use the council taxonomy to find particular experts and to know what their general expertise is. We also have their employment history and have a taxonomy classifying the types of companies and types of positions they've worked at, as well as a biography that's been written up, a few paragraphs, and the profile questions. So it's a combination of full-text, kind of Google-style search in addition to a faceted navigation kind of Amazon.com-style search.

S. Donaldson: Do the people get paid "by the drink" in terms of consulting.

Ballard: Yes.

S. Donaldson: And are people on retainer to you, or do they get paid by engagement?

Ballard: They get paid by engagement, so the economics are actually one of the best things about it. Say you're an executive at a big company or an executive at a hedge fund and you want to consult with hundreds of individuals a year, one of the big benefits of going with Gerson Lehrman is you pay us and we deal with all the billing and downstreams and we'll make 100 small, individual hourly or half-hourly payments to the experts and spread that over a large number of clients. So there's a huge operational convenience, particularly if you're a hedge fund, where you have a large amount of money to manage and not terribly many employees. The individual council members get paid and our payment system is pretty sophisticated and automated. We actually pay every council member every day if they've engaged and finished an engagement, which is an industry-leading payment system. I know, by comparison to Demand Media, where we also used an outsourced network for writing, we would only pay twice a week, so what we've got going at Gerson Lehrman is sort of state of the art.

S. Donaldson: Who do you consider your competition in your space?

Ballard: Competition is almost co-opetition as well as competition. There are all types of ways professionals conduct research – online and through consulting firms, for example. There are also other expert networks. The vast majority of them are small in comparison to us.

S. Donaldson: It sounds like a McKinsey, though, would be engaged on a longer-term engagement with a customer. Yours sounds more like you're giving spot expertise so a decision can be made to go left, right, or go deeper into detail. Is that accurate?

Ballard: That's accurate and is actually a good way of thinking about it. We will do what we call "breakout engagements," longer-term projects. But the vast majority of the delivery is phone calls and consultations, not unlike this conversation, where, if this wasn't an interview and instead you were asking me, "I'm starting a company and I want to get your idea about what kind of CTO I should hire." I would be the expert and you would be the customer in that scenario. Gerson Lehrman would connect you with 6 to 20 CTOs for you to speak to, and then we'd get the feedback.

Siegel: I noticed looking at the background on your company that it has been around since 1998. How many permanent staff do you have and do you advertise your company or do people actually come to you for helping them?

Ballard: We're a little over 800 people right now and we have grown in the last few years. The product is sold by our direct sales force both inside and outside. A lot of the business comes from referrals and people moving around the financial services industry. There are a lot of business benefits from being in New York and having a relative concentration of the financial services industry.

Siegel: How closely do you interact with your business development personnel?

Ballard: I interact with the head of sales closely and meet with the various sales managers on a regular basis. At the moment, we are rolling out salesforce.com, so we have a relatively high level of interaction with them at the moment. In general, I don't go out on sales calls.

S. Donaldson: Will, how big is your staff?

Ballard: The engineering staff is a combination of IT, development, QA [quality assurance], and some administrative. I have 82 employees on the roster this week. That's out of, let's say, just over 800 employees in the company. Of the 82 employees, about a third are IT, and the rest are divided between development engineers and quality assurance engineers.

S. Donaldson: Where do you look to recruit folks?

Ballard: Recruiting—I like to look across multiple markets, which is one thing that I've been doing much more of in the last few years. In my current job and my prior job with Demand Media, I have looked in multiple markets. At the moment, I am looking in Austin, Boston, New York City, and recruiting with multiple recruiters, as well as doing technology events and networking through folks who I know in those various cities. I found that the talent is where it is and it's difficult to get everybody to relocate to one location. Given the high demand for engineers, I've recognized that they are where they are, and I hire the people best where I can get them.

S. Donaldson: How many engineering offices do you have?

Ballard: We have three engineering offices in the U.S. and one in Dublin, Ireland.

S. Donaldson: Are the offices spread across the country in each of the major time zones?

Ballard: No. They are located in the markets we're in—Austin, Boston, and New York City—and tied to our expansion. Originally, we were very New York-based and worked in the financial services industry. We expanded in Boston where we have a decent-size financial services industry. Then the Austin office was opened several years ago. I'm very familiar with the Austin market and that's how I got connected with the Gerson Lehrman Group originally.

S. Donaldson: What do you look for in the people that you hire? What qualities are you looking for?

Ballard: I'm a big believer in hiring talent, not skills. I'm fundamentally looking for smart people who are adaptable and can get things done. I'm not looking to fill really narrow roles, I'm looking to fill roles with folks who have ideas and who are willing to do things. For example, at Gerson Lehrman, when I took over, it self-identified as a .NET [dot net] shop, which is neither right nor wrong, but had the consequence of limiting the total recruiting pool you can get to, because not every engineer wants to do .NET. A change that I've made is to open up the technology so that there's not an official or designated platform and that multiple different platforms can be used, strictly for the purpose of being able to recruit more broadly.

S. Donaldson: What do you see as major issues confronting your customers today?

Ballard: When you're making business and investment decisions, sometimes you need to know right now. I think getting our clients the right experts, getting the right answer to their question when they need it and doing an excellent job of matchmaking a person's business problem with the expert. We have to over deliver that to stay in business.

S. Donaldson: Do you see the regulatory nature of the business increasing in the future?

Ballard: Our business isn't regulated, but our customers often are, and so we're working with sort of a transitive theory of regulation. We end up complying with the regulations on their behalf. I see it as being an ongoing and important issue. And there have been some high-profile prosecutions on insider trading this year that are not related to us. That's been a distraction to many on Wall Street.

S. Donaldson: So Martha Stewart wasn't one of yours, huh? [Chuckling]

Ballard: No, no.

S. Donaldson: Right. Okay, let's shift gears here and talk a bit more about your day-to-day job. What are your main CTO responsibilities?

Ballard: The main thing is to build technology projects to make the business go. I describe it as make money for the investors, make the business go, and do so by applying technology. That tactically means managing several groups of engineers working on several products, some of which are externally facing, some of which are internally facing; sitting down and problem solving with those engineers, whether they have a technical problem or a people problem or a requirements problem; keeping communication flowing between business stakeholders, product managers, and the engineers doing the delivery. That's the bulk of my CTO responsibilities.

Siegel: Could you give a specific example of what you just described?

Ballard: Sure. Down to the technology level, just this week, I had to sit down with one of my engineers who was having trouble automating the installation of a Ruby on Rails app because he's never actually done it before. I helped him write a shell script and a make file in order to configure his environment. I help with very low-level programming detail, all the way up to thinking through product features. We've had conference calls and preparations for board meetings where we were talking about which product features we designed and are implementing in 2012, to a meeting I had with a product manager just yesterday talking about the workflow, to how and when we prioritize certain tasks.

Siegel: It's apparent that you have a broad range of responsibilities, as it were, from guiding your senior management to helping your tech guys implement things.

Ballard: Oh yeah, absolutely. For the senior management, I can be a teacher to let them know what's available with the technology and a problem solver; and the same thing for the staff, teaching different programming techniques or giving them the benefits of my programming experience or sitting with them and figuring out a technical approach in a problem-solving setting. That's really what the job is about; it's coming up with answers and solving problems.

S. Donaldson: Is there a CIO or do you handle internal systems as well?

Ballard: I handle internal systems as well, so there's no distinction between a CIO and a CTO in the company. It's all covered by technology. I have the IT function inside the technology; or I have the head of that group that's primarily focused on those issues. But we have a business-focused executive team, not really a role-focused executive team. There's a senior vice president of product who is the head of product management and design who I work with a lot. I work with the senior vice presidents and managing directors of the various business segments directly.

S. Donaldson: Understood. If you have a typical day, what's it look like?

Ballard: Sometimes my typical week is I wake up Monday morning, get on a plane, go to New York, review notes from projects and program a bit on the plane, usually with prototypes and experiments with ideas from different engineering groups. I land, go to the office in New York, have meetings with the engineering directors, as well as regularly recurring meetings with each engineering team: sitting down with the groups, talking to them about which parts of our process are working, which parts aren't working, what technology problems they're having, what communication gaps they're having. Usually, I am meeting with one or more executive stakeholders, talking to them about projects that are not in the immediate future, but right over the horizon future and working out the relative prioritization. Most of my day is involved in communication activities, making sure that people are talking, information is flowing, and that they're not stuck. I'm a big believer in meeting with all the engineers, so like a staff of 80, I have managed a staff of about 80 to 150 or more. At that level you can take the time to absolutely meet with everybody. I did a series of one-on-ones with every engineer earlier in the year, and I'll do small group meetings with them to review regularly. I think that's an important part of the everyday or every week, to make sure the communication is available. And the people can talk to me about, "What is our product strategy right now? What is our business strategy right now? What's the most important project? How can I learn new skills in order to be better at my career? Am I working on the right thing? Am I taking too long? Am I spending too much money?" Being able to have that real-time feedback, as much as possible, is very important.

Siegel: Picking up on what you just said, how do you see that role evolving over the next five years?

Ballard: In general, in the context of the company, what I would expect is that there would be more individual teams. We will have more projects, more teams, and more coordination across those teams. In terms of the overall industry, I have to say I haven't seen that aspect of the job change or evolve in the last five years. While the technology changes pretty rapidly, people are still people and making sure that they're still talking and communicating and not getting sullen is important. Engineers have a tendency to get a little passive-aggressive when they don't agree and they'll huddle up like a turtle and not talk to anybody. Those things are fairly constant, so I wouldn't imagine there would be less of an obligation for a CTO to be a communicator and to coordinate people in order to make sure that problems are getting solved.

S. Donaldson: What external organizations do you interact with? For example, do you have affiliations with outside universities?

Ballard: No, we're not really doing any of that right now. We will go to technology and training events. Like MongoDB is really popular right now and a really good product, so we go to those training events and go to vendor-sponsored training events. But there's no formal affiliation with universities or recruiting programs along those lines. In practice, I've not been one to hire directly out of school, particularly since I'm working at relatively smaller engineering shops, say 80 to 100 engineers. I'm actually much more inclined to hire people when they've had two, or five, or 10 years of work experience, especially when somebody else has already taught them how to be an employee.

S. Donaldson: What key CTO lessons would you like to pass on to other CTOs?

Ballard: The most important thing to realize is that the vast majority of stuff, whether it's projects or technologies or steps or process that you're told to do or assume is the right thing, is just a complete waste. I had one of my security engineers lamenting to me one afternoon that he really wants to be able to do the right thing, but he always just has to do the minimum. And I looked at him funny and told him, "Well, from an economics point of view, the minimum, if you've truly found the minimum, the minimum is the right thing. It's optimum. It's the least amount of cost for the maximum value."

I'm concerned that the industry as a whole has gotten so complicated because people have taken the engineering solutions and products to try to prevent any bad thing from ever happening and being beyond reproach, but this essentially will end up being uneconomical at most folks' scale. I would encourage everybody to look at the economics first rather than look at the technology, rather than look at the best practices. Start with the economics and think about it from that flow. Figure out if this project or product has an opportunity to make money or save money, and make a guess as to how much money that is, then write that number down, and don't let yourself design a solution that costs more than that number.

This situation shows up constantly in projects, where you're making a change to the accounting system and the idea is that you can improve the workflow and make accounting's job easier. That's fantastic. Making accounting's job easier is doing them a favor. It's making their lives better. But it's not necessarily good business unless you can reduce the cost in accounting by less than the cost of the engineer. That is something that consistently gets lost from what I've experienced.

For engineers, particularly if their staff-salaried engineers, when other staff and mid-level management want projects from them, they lose sight of the fact that the engineers actually cost money. In the vast majority of cases, the engineers cost more money than the business people or business process workers being automated. There's the reverse financial leverage there. So unless you're making a real dent in the total amount of manpower through an automation activity or a system activity, what you're probably doing is making it cost more by investing in software rather than buying off-the-shelf software and not programming at all.

My main advice to CTOs and CIOs is don't just do whatever the project is. It's probably not a good idea and it's probably not cost-effective when you take a step back and do the math on it.

S. Donaldson: That's a good segue for talking about technologies. Are you saying that you try to buy out-of-the-box and stick to the functionality that comes with the box? Configure the software and stay away from custom application development?

Ballard: As much as possible, and this is always, to varying degrees, a losing battle. While I know it is the case that businesses deeply believe that customizing the software, customizing their workflow, is part of what makes them special. Having worked in a lot of different businesses, the customizations that most folks make to their software are arbitrary rather than special. The customizations could be very important to the person asking for them. But in the grander macro context, such customizations tend not to be very important and not very economical. And that's always sort of a hard conversation to have and to tell someone in a polite way that their optimum idea doesn't matter. But that's definitely part of the trick: to get good at telling people, as politely as possible, that their awesome idea is probably not going to differentiate or help.

The other thing about off-the-shelf software is you really need to buy the off-the-shelf software that actually really works out of the box and not the off-the-shelf software that isn't done yet and you're paying the vendor via consulting and services to finish it for you. I know there's a lot of software that straddles that line, particularly with early-stage enterprise software startups. I have done some of those software applications myself, where the product is more a set of capabilities than it is a set of deliverables. You try to align those capabilities to the target business when you get there. I've actually found that people just generally overdo it. They will automate and customize processes that aren't running well manually, rather than focus on making a good process, running it manually, getting it well understood, simplifying it, and then automating it. There's this tendency to customize software in order to capture a complex business process because the process is too complex to do it correctly manually. The idea is that somehow doing the process with computers will make it better. However, the root cause is the complexity of the process, not the lack of automation, and so you've got to attack the process complexity first.

I still write software and definitely there are pieces that you can't buy, particularly when you are working with data. The vast majority of the work I've done in the last three years has been about applying data either for searching, data mining, machine learning, prediction, formatting, and reworking. You can think of these as sort of ETL [extraction, translation, and loading] activities manipulating your data to get the data in formats that you can exploit. There's always programming involved in that scenario and it's always customized to the individual data formats that you are working with. That kind of programming is needed so you can differentiate on data and decisions. Differentiating on application development to me is that it is difficult to see the economics.

S. Donaldson: What kind of databases are you using?

Ballard: Multiple different kinds. I'm really into it. I think of it as eclectic computing. I will routinely use relational databases, mixed platforms. For example, right now we've got SQL server and MySQL in regular use. MongoDB is a personal favorite because it really embraces the reality of web application development, where JavaScript and JSON are data models on the browser, so why not keep that data model end-to-end? I use full text indexes as databases routinely. So, products like Xapien from the open-source community work really well. Plain old tab-delimited text files are a really good database technology when you're doing set processing. Using just plain UNIX, pipes and filters and make files and shell scripts, processing large amounts of text up to hundreds of gigabytes of data volume is actually an extremely cost-effective way to do data mining. There's a full spectrum of tools to pick from—pick an amount and pick the smallest tool for the job possible. There are definitely guys who come from the point of view that they want to have standardization and pick the one right tool. I personally don't think that you can get a tool that does everything in all scenarios, so I tend to be much more eclectic in my selection.

S. Donaldson: What other types of technologies are important?

Ballard: To me, the most important technologies that have been moving along here recently are memory and solid state. If you think about how applications have been architected since I would say the mid-'90s, when you have this multi-tier setup, that is, application server or presentation server or database server, and spinning across all these different tiers and these different computers, where a normal line of business app is, say, going to process thousands of users and gigabytes to low terabytes of data. These systems are engineered across multiple computers broadly out of a concession to 32-bit memory addressing. You simply couldn't get a big enough app on a single machine in the '90s to address these user populations, so this style of development emerged where you have these tiers. These tiers lead to meaningful redundancy in the code because the data crosses the tiers. So every good programmer is going to validate data, check for security, and the stuff is repeating over and over. The typical application goes through my song of repetition, which is, "Web browser transmits to a web server and it processes through an object-oriented layer, which goes to a data mapper, which then talks to a database driver, which then talks to your network card, which then talks to your database server, which then talks to your SAN [storage area network] adapter card, which then talks to your SAN," and you're saying, "Wow. I just made a lot of copies of that data by the time it got to the web page. It's kind of crazy."

So that setup definitely works, but when you think about it end-to-end, there's a huge number of pieces involved—there are technology subspecialties whether its object-oriented programming or storage area networks, a web server applications development or JavaScript or HTML [Hyper Text Markup Language]. So you need a really high level of technical complexity to do a basic web Internet application, which is typical in the enterprise setting. So that's the background.

Going forward, the world has 64-bit computing and solid-state storage. You can absolutely, and I have done this over and over again, build applications that serve substantial user populations on single machines storing the data in memory that's your working set and spooling it out on the solid state locally and essentially replicating that entire system for availability, such as disaster recovery, like replicating it to a remote site. I refer to it as a fractal architecture that's self-similar all the way down, so there are no tiers or layers. It's going back to the classic mini- or main-frame self-contained architecture, and replicating that mode. And that is a much simpler programming model compared to what folks are doing with the layering, so paying attention to what you can get away with on one decent, say, $15,000 server. That's the most important technology difference to me.

You can use these modern data management products, for example MongoDB, to implement this fractal architecture. Let's say you're building an intranet portal application to search one of your proprietary databases. You can load MongoDB data in a full-text indexing package such as Apache Lucene. Let's say that you're using Ruby on Rails and Nginx. You can pack that all onto a single machine and then you have the benefit that the application doesn't incur any network latency internally. The web request comes in over the network and everything stays on the machine from there, and so you can have much lower latency, which is a quick and easy way to get much higher performance on an individual user basis. Given MongoDB's replication set capability, you then set up another server that sits there, replicate the data, and use your load balancer as your fundamental fail mechanism. Rather than a very complicated web server–web server farm–application–application server–cluster server failover–database server–database cluster–shared SAN storage technology, I just described a million dollars' worth of equipment in order to build a high-availability system with a traditional RDBMS [relational database management system] architecture, you only need to buy two decent PC servers with a networking software disk and build high-availability application equipment. Radically different economics that are all enabled by 64-bit memory and solid-state storage. That's the big change that I think everybody should embrace.

Siegel: Will, what autonomy do you have in implementing, particularly customizing, your infrastructure?

Ballard: Oh, I have complete autonomy on that side of the department. I certainly don't decide by myself. I have a good set of engineering directors and engineers, and we consult together in order to arrive at those conclusions. But I don't have, for example, contractual relationships with customers that prohibit a technology or constrain those technology choices. I'm obviously constrained by budget, like everyone else is. But given my focus on these minimal architectures, I find that I'm a CFO-friendly CTO because I'm usually asking for a lot less money than others.

S. Donaldson: [laughing]

Siegel: Do you have to get approval up your chain of command before you get involved with changes to your infrastructure?

Ballard: No. I work directly for the CEO. In my current job and the prior job and the prior job before that, my responsibility was to take care of the technology problems, make the right decisions, and implement them. I certainly communicate what I'm doing and describe it, but my job is to make those problems go away.

S. Donaldson: Will, given that the company provides lots of expert advice and I'm assuming that there's technical advice in that expertise, do you leverage the expertise that you provide to your customers for yourself internally to help you make those technology decisions?

Ballard: I sure do, and without this sounding too much like an advertisement, our major activity is "search." We're helping to find experts to give advice to business folks, so I'm always looking to improve our search capabilities. I will talk with one of our research managers, and our research managers are generally really smart early career experts who are really good at researching and figuring things out. I ask them, "Which of our council members can we talk to to figure out how to make it easier for you to do your job to make a good match?" They give me a list of experts who I will call. For example, I talked to a series of computer science professors, CEOs of software companies that make search products, and human factors experts about search techniques and technologies. Searching is as much about presenting the search to folks and making the search fast and interactive as it is about algorithmic brilliance. Some guys we talked to about collaborative filtering as well as latent Dirichlet allocation (LDA) and latent semantic analysis (LSA), relational math and indexing—basically finding clusters in data and data mining. I was able to use our own network of experts to come up with a really good list of improvements to make to our search engine. It was sort of self-serving for those experts because they want to get found so they can do consulting projects. It was sort of a "self-referential" project about asking the experts how we can make our system better to find experts like them. This part will unfortunately sound a bit like an advertisement, but I really think that a normal CTO/CIO out in industry is called upon to be responsible for a huge number of things that he/she can't possibly keep track of, who needs a large amount of consulting, and who could really benefit from access to direct expertise like I just described.

S. Donaldson: Right.

Ballard: Consulting with other CTOs or CIOs on an a la carte basis, as well as talking to academics and industry experts in order to get different ideas without having to go out and do the recruiting to find all these people is valuable. We've already taken care of those steps. We can search our database, match clients with experts and set up the calls. To me, it's been a really great, compelling business in that I can see how the business we're doing helps me do my job at that business better.

S. Donaldson: How are technologies like social networking impacting your marketplace?

Ballard: We released a new website in the last year, gplus.com, which is a social networking and question and answer (Q&A) product. Social networking is impacting us in that certainly there's a lot of Q&A online that is free. The existing research model, or Q&A that we deliver now is mostly via phone consultations—although we also offer surveys, roundtable discussions and other ways of connecting to outside expertise. Now we're seeing social networking as a spectrum of engagement that ranges from (1) really lightweight engagement, for example, searching Google for an answer quickly, anonymously, and hidden, to (2) online Q&A where you're probably going to be identifiable via an account, but your questions are out in the public forum, to (3) Q&A experience or online chat experience that's private because you're discussing business confidential matters, to (4) phone calls and consulting projects like the development of black papers or business strategy papers. Social media to us is extending the Q&A spectrum. It's also a way to recruit. Tools like LinkedIn and Google are incredibly useful in finding the right experts, building a network and having access to the best and the brightest to answer people's questions. Having been the CTO of Pluck and Demand Media, I have a lot of background in social media, which was fundamental to those businesses. I don't even really think of social media as separate or new. At Pluck we built our social media application server in 2005. I've been in this space for a while. I guess social media may be new in some quarters, but I think it's just part of what we do.

S. Donaldson: Is mobile computing impacting what you're doing?

Ballard: Businesses are certainly able to get more business due to mobile. I think Q&A on mobile is at the stage where we'll get more engagement, like the ability to route questions to experts if they're going to be able to answer quickly on their phone or in text. Capabilities will expand from what we have right now, which is a web portal, to a mobile-friendly web portal experience. There are two more broadly valuable areas in computing, mobile and large-scale data mining, where you can still find meaningful economic opportunities to compete on. Less interesting to me are application development types of areas, which I think is a bit saturated at the moment. I don't see how you can be competitive in the application development space.

S. Donaldson: Right. How is cyber security impacting what you do? Do you have to worry a lot about people illicitly getting into your data or eavesdropping into the consultations that are taking place online, etc.? How do you protect against such situations?

Ballard: We actually practice a pretty rigid form of perimeter security. For example, we don't even run a VPN [virtual private network] right now. People have remote desktop capabilities, and as a result of that, the data doesn't leave the network. And the consultations and conversations that are going on online on GPlus are publicly visible and available, so the only security issues are denial of service and defacement.

S. Donaldson: I see.

Ballard: We do external penetration test and scanning, sort of normal practices. I think a pretty good distinction between things that you are usually allowed to see anyway, in which case the security terms are quite light. We just need to get to our service and data that we really want to keep private, in which case it's probably not going to be on the Internet at all.

S. Donaldson: Right. How's cloud impacting your services?

Ballard: Cloud is actually having a really positive impact on how I can run the engineering process. I'm a big proponent of full system automation, and that means systems should be considerable in development, QA and production from a bare machine by my typing a single command line to kick of a series of scripts and that automation is used end-to-end. The big benefit of cloud is not so much the economics of it being in the cloud to me because the systems I run tend to be 24 by 7 systems, and when you work them out in cloud, it's really not cheaper for those systems. But the fact is that it's application programming interface-accessible, -programmable IT infrastructure has transformed the IT operator's job from being a fairly blue collar job to a very white collar engineering job. I think cloud made a better job for the IT operator who can focus on automation and programming the infrastructure rather than being the guy with the bolt driver shutting down stuff that doesn't interact so much.

S. Donaldson: Absolutely. Do you have any big projects right now that you're dealing with?

Ballard: The biggest projects we're working with right now is salesforce.com. We've been running a SugarCRM and have outgrown it now that we have worldwide sales and multiple sales revenue plans. Another project is a product called ZipDx, which is pretty compelling; it's on the Internet and it enables conference calls systems: We can schedule a consultation call and the call will go outbound as if multiple lines were dialed into a conference call bridge number. This capability is the exciting thing that turns us upside down. The conference call bridge number would call the scheduled participants at the time of the call and say, "Hey, you're on your conference call," so ZipDx has an automated reminder that calls you. ZipDx is a company and product. It's pretty cool. The other functionality it provides is the ability to electively have transcripts of the calls, which would be useful right now because you're going to transcript this call.

S. Donaldson: It would be very useful. [Laughter]

Ballard: It would be very useful, and it would work exactly in this scenario. Another really important feature is the ability for compliance officers at our customers to be able to selectively call in to these conferences and listen in and observe their employees' questions, or listen to their employees' questions. We also think this technology can make lives easier for our experts because when you call in to the conference room system, it counts the minutes for you and it fills out the bill and the time card. As an individual expert engaged in consulting with us, that's just one less thing you have to do, so you can automatically get paid without having to log into our web portal and submit your time.

S. Donaldson: Very nice.

Ballard: Yeah, ZipDx solves a lot of problems and that why we're really excited about implementing it.

S. Donaldson: What are your favorite technologies, those technologies that you keep a personal eye on?

Ballard: Personal eye on? I do a lot of work with machine learning, particularly with support vector machines and mathematical, linear algebra-type approaches. I use a lot of Python and C code and FORTRAN code that's been lying around since the beginning of time, using really simple, ancient programming styles. I should say UNIX is my architecture for building new applications rather than big, object-oriented architecture. MongoDB is really compelling to me in that you can build very fast, very simple operational-shaped Internet applications. On the data center side, again, the 64-bit large memory computers with 300 to 500 gigabytes of RAM and solid-state local storage are really compelling to me. I keep an eye on automation technologies running an internal cloud like VMware's product vSphere. There are open source alternatives as well, especially to have the Amazon.com-level API automation they have. Programming tools- and languages-wise, classic core scripting languages that are now in fashion again, Python and Ruby in particular, JavaScript is extremely resurgent and given that everyone more or less has to go the web app, JavaScript is wonderful whether you're an engineer that likes JavaScript or not, you need to know JavaScript and be engaged with it and server-side JavaScript. Things like NJS JavaScript Interpreter are really compelling. We have this one project going on with NJS. We're drifting away from the classic C#-, Java-, C++-style of object-oriented programming into more of a functional transformation style of programming, running data through transforms and templates that ultimately result in a web page. But that's definitely resulting in less code and simpler programs.

S. Donaldson: Very interesting.

Ballard: Functional programming is in a paradigm whether you use an explicit functional programming language or not, I think is important.

Siegel: Let's shift gears for a minute and talk about technology investment. How does your company invest in technology?

Ballard: We invest on multiple different levels. I alluded to this topic earlier when I was speaking about the ROI [return on investment] on a per-product basis. There's base-level technology that we need to get the job done. For example, in our setup, the most important piece of technology is our phones. Telephony systems that are available and keeping those phones working and expanding them so that there's enough phone capacity for all the phone calls we need for talking to the experts is critical. On a product basis, we charter the projects broadly based on a business unit stakeholder belief that there is an ability to make or save money. We work to build a solution that we try to fit inside of that economic manifold of, "Here's the money I think I can make. We need to spend less money than that in order to make it." So there's certainly not technology for technology's sake. Then we have products like GPlus, which are substantially more strategic and are based on a market observation that this consultation and question-and-answer and expert network business is going to have an online component. We need to have an engagement of mechanism beyond phone calls. And right now we're doing that with online Q&A. The investment there is to increase our ability to connect to experts or with customers on sort of a different channel.

Siegel: What is your role in this investment process?

Ballard: The main thing that I end up doing is being the guy in the room reminding everybody that engineering costs real money and we need to figure out what the upside opportunity is and that the upside opportunity needs to be reducible to actual hard dollars, not simply to things like a convenience or "it would be nice" type of activity. Then again, we're going back to the fact that engineers are actually tons more expensive than people realize, particularly if you're looking at doing any kind of customization at all. I'm always the guy asking, "How does this make the company money?" And, conversely, working with the engineers, reminding them that the project that we're working on is being done within the context of the company and that there is a finite amount of money to be captured with a successful project, and that they need to design a solution that fits inside those economics rather than design the solution that intrigues them or that they want to try or that they want to learn on the job. I'm not against people learning on the job, but not to the extent that it wastes the company's money.

S. Donaldson: Do you get involved in mergers and acquisitions?

Ballard: Not in my current job and that's really refreshing because previously I was involved in scores of mergers and acquisitions, and bringing together different teams was actually part of the challenge. It's amazing how much less complexity there is when you don't have a lot of mergers and acquisitions. Having switched from Demand Media to Gerson Lehrman Group, I've got real time this year, which is a big compare-and-contrast to my previous job. Mergers and acquisitions are really hard.

S. Donaldson: Not having to deal with mergers and acquisition has freed up time for you to spend dealing with the question, "How does this project make the company money?"

Ballard: Right. With mergers and acquisitions, lots of people are brought together who might not actually have been picked to work together due to their circumstances, their culture, and the mixes. You spend a huge amount of time getting people to get along and working on communication gaps. You really don't have to spend anywhere near as much time getting people to get along in a company that's grown organically versus a company that is acquired.

S. Donaldson: Right.

Ballard: In the organically growing company, the internal systems end up being more stable than when you grow through acquisitions. With acquisitions you end up with lots of stuff that does not work well together. For example, it's surprising how difficult it can be when you turn off an acquired company's accounting system. Integrating the new company is a pretty good project, and not having to do the "turn the XYZ system down project" is actually liberating so we can focus on top-line activities and making the business better rather than always have to work so much on streamlining.

S. Donaldson: When you turn "things" off you find out how they're really connected to a lot of other "things" you didn't know about.

Ballard: Yeah! Absolutely! Again, it's never easy. I think presumably you could just force it to be simple by just turning off the acquired systems, but there's an actual group of people who depend on those systems, and if you just blow up their world, then you just turn the technology problem into a psychology problem.

S. Donaldson: Right. Let's switch gears once last time. I'd like to spend some time discussing your vision of the future and what future changes you think will have the most important effect on Gerson Lehrman?

Ballard: I think the ever-increasing acceleration of open source is going to provide companies like mine the ability to fulfill what is thought of as custom software, but without really having to do that much development. In the last five years, use of open source seems to have picked up. Part of the adoption is due to the startup movement. Part of the adoption is the collapse of the dominance of Microsoft and Sun and IBM on the developer mindshare. I think that's going to give us things that I can't tell you what they're going to be, because there's a new thing every week. You go read Hacker News, and there's a new library or a new programming language or some new tool, but it's almost like a Cambrian explosion of new ideas. Staying on top of that and being aware of those things as they come along, and picking the ones that work for you—there are a whole lot of choices—and that to me has been the biggest technology impact and change.

On the delivery side, I have been doing continuous deployment cycle with dozens of releases a day over the last few years. Getting all of our product teams to be working at that velocity, where the unit of release is an individual feature rather than a large batch will have a large impact on us because it will lower the cost of failure. Not every feature of a product is a good idea, and many times you can't tell until after you've done it. So what you need to do is to be able to get it out into production as quickly as possible and figure out whether or not it's a good idea by actually doing it. I think that's true for us. I think that's true for many companies, going into a faster cycle time and lowering the cost of failure, and really adopting a startup experimental style of development for projects that aren't exactly experimental and you're trying to figure out if you have a new market opportunity or a new feature opportunity.

I think the things I mentioned earlier about 64-bit architectures, I've been doing those for a few years now. There are definitely groups inside the company that need to get switched over to that because we have systems going back to 1998. I think embracing the fact that the hardware has changed in a fundamental way and programming changes to accommodate that really opens different application avenues. For example, we have a search engine internally right now that we use. It's pretty good, but it's not very fast. I was able to use memory on a single server, 64-bit, off-the-shelf, open-source to build an internal search engine prototype that answers queries three orders of magnitude faster. In the course of doing that, essentially you don't have to hit the search button anymore. It works almost like Google instant. The research managers can engage in more searches per minute. It embraces the fact that search and discovery results are going to an expert in an incremental process. That's because if you knew what you were looking for, you would just type in the guy's name, then search and explore the data. Building really fast applications that let people explore and do real-time data mining and getting those results out to the desktops to let end business users drive their decisions with real-time data has really been the promise for a long time. I know having such a capability is doable with the technology that's available now. Of course, five years ago, I wouldn't have believed that you could do it.

S. Donaldson: Right.

Ballard: It wasn't real time enough to be real time. By "real time," I mean like video games level of latency; you push a button and it happens right now. There's no "count to 30" or "count to 6" kind of thing here.

S. Donaldson: What do you like best about being the CTO? And the follow-up question is, what do you like least about being the CTO? Not that we want you to say bad things about your job. [Laughing]

Ballard: I'm actually thinking about the questions not so much in terms of my current job but in terms of the role that I've had in multiple different companies. Being the CTO has this really awesome benefit in that in many circumstances, if you're good at it, you get to be the internal consultant that gets to help solve everybody's problems. Your reach and scope inside the organization can be really broad, and you can develop really good relationships, and you can have impact across every line of business.

I'd also say in a sense that's the downside because as the CTO you're sort of intermingled with everyone. Your accountability is diffused across all the business units, so it's very easy to get into the trap of building the projects that everybody's asking for, getting to the end of the year and realizing that all of your projects were a complete waste of time. And that hasn't happened to me in this job, but that's definitely happened to me before in life, where I did everything everybody asked and it was all the wrong things. Wow, that was a shame. And because you don't have your own P&L [profit and loss], your success and failure is intermingled very heavily with your customer satisfaction, probably to a fault in most organizations, where the success and failure metrics really should be a lot more about economics and much more about business. However, in practice, because you don't have a P&L, your metrics end up being, "What have you done lately?"

S. Donaldson: How do you see the CTO role evolving?

Ballard: There is a split horizon on the CTO role. There are CTOs that aren't VPs of engineering or CIOs in any way and are almost completely product- or visionary- or outward-facing or market-oriented. There are CTOs that, like me, are very operationally focused. My goal is to find technology and apply technology and build product with it.

Then there's the CIO role, which pre-existed the CTO role and worked in larger companies. I really don't understand, at least from how I do the CTO job, why there's still a CTO/CIO distinction in a lot of companies. I would expect a lot of people to be asking that question as well. Do you need multiple heads of technology in companies, particularly ones that aren't technology-focused? I think there's potential for some streamlining there.

I'm of the mind that CTOs should have operational responsibilities, staff management, delivery of project, operations, because if you don't have to run your product and actually service customers with it, you're not really forced to confront all the issues of technology and design. You're able to skirt around the harder and nastier parts. I would expect a lot of businesses to be asking this kind of question.

In terms of scope and impact on the business, it's my hope, although I don't necessarily have any reason to believe it, that the CTO job will be substantially more focused on economic impact using technology rather than addressing technology issues. So it's not an IT type of job, but that it's far more of a problem-solving consultative role.

Siegel: Will, we want to wrap up here with two final questions. What's next in your career and what keeps you up at night?

Ballard: So for me, I've fortunately risen to the level of my competence while I'm relatively young. I don't actually aspire to be anything other than the CTO. I think that there's a lot of room for me to get better at this job, and I've been trying to get better at this job. I expect the scale of it to grow in terms of economic impact, a bit in terms of staff and budget, but in terms of career aspirations for me, I would like to see me being a successful CTO over an array of companies over time where I can really make an impact on the business. That's my career plan.

With respect to what keeps me up at night, I worry about the people a lot, maybe even to a fault. There's no process or magic technology that's a substitute for smart people working hard. I spend a lot of time worrying about my employees' relationships with each other, their satisfaction with their career and their boredom level. Is my hyper-focus on economics optimization making the work stale and boring for them? I worry about recruiting because there's a meaningful war for talent out there, and ready capital for smart young folks to start companies. I've started a few companies myself, and competing against that allure is very difficult for an established company. Finding the way to pitch your business to somebody who has the opportunity to start their own company and is going to be successful at it is difficult. Such a person is the person you want as an employee. You want to be able to convey to them how they could go start their own company, but going into an established company, you can get a ton more leverage on your work and you can achieve a bigger financial outcome or bigger impact on society.

Those are the things that I have always worried about.

David Kuttler

Johnson & Johnson, Vertex

David Kuttler *currently consults on the use of technology driven innovation for business growth, IT governance, technology life cycle management and aligning IT to different business models in complex organizations. Prior to this consulting role, he was the SVP & CIO at Vertex Pharmaceuticals. Before Vertex, he was the world wide VP of technology and architecture at Johnson & Johnson. Early in his career, he worked within financial services and technology organizations, the latter including IBM, where he started in the development organization, becoming a technology leader for the insurance industry solution team as part of the marketing organization. He has a BS in Psychology, and a master's in Information Systems Management.*

David has worked for a variety of different companies each with their own business models. This experience has given him the ability to apply organization and technology solutions to real world situations. He has accumulated realistic experience about what's available, how things work, how different companies think and do things and how they work with technology, shaping what is needed to deliver the best results.

He defines the CTO as a core partner to the CIO, helping establish and market the IT organizational strategy, finding and fixing operational gaps, and looking for innovation opportunities. He sees the CTO as a developer, operator, and/or partner with others for the strategic platforms which become the core foundation of all IT execution.

Scott Donaldson: Let's begin with what you're doing today. I understand you've held various technology positions during your technology career, and most recently you were at the SVP and CIO at Vertex Pharmaceuticals. And before Vertex, you were the world wide VP of technology and architecture at Johnson & Johnson. And so what would be useful is if you could provide us with an overview of your professional background and how you came to work for Vertex and Johnson & Johnson.

Kuttler: Sure. So it's funny. For a long time I referred to my career history as my "assorted past." And I call it my "assorted past" because it was a variety of roles and jobs in different industries; I was not always in the pharmaceutical industry; I was also in financial services, and technology companies. I've worked for a whole variety of different companies each with their own business model. Each company offered a different way to learn about technology and how technology operates in the world that we live in. And by joining and becoming part of these different companies, I built up a really good understanding about what's available, how processes work within businesses including vendors, how different companies think about things —and how they work with technology.

I was at Stevens Tech in Hoboken taking my master's and the head of the master's program there, recommended me to Johnson & Johnson. Johnson & Johnson had a very unique policy which allowed them to hire people opportunistically. That meant that if someone was recommended to them from an internal or external source – that could provide value now or in the future, J&J would hire you with the discussion being, "Listen, there's no confirmed role, but we'd like to bring you on board because we believe that you could bring value here. We believe you're interested in the same things we are." As a result of their hiring process I was brought on board and spent about nine years there, working as part of the IT leadership team. They were some of the most exciting times of my career; however, over time I missed being part of a smaller growing business where I could have one-on-ones with the management team, and engage in a conversation about how IT could help the business grow. It was during this time that I was contacted about Vertex. Vertex was a biotech that was in the process of going through a major change, transitioning from an amazing research organization to a fully integrated biotech adding supply chain, medical, regulatory, financial, compliance, safety, sales and marketing capabilities to support bringing its first product to market. The founder believed that information technology was a core part of making that happen and believed that with my experience I could make that happen for Vertex.

Donaldson: It's a unique approach that Johnson & Johnson has. We call it "putting people on the bench," and as the opportunity arises, you fit them into the opportunity. Well, what was your educational background, and was it tied to your career in any way?

Kuttler: I believe that all business owners have to be leaders in the part of the business they are responsible for. As a result, my education and early experiences were all about gaining as much broad based experience as I could. My masters came later in my career, in 2000, because at that time many things were changing and there were new approaches that IT needed to take to continue to be successful. My time at Stevens helped shape new directions I would take. Throughout my career I used my undergrad degree in psychology to help me better work with people and processes. It was not something I originally intended but I am sure glad I did.

Donaldson: So as you traversed through your career, were there mentors or people who advised you, to help shape your career along the way?

Kuttler: I don't think you can take on a role today and not have had people help you and point you in the right direction at different points in your career. For me there is no one individual—that I could point to directly and say we established a formal mentor and mentee relationship. I worked for IBM for a long time, early in my career. And I worked independently before that in one- and two-man operations and startups. In each of those cases, there was either the leader of the company or someone I respected who was a partner of mine who I would always spend time with and say, "Do we believe there's a different way to do that? Is there an approach I could take that might do that better?" because I'm not inclined to think I have the answer to everything. I would tend to seek feedback as part of my development in hopes of growing and doing things better. And because I have that assorted past, where I've gone into different businesses, I always needed to learn something about how each business operates, what's different in the model, what are its challenges, and how can we use technology differently to help solve it? That's always caused me to get engaged with people in the organization. And as a result of that, there's always been someone in the organization who's turned out to be a strong supporter and a strong, guiding force for me. So throughout my career in each role I have had there has always been someone that I learned a lot from and that helped me in my career as I moved forward.

Donaldson: When you were at IBM, where were you located? What did you do?

Kuttler: In three locations because you can never be in IBM and just be in one. Inside, they would always say that IBM stood for "I've been moved." I started in White Plains NY, and then my group. The development organization, moved up to Norwalk Connecticut. The target location for that team was eventually Southbury Ct, but prior to that final move I made a change in my role and transitioned to the systems engineering part of the marketing organization at 590 Madison and spent the majority of my IBM career in New York City.

Donaldson: So in your "assorted past" here, as you say, what did you enjoy most about your positions?

Kuttler: For me, part of the enjoyment in life comes from learning new things, and with each position I have always grown, whether I was accepting more responsibility, moving up in the organization, or I was doing something different, I was always learning something new about a business. So for example, J&J was 200 plus companies. You can imagine it was very exciting to spend time learning the different businesses and different business models, how each operated and what made them successful, kind of what drove them. So that's one aspect. Another was the people that I met along the way; there have been managers, leaders and partners that have I found absolutely fascinating; they were all engaging people to work with. Another part of the role I enjoyed included our vendors. At J&J, as an important customer to many of our vendors, we would meet their leaders and, I learned how these relationships were very important to us, and how they helped us be successful. In some ways, partnering with companies, working on direction, setting joint strategy and helping each other get there at this scale was something new for me. But it wasn't what I remember most about go to work every day. What made it exciting was learning new things, delivering great stuff and the people that I got to work with.

Donaldson: I can relate to that. I think that's true in a lot of our careers where we've had an opportunity to have continuous learning and with people that are smart and enjoy similar things. So let's shift gears a little bit here and talk about Vertex for a few minutes. My understanding when you were at Vertex is that you were the CIO, but you also had CTO responsibilities. So to help set the context here, could you spend a couple minutes explaining what Vertex does and what some of the marquee products and services were?

Kuttler: Sure. Vertex is a biotechnology company located currently in Cambridge, Mass. The thing that's absolutely fascinating about Vertex is that the founder ran Vertex for 20 years without a product of its own that it sold and marketed. So here was a solid, important and relevant research company, a fascinating place from that perspective that made a decision to become broader and to transition from that model to one in which they would become a commercial organization by bringing one of their potential products to market.

Donaldson: Okay.

Kuttler: To do that, we needed to establish the technology foundations and broaden some others to help to support Vertex's business plan. Medical, compliance, sales, marketing, supply chain, and all of the other functions—financials, HR—that enable a company to actually bring its products to market, were all areas we invested in. So, in the end, when we brought our Hepatitis C product to market, the necessary foundations were in place to manufacture, deliver, sell and support the product in the marketplace. What Vertex did that was so important was to change the standard of care for Hepatitis C by bringing to market a product that now can potentially provide a cure.

Donaldson: So in that role, did you handle any of the internal research and development?

Kuttler: Yes, the founder truly believed that information and information technologies could change how research was done and could bring value to it. Hmm, I don't know. "Change" may not be the right word, but to enhance, drive, and support research in pretty sophisticated ways. I had responsibility and staff allocated to research, sales, medical, compliance, supply chain and G&A departments within Vertex. So internal R&D had IT folks assigned who were in some cases scientists themselves who were conversant in what a scientist needed to do and they worked with them helping build IT capabilities that could aid early research and development.

Donaldson: Was that a large budget?

Kuttler: Large is always relative to the company that you're talking about. In our organization it varied year to year but on average 20% of my budget was allocated to the research organization.

Donaldson: I think that's substantial. Did you have an opportunity to be involved in customer engagement and be more customer-facing instead of internal facing?

Kuttler: Sure. IT participated with HR in building out the training program for the new sales force that was going to become our customer-facing organization. They would be the ones to talk with the doctors, caregivers, hospitals and pharmacies, so, we did not have direct customer contact, but we created the platform the sales and marketing teams would use and supported them during their training process and into the field as they worked with our customers. When bringing a product to market there are strict regulatory limits about who you can communicate with, and what you can say in advance of a product being in the market, so I did not have the opportunity to be directly customer facing. In my prior experience with J&J we had many products in the market and I would go out with the sales team to visit the doctors and hospitals that used our products.

Donaldson: Okay. Did you have a large staff of developers? Did you outsource a lot of it?

Kuttler: It was a real mix. The way that I like to think about it is that there's a pyramid model that can represent needed services. The foundation of that pyramid is commodity services which don't need to be built anew because they are well understood and are better delivered as an industry standard rather than being re-invented, these we are better off purchasing than building.

Donaldson: Right.

Kuttler: They're, simple and easy to identify for the most part. For example you don't really want to redefine a purchase req., everybody's got a process for doing that, and if you can do it effectively and efficiently, that's really what you're after.

Donaldson: Right.

Kuttler: The second level of the pyramid contains solutions that need to be modified to fit the business and the business model you're in. Today's technology choices include sophisticated configurable tools. These tool/software manufacturers, SAP and Oracle for example, perform commodity functions really well and offer the opportunity to configure their platforms so that if you have an industry specific process that needs to be followed you can configure the system to do what works best for your organization.

The third level of the pyramid is for innovation or experiments where there isn't a good partner or solution available, these include functions that are considered competitive advantage; and there is a necessity and value to building these capabilities on your own. Our development organization represented and supported all the levels of the pyramid, we partnered and leveraged where appropriate but in all cases took compete responsibility for any solution we provided to our Vertex partners.

Although the pyramid helped us with many of our decisions, it did not help as much with resource (people) capacity. One good example we had to resolve was what to do about reporting capabilities. If you're bringing a new product to market or a variation of an already released product, there are many things you want to report on. And what happens is that there's a whole series of requests that start getting funneled into the IT department really, really quickly that need very quick response: How are we doing? What do our markets look like? Can we get data delivered in order to understand why people are buying? Why they're not buying? Why aren't people renewing? Why are they renewing? What's making this segment of the company operate better than the others? What are the financials? How is that working? These questions come up for everything from the supply chain all the way through the sales side. All of that really gets pushed very hard when you're doing something new and you're bringing a new product out into the market. So reporting is an example of where you need to be able to flex and deal with that flow coming in. It's kind of like the storm that hits. But then it settles down, and the streams calm down again. You need to be able to deal with that. Knowing this in advance allowed us to establish partnerships with companies to help us deal with those situations where we thought we might get a substantial push and become overwhelmed. We'd be sure we had them on standby, so that we could work through that with them. And then there were other times where we were just doing things from a commodity perspective, at the lowest end of the spectrum, where we just needed to be able to execute over and over and over again in a reliable way. One imperative we always needed to keep in front of us was that we owned the products. We had responsibility for any product that we provided to or for Vertex. Because of that, we had to know a lot about what was going on and keep track of it. It created the need for a new skill and process for vendor management and governance.

Donaldson: It sounds like a lot of the configurable applications. When you do that, you end up implementing the business rules that "come out of the box." Did you find that to be restrictive in any way?

Kuttler: The challenge is to understand what you're trying to get done and its priority. One aspect is "This is how the vendor perceives this to work, and if we do it this way, we can do it very quickly."

Donaldson: Right.

Kuttler: There is usually a conversation around, "Well, we have been doing it this way, and this is really important to us. So we want to be able to continue to follow our process." And as a result you may look at it from a configuration perspective and say, "Okay, well, that aspect of the solution/tool is configurable, so we can make some changes to that." Our strongest pushback came when there were things that weren't in the configurable parameters; so, if you were asking for something that was out of what was configurable, we would look for a business justification to say, "Okay, how does that really help us?, Because it's not only the configuration change we're going to make for you here, but it's also that we have to integrate that into the other business functions that may need the data or information that comes from this process." So that would become a very robust conversation. We'd try to drill into those pretty hard.

Donaldson: Right.

Kuttler: If in the end we all agreed to accept the changes we worked very hard on the configuration changes, integration into other systems, and a way to include these changes into the life cycle management of the solution/tool we were using.

Donaldson: Did the people that reported to you have a unique set of skills? Were they germane to the industry associated with information technology?

Kuttler: So it's funny you ask because we made a change in how we looked at hiring. The tendency is to only look for somebody who's done it before, not necessarily somebody who can really think about the problem and potentially address and offer you different ways to do the same thing. What we looked for when we hired, depended on the role. We had positions that had requirement which included specific substantial knowledge about an area. But if they were a business analyst, for example, they needed to be much more broad-based than narrow. They needed to understand the current business need, predict what short term changes might come, match that against what was available already within Vertex and help us determine if we needed something new. This requires a person with good industry knowledge, excellent understanding of IT process and capability and great intelligence and partnership that can help the IT organization deliver the complete solution. If we are hiring someone to perform backup support, the area they are in is narrow and they need to understand the tool sets and things we were looking for, but we still looked for a person who was a thinker and who was energized by new opportunities, because you always want folks to be able to grow in an organization and do different things. For the senior people, we stressed strong management experience. They needed to come from an industry that had to deal with compliance or government regulation. Big industries in this space included pharmaceuticals, medical device companies, and financial services, just to name a few.

Donaldson: Mm-hmm.

Kuttler: Each one of those organizations has to do a substantial amount of government reporting as part of normal business. Appreciating what that means helps define and decide the process you follow so that you can always meet the regulatory objective. Without that previous experience, it is very difficult to understand the impact in everything you do. Another senior skill we thought was very important was governance. We assumed that we would always be building and developing new things in the IT space, so it was always about continuous learning about IT and business developments. We wanted to keep reinforcing good foundations: that made us look for strong skills in change management; you knew why it was important; you knew how to deal with a customer and an internal partner within the business and what that meant; that you worked well with other people both across your organization and outside of your organization; and that you knew that vendors were a part of your team. It made hiring very tough; these skills are the things that we looked for overall. Last but not least everyone we hired had to be excited and interested in what Vertex was accomplishing and there had to be a cultural fit that would help a person be successful in our organization.

Stan Siegel: What was your role in actually selecting candidates to be interviewed?

Kuttler: Because we were making a change in the organization and the types of people we were looking for, I asked to see anybody who was manager or above that we hired into the organization. I had a team get together and talk about how we would do hiring differently than we had done it before to help with our different needs and the changes we were making to the model of how IT executes. We used those recommendations as part of our hiring process.

Siegel: How did the new hiring approach work out regarding who stayed and who didn't?

Kuttler: We actually did pretty well, I think. We went from a fairly substantial turnover rate to a lot less in terms of year-on-year changes. The people stayed because they were much more knowledgeable about what they were getting into and they understood where we were going, so there were very few surprises on that end. We had a better sense of the people coming in because we spent more time with them and used a broader array of people to help us with those assessments.

Donaldson: Before we get into your experience at Johnson & Johnson, how did you balance your CIO and CTO duties at Vertex, or did you see them as one and the same?

Kuttler: In my CIO role, I have to understand what the organization is doing, set a strategy that aligns with the overall business direction which can be dynamic during the building, creating, and running of the business. In the IT operating model for Vertex the CTO is the person who runs the infrastructure and enterprise platforms for the organization. Anything that application development does: connections with outside partners, overall IT security, email, phones. All come through the CTO role. These are the foundations that everything else rides on. The better those functions work, the better the rest of the organization works because they're all so heavily interdependent on each other. We made sure that the CTO was integrated into the decision process for new applications, changes in the way we were going to do things, how to streamline and become better and more efficient and effective at being an IT organization. Without synergies between the CTO role and the rest of the organization we could have never done things as quickly and effectively as we did.

Donaldson: Okay. I'd like to move on now to your role at Johnson & Johnson. Your title, as I understand it, was VP of technology and architecture. Is that essentially the role of the CTO that you had?

Kuttler: So, the way I defined the CTO for Vertex, being a much smaller organization was very focused around the infrastructure. At J&J, it wasn't focused so much around the infrastructure but around the strategy and the planning and the direction for what technologies would be used, how they might be deployed, and how we might do some things differently, and how we might fill gaps and white spaces created by the new needs that the companies might have going forward. And although there was an infrastructure component to that in terms of how I might apply or use or deliver that service, it was much more at the strategy level, the selection level, and the integration level into the Johnson & Johnson companies and our partnerships.

Donaldson: Okay.

Kuttler: So a change from infrastructure, some might say on a different way of thinking about it.

Donaldson: I see. Did you have formal processes to help you make those decisions on which way to go with strategy and how to plan out what the future vision was going to be?

Kuttler: Sure. The thing that was different was in a company as large as Johnson & Johnson, it's difficult to take a piece of paper and in 10 boxes or less, put a strategy map up on the wall and say, "Okay, this is our strategy. This is going to work for a whole lot of decentralized, highly independent, individually focused companies. And, you know, people might actually ask for that. They might say, "Okay, so what is the strategy?" especially vendors that we would talk to. They would say, "Where are you guys going?" The real challenge became how we used and developed a series of functions to help us plan and create a future vision. It started with a standards and strategies function within the organization that helped make decisions and look at what different groups of companies might be doing, and how they might be doing it, how we might become more efficient over time as we added an architecture function within the organization which gave us more of an end to end view of our business processes and the technology that supported them. . And from those organizations we began to examine what needed to occur or what might occur better. For me there was a major event that helped put all this in place. So early on in my J&J tenure, the operating companies were asked by the executive team to take a look at how they might use the internet differently and how they might change the business plans to adopt and leverage and drive utilization of the internet. And funny enough, at the same time, the IT organization was being driven to be very cost-effective and cost-conscious, so what they were trying to do was to shut down the use of the internet. They were trying to limit it and saying, "Okay, we shouldn't be doing this. We shouldn't allow shopping sites. We shouldn't be doing these other things." So immediately you could see that there was a positioning that wasn't going to work. So we put a plan in place and said, "Listen, this is not the most appropriate way to go. There are business plans being developed right now on how to use the internet very strategically and drive its utilization. So we're going to need to not only build that function more substantially, but we're going to have to figure out what functions we want to own strategically to support the organizations and where we will look at partners more strongly for those business needs we have chosen not to do internally and connect to the partners in a much more substantial way so all meet the business objectives better, faster, and cheaper." So that's kind of how we approached it. If you ask the question, "What technologies did J&J have?" the answer is, "All of them"—probably not uncommon in a large company. But we were getting better at focusing on the things that we really needed. We would then develop the skills and dedicate the resources so that these services became robust and provided real value to us. We made sure to do this with partners as well. We would talk to vendors and say, "Listen, if you want to sell more licenses and drive this functionality within our organization, here's a way to think about where we're going and what we needed." So we used the standards and strategies folks to help plan and help build and gather input from the companies to set our standards in the end allowing for more comprehensive contracts. We also did advance reviews with the architecture organization so we knew how those things would work together before we brought them on board.

Siegel: When you worked at J&J—I see it was 10 years, from '99 to 2008, was your office in New Jersey?

Kuttler: It was in New Brunswick.

Siegel: Given that you were in New Jersey and in proximity of Rutgers and also to Princeton, did you have any relationships with those two particular universities regarding technology issues?

Kuttler: The answer to your question is yes, but let's not limit it to just to Princeton. The IT organization operated as part of every J&J company. J&J operated in 51 countries with major build-outs on each of the continents. We had to think about what new developments we were looking at and bring the best people on board. So we would align the leadership of the IT team with universities around the world. Each one of us took on responsibility for a university. And mine, was Stevens Tech in Hoboken. So I would go out there and talk to them both on the recruiting side and the course development front. In addition, my organization held a relationship with MIT. We invested in some areas where MIT was doing unique development and programs at MIT that fostered innovation. MIT was an amazing place to spend time!

Donaldson: How large was your staff, and how many direct reports did you have?

Kuttler: So I had a number of roles in J&J. Across all of my roles it was a little over 200 people. We had a very strong matrixed organization, so if we were working on a project that might affect four or five companies, with the medical device group, for example, there might be a group of 40 or 50 people working with vendors on design and configuration. There may have been five or six of those projects going on at any one time, in addition to other things going on. Those were part of my matrixed responsibilities. There was always a flux of things that came and went. But I had fundamentally about 200 folks working on stuff

Donaldson: And they were spread across all the companies or were they centrally located?

Kuttler: They were centrally located.

Donaldson: Would it be fair to say that with the 200-some companies that make up J&J, did they all have a CTO function? Did those folks report to you in a dotted-line way or were they given autonomy to do what they needed to do locally?

Kuttler: So the CTO function at J&J within the companies was not a defined role. What we did to foster the CTO role is establish architects in each of the organizations; people who would help work with business and IT owners, to help build IT strategies and IT models that would be long-lasting, that would integrate well and fit in with the rest of the enterprise easily and cost-effectively. And we thought that that would help make things flow smoother and easier and help reduce costs in the long term. There were other things that we would try to do such as how we did contracts with major vendors that we were working with. At one point those were all handled by the operating companies, but, as you can imagine, that turned out to be very inefficient because we never got the benefits of scale. We pulled some of that in and began to build some enterprise IT contracts.

Donaldson: Right, right.

Kuttler: It sounds simple to do, changing the contract with vendors but to get it done we had to talk to the operating companies and make sure that whatever needs they had were being addressed. Although each J&J company did not have the CTO function each one had a CIO, or a VP of IT, who was responsible for the IT service delivery for that company. Their objective was to be the IT leader that aligned IT with their business and make the local decisions necessary to make the company successful.

Donaldson: I see. Were systems standardized throughout the operating companies or were the connections, back to the architecture, the glue that kept them together?

Kuttler: It was for the most part the connections through the architecture that brought everything together. J&J's history included a substantial amount of acquisitions and divestitures. Each company that became a J&J company brought its own technology, and the question was, "How do you integrate them?" What choices do you make, and how do you make those choices about whether you keep their applications and infrastructure or transfer to in-house technology? We used the architects to help make our decisions, they might say, "Listen, we have a product internally that covers 80–85% of what we understand your business to be. Let's take three or four people to drill through the rest of that. You were independent before and you didn't have the option to use the kind of platforms that we have." That really started to take hold later on as we began to adopt and bring in to place more substantial robust systems and then create core services that people could leverage and use as long as they met their objectives. But each operating company still made the decision about whether they would come on board or not. They were incented to get the businesses on board because it almost always was cheaper to run it internally, but there was no requirement for them to do so.

Donaldson: Right.

Kuttler: So it was our job as good salesmen and good providers of services to be able to say, "This might actually be able to work better." In the end, people began to share and leverage systems, which made sense. That said, at J&J you can probably still find most of everything.

Donaldson: Who were your peers and who did you report to?

Kuttler: My peers were the executives of the IT organization. I reported to the corporate CIO for J&J world wide. And she had a leadership team under her who were responsible for the medical device, pharmaceutical, corporate, and consumer goods businesses. In addition we had a head of infrastructure, IT finance, IT HR and IT security.

Donaldson: I see. With respect to the technical people that worked with you, where did you look to recruit them? Was it a different problem than you an encountered at Vertex?

Kuttler: It was. At J&J we looked for people from all over. We needed to fill voids from everywhere, and we were trying to build change into the organization. Again, funny enough, the challenge wasn't any different; it was finding good technical people, people who understood the function of IT. During this time, there was a transition going on everywhere in IT, first ᵗ was the internet boom and when companies weren't stealing people from each other and second it was business partners complaining that IT people were too geeky, that they didn't speak a business language, that it was difficult for them to communicate and explain how a process might work and what a change might be. So we were always looking for people that we could develop with good business acumen and a good conversational style where they could both represent a part of the business but have strong enough technology skills not to make major planning mistakes, like over committing or under delivering, right?

Donaldson: Mm-hmm.

Kuttler: So when you're in the business relationship function within a company, we wanted those folks not only understood their business and become a trusted partner, while still representing IT for J&J as a whole. We also worked very hard at developing people and moving them through a variety of channels, so they would get a broader view of J&J and bring educated and innovative solutions to the companies they worked in.

Donaldson: What is the turnover rate in that industry? Is it, is it comparable with your other experiences, or was it lower or higher?

Kuttler: In those days, it was all about the new technologies that were becoming available. So in the years '99-2008, it was all about the internet; the internet being a boom; people were changing jobs if they could manage to find anything related to the internet; People left: they went to new companies to take advantage of higher pay and newer technology. Companies were paying very highly for skills. So there was a real challenge in terms of keeping really good talent in-house. The differentiator with J&J was that we were in the business of really developing people and staying current and doing the right things. We were developing people in-house and giving them opportunities to change roles so they always had the ability to learn, and to see things differently and from a different perspective within the J&J family of companies. So our rate of loss was fairly low. But it was higher than we wanted it to be.

Donaldson: I see. Well, aside from those types of challenges associated with personnel, what do you view as some of your biggest challenges that you've had?

Kuttler: There's stuff that's happening both to us and with us. There's consumerization of IT, which is really about people having adopted IT and making it very much part of their lives. .On the business side there's this tendency to say, "Well, there's IT and there's the business." In my experience, IT has made up 7 to 10% of the business. If you're that much of the business, then you're not just a service, but you're part of what makes the business work and function. So you have to think about yourself in those terms. You have to appreciate the fact that we are very much a component and a working principal within the business and that what we do is as important as what product manufacturing does and what supply chain delivery and what the sales organization does. **Donaldson:** Right.

Kuttler: Today, because of the proliferation of mobile devices and imbedded technology in car's etcetera, the expectation for IT has changed. There is this expectation that IT is easy. I'm not even going to argue that. It should absolutely be that easy, and yet we still haven't made it that easy. In IT departments and corporations, communication, communication, communication. Change, processes and alignment can still be difficult things to do.

Donaldson: Yes.

Siegel: Dave, you mentioned that IT is, in your view, considered part of the business. Do other parts of the business at J&J, the product developers, share that view?

Kuttler: No, what I've learned is that there are enlightened individuals in this world. There are people who work really well with each other and within the organization. What I found is that there are people within organizations that clearly understand that in order to get something done and to get it done well, they need to work together with respect for each other and the team. To get something done one of those groups is almost always IT. And when people work well with IT, stuff gets accomplished. So at Vertex, when we needed to submit an application to the FDA for a product that we were putting together, we didn't have a huge amount of time to do that; we needed to it well. It had to be perfect. It had to go through the right channels. It had to do the right things correctly, and there was nothing we could buy or do that would make that perfect. There was a team of people who understood that the only way they were going to get this done was by working with their IT partners hand in hand. And that's what they did. They sat down and they said, "Okay, these things are broken. These platforms we can buy. These things work. This is how we're going to do the workarounds." And they managed that together. And as a result of doing that together, they accomplished a really tough goal in a really short period of time.

Donaldson: Right.

Kuttler: When you're doing accounting and you're doing processing of transactions or you're looking at supply chain and flow, and you're, you're processing orders through the system, if you have a system that's processing 10,000 transactions an hour, you should be able to make that system do 20,000 transactions an hour, and that shouldn't be something a business owner should have to think about or, quite frankly, the IT team should have to think about. It should have structured and built it in such a way that those things can happen. And the challenge for us is making sure that those aren't the conversations we have. The minute you sit down and you say, "Well, you know, we increased the volume because the product really started to sell. Because Vioxx went off the market, Tylenol went up and began to sell like hotcakes, so our supply chain systems broke because we couldn't handle the volume." That's

Donaldson: That's a challenge.

Kuttler: My take is that it shouldn't be a challenge. It's a mistake.

Donaldson: Right.

Kuttler: It's a mistake that occurred because we didn't do the job well enough to know that we only wanted to do that part of it once. When we wanted to sell more and we wanted to approach the market differently, we needed to be able to think about doing that in new and inventive ways. And if we're still spending the time internally thinking about how to do things well, being able to handle volume, rather than taking the time to think about how we might be able to do new things, we are making a mistake. We must look at how we can bring change into the organization and make things better and change with the growing world we live in. So in answer to your question, I think the problem is that when you don't act and you don't take the position of a business within the business and don't command and demand that kind of respect, you don't get it. If you can't deliver the basics, then you don't get it.

Donaldson: Let's shift gears here and spend a few minutes talking about technologies. I understand that, as you said, J&J has all of them, a corporation of that size. But we want to narrow it down to a few technologies, such as social networking, Facebook, YouTube, Twitter. Did those technologies impact the marketplace when you were at J&J?

Kuttler: The question becomes, how can a pharmaceutical company communicate with the people that use its products? And does social networking really help bring those things to bear? And the obvious answer might be yes, immediately. Why wouldn't you want to see these things? And the answer that we actually come back with is that there have been some struggles with the regulatory agencies, the FDA, about coming to terms between the pharmaceutical companies and the FDA about what is good, positive, acceptable practice using social media when dealing with a broad, unknown constituency. And so far it's been a very difficult question to answer. And as a result, what you see is product material being promoted out so that people can see it and understand it and use it, but you don't see a lot of use of interactive social networking. Partly because the regulatory responsibility is still uppermost in people's mind, and that issue hasn't been solved yet. If I could put that in clear terms, if you had a Facebook page, for example, for a painkiller and you asked customers, "tell us things about it." People could say anything. Someone might say "I'm having a problem with this drug." You can't let the community monitor that for you as a drug company. You have to monitor it.

Donaldson: Mm-hmm.

Kuttler: You'd have to have organizations there cleaning it and looking at the interactions to make sure that if someone reported something that was thought to be a problem with the drug, that you actually understood that and that you could incorporate that and get more seriously engaged so that you knew if it was a problem or wasn't a problem with that particular drug and how it was working. You can see where that creates a risk, and you can see how difficult to understand those things are in social-based strategies, where you would get a lot of other people potentially commenting on what that was, like "I got a rash on something," or "I didn't get a rash on something."

Donaldson: Okay.

Kuttler: "Something happened." You have to be there tracking it, understanding it, and getting a real handle on it. And that's just really difficult to do. So as a result of that, the risk vs. the benefits limits how these tools can be used in the pharma industry. So from the marketing point of view, it's easy to get information out, but to be able to set up that two-way conversation or make it relevant is actually difficult.

Donaldson: Okay. Do you see any transformative technologies – cyber, cloud – that might impact the business?

Kuttler: I think IT is continually evolving and as part of that evolution, what we see are service providers running services on your behalf. And I think that's interesting. It takes some stuff off the table for the IT organization as a whole. That means the operational running of something may not be as necessary as it was. I'm hoping that those companies will also become good at adapting and adding functionality as they work with their business partners to determine how to both configure and change their products and move them forward. So I think that the cloud is actually a really positive step and I hope what it does is to begin to tie the IT function and the vendors closer together. That in turn, would create transformations in the vendors' products to hopefully make things work better getting to this ease expectation that is being set in the consumer space. GPS, mobility and image are all growing and transforming quite substantially. The fact is that we're actually working through the very early stages on 3D where hospitals and other places are tied into substantial networks where they see and manipulate high def 3D images helping with diagnostic decisions, remote surgeries, and related procedures. So I believe all of these technologies, be it image, high-def, or mobility mash together to bring new ways for us to leverage technology and support real advancements.

Donaldson: Do you have a personal technology favorite that you keep your eye on?

Kuttler: I keep my eye on networks and imaging. Obviously, it's something I think that is going to bring a real change. And I also follow startups, not a particular technology per se, but I see a lot of startups and investments where people are focused on new ways to represent and present information. So I follow reporting capabilities a lot: what are new ways to report and translate data into information? What are new ways to allow people to actually look at something and be able to make a decision out of the data that they see in front of them? I see that capability growing and becoming very important to everyone, so I'd say I follow that, I follow image, and I follow mobility.

Donaldson: Okay. You did talk about technology investments and some of the ways that you worked through those issues throughout J&J. Another area tied to that would be mergers and acquisitions. Did you play a role in mergers and acquisitions and due diligence, for example?

Kuttler: Yes. Within the organization we needed to be able to ascertain how easy it would be to onboard a company, what we would be able to do for them, what we shouldn't do for them, what was unique to them that we wouldn't want to change or affect, how we might integrate them into the company, and what things we could do to make things better for them. Also, what things we just needed to absolutely have for ourselves and to make sure we got those things, so we could provide financial integration for that company and do basic other things for them.

Donaldson: I see. Okay, so let's now go to talk about what you see happening in the future. What changes do you see in the future that you think will have the most important effect on companies like Vertex and J&J?

Kuttler: I think that skills will continue to evolve and get better. In terms of what we need to be able to do for the future, simplicity and people—as I said before—the consumerization of IT sets expectations about how simple IT should appear n a time where we are asking that IT produce and deliver much more sophisticated and integrated capability. We use our technology to help guide us and understand what is working and what's not. We have to be able to represent the data we gather as information that can be easily understood by the CEO who looks at things one way, and the CFO who looks at things another way.

Donaldson: Right.

Kuttler: The head of supply looks at things a third way; logistics manager, another. So how do we represent the conversation back to all those folks, because in essence we have the data and information about how the company is running, performing and engaging with its customers. I think that's where we're going, with applications that are easy to use, not like EIS systems of the past.

Donaldson: Okay. How do you see the role as CTO evolving?

Kuttler: I think more of a strategy-setting function in large companies. I see it more as both a strategy and operational mode, becoming more of a COO. I think the CTOs eventually roll into a function where they become partners; with the CTO focusing strongly on executing the strategy and the direction. The two roles together insuring that the IT organization is aligned and prepared for the changes and growth that will help the business stay one step ahead of the curve and make the right things happen.

Donaldson: What did you like most about being a CTO? And then the follow-up question would be, what did you like least about being a CTO?

Kuttler: From a strategic perspective we were trying to examine a new problem in a different way; so we were trying to do something different. It's always exciting to be able to spend energy on doing stuff like that and to say, "Okay, here's what's going on in the marketplace, so what tools or capabilities do we need to make that happen?" and to begin to evaluate that and see how we could use the organization to bring about that change. Making that stuff happen was really cool stuff. Working with vendors to enable those kinds of changes in either products or services or just to be able to create them on our own was also a lot of fun. In one example I remember we had a contract with the government in which we expected a certain amount of business to come our way. For that contract, I actually very early on created something akin to a robot of processing engines. I had a series of CPUs, each one doing a particular function that they would hand off to each other. And that's how we would process the government's work. It took us a little while to get that together, but it was a unique way to solve a business problem using technology that wasn't really being used that way, but was clearly capable of doing that kind of work. Today we look at it as virtualization, but then virtualization didn't exist. So it was both the enjoyment of being able to use the technology really well and apply it in ways that hadn't been thought of before. I enjoyed setting the strategy for the longer term because you get a broader perspective on where things are going. Here is an example: "if 40% of our business is going to be done through outside parties, then what we really need is to do is do business-to-business integration really, really well. How are we going to go about doing that?" That kind of problem solving was an aspect of the business that I really enjoyed.

To answer the other side of your question, if I were to look at the part of the job that is harder, it's being able to sell a capability when the organization you're trying to sell to isn't interested in hearing it.

Donaldson: Understood.

Siegel: Dave, to wind up here, I read on the Journal of New England Technology you're currently leveraging your experience in IT leadership as a consultant on IT governance and so forth. What's next in your career, or is that what you're going to continue to do?

Kuttler: So for my career, I continue to like to learn things. I haven't given that up. So for me, it's about what opportunities come along that allow me to continue to do that. And that might be another CIO role. It might be CIO for more than one company. These days there are lots of small companies that need help. Or it just might be in terms of helping people out on smaller jobs and seeing what they need. But whatever it is, it's always going to be about something where I'm learning something and helping bring my assorted past to bear, whether I can help people see something a different way, potentially take a step that they might not have taken before, and feel better about IT because it is information that helps us make the world go round. Translating data into information is not a job that's done yet. It's a job that always needs doing. And I think there's room in there to continue my career.

Siegel: What kept you up at night while you were at J&J, and what keeps you up at night now?

Kuttler: What kept me up at night at J&J was that we would sometimes experiment with technologies that weren't ready for prime time. And in order to do that, you need fabulous partnerships and people with really, really substantial skills. And that can be difficult. Fabulous partnerships are not always easy to have and to get. And they go through a process where you learn about each other and you spend energy and time, and you get people up to speed, learning about their ways of doing things. So how to effectively do things when you might be in an area that people haven't been before always gave me cause for concern, and carried a high profile of risk. Understanding how you might mitigate that risk in a known world, where you're tackling something that you already clearly understand, is addressable, so you can sit down and figure it out. In areas where you're not really sure how it's going to go or you're testing a hypothesis, and worry about the impact it may have on the IT organization and the businesses. Innovation and change management around innovation are never easy, and it kept me up nights, but I never gave it up. And today, what I worry about is that the consumerization of IT and the expectations for IT as a result of that consumerization will set demands that our partners and our capabilities just aren't living up to and that IT and our delivery of that service won't meet those expectations, If that becomes the case, people will look down and stop doing things with IT and look for other mechanisms and methods to do things that won't potentially be as effective or help us in the long term.

Index

CPSIA information can be obtained at www.ICGtesting.com
Printed in the USA
LVOW111303110212

268236LV00002B/1/P